SONGS OF FELLOWSHIP

Songs of Fellowship 2

MUSIC EDITION

KINGSWAY MUSIC
EASTBOURNE

The words of most of the songs in this publication are covered by the
Christian Copyright Licence.

United Kingdom
CCL UK Limited, P.O. Box 1339, Eastbourne, East Sussex, BN21 4YF.

United States
CCL Inc., 17201 Sacramento Street, Portland, Oregon 97230.

Australasia
CCL Asia Pacific Pty Ltd, P.O. Box 26405, Epsom, Auckland 3, New Zealand.

Africa
CCL Africa Pty Ltd, P.O. Box 2347, Durbanville 7551, Republic of South Africa.

ISBN 0 85476 770 3
Words edition ISBN 0 85476 771 1

Biblical quotations are taken from the New International Version,
© 1973, 1978, 1984, by the International Bible Society.
Published by Hodder & Stoughton and used by permission.

Music setting by STM Publishing.

Designed and produced by Bookprint Creative Services
P.O. Box 827, BN21 3YJ, England, for
KINGSWAY COMMUNICATIONS LTD
Lottbridge Drove, Eastbourne, East Sussex, BN23 6NT, UK.
Printed in Great Britain.

Contents

Important notes

Order of songs

The songs appear in alphabetical order by first line (letter by letter), not necessarily by author's title, for easy use in praise and worship meetings. An index of titles and first lines is included at the back, along with other useful indexes and chord charts (see Contents page).

To further facilitate the use of this book, all two-page songs and hymns appear on facing pages to avoid turning over, while maintaining the alphabetical order.

Numbering of songs

The songs are numbered from 641 to 1150, continuing the numbering sequence from the companion Songs of Fellowship 1 Music Edition. This numbering and song order is also reflected in the Combined Words Edition, and the enclosed computer disk (see below).

Scripture references

References – listed in biblical order – are to the key Bible passages quoted or echoed in the songs, and to some passing references. In many cases the whole Bible passage will repay further exploration, beyond the verses listed. A full index to the Scripture references is provided at the back of the book.

Computer Disk

The computer disk contains the words to all 1150 hymns and songs in the two Songs of Fellowship Music Editions. For instructions on how to install the disk on your computer, please read the label on the disk itself, and refer to the 'Using The Computer Disk' pages at the back of this book. More detailed operating instructions are given in the README.WRI file on the disk.

641.

Abraham's Son
(Hail to the King)

Gen 3:15; Is 25:15; 1 Pet 2:6;
1 Pet 2:6; Rev 17:14; 19:16;
Rev 21:2

Steadily, building to chorus

Bob Baker

1. A-braham's Son, Cho-sen One,— Zi-on's cor-ner-stone;—

Pass-ov-er Lamb,— Son— of Man,—

Chorus

seat-ed up-on— Your throne.— Hail to the King,—

hail to the King,— hail to the King— of kings.—

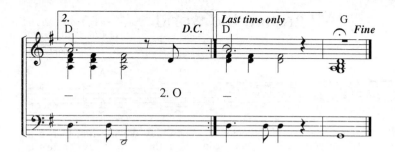

2. O

2. O promised Seed, beneath Your feet
Sin and death shall fall.
Now through us tread the serpent's head
Till You are all in all.

3. The world's yet to see Your glory,
But You'll be revealed in power,
And You will reign with the Bride ordained
For Your consummating hour.

642.
All around the world

Ps:85; Is 61:1; Mt 11:5;
Lk 4:18; 15:18; Rev 10:3

Paul Oakley

Driving

All a-round the world there's a new day dawn-ing, there's a
Ev-'ry where you go you can hear this sto-ry, there's a

sound com-ing round, there's a new song ris-ing up,
pow-er com-ing down, there's a glimpse of glo-ry now,

ah, it's a new day!
ah, it's a new day!

1. There's a sound of praise, there's a sound of war,

yeah; lift the ban-ner high,

2. Let the lame run, let the blind see!
   Let Your power come, set the captives free!
   Let the lost return to the Lover of our souls,
   Let the prodigal find the way back home.

Come let us bow down in worship, let us kneel before the Lord our Maker.

PSALM 95:6

643.

All consuming fire

Ex 3:14; Deut 4:24; Heb 12:29

Capo 1 (Bm)

Randy Wright

With awe

All con-sum-ing fi - re, You're my heart's de-
You're my me - di - ta - tion, and my con - sol-

si - re, }
a - tion, } and I love You dear - ly, dear - ly

1. Lord.
2. Lord.

Glo - ry to the Lamb, I ex-

644.

All creation bows

Nahum 1:7; Rev 1:16; 2:1; 3:1; 5:9

Mike Blow

Bright and rhythmic

1. All cre-a-tion bows___ at the name___ of Je-sus,___ ev-'ry star___ is in His hands. Yet the glo-ri-ous___ mys-te-ry___ of a-ges,___ He de-lights___ in fra-gile man.

2. There is mercy in the name of Jesus,
   Mercy to forgive our sin.
   The mighty King of heaven became the humble servant,
   To bring His children back to Him.
   And this is why I will sing:

3. There is shelter in the name of Jesus,
   He accepts the refugee;
   And His mighty strength will never fail us,
   His arm is always close to me.
   And all my life I will sing:

645. All creatures of our God and King

1 Chron 23:30;
Ps 55:22; 148:1-4,8; 150:6;
1 Pet 5:7

Tune: LAAST USN ERFEUEN

Capo 1 (D)

Melody from *Geistlich Kirchengessang*
Cologne, 1623
Arr. R Vaughan Williams (1872-1958)

1. All crea-tures of our God and King, lift up your voice and with us sing: Hal - le - lu - jah, hal - le - lu - jah! Thou burn-ing sun with gold-en beam, thou sil-ver moon with soft-er gleam: O— praise Him, O— praise Him, hal - le -

Unison
F(E) Bb(A) Cm(Bm) Eb Fm C7 Fm(Em) Ab(G) Bb(A) Eb(D)
(D) (Em) (B7)

lu - jah, hal - le - lu - jah, hal - le - lu - jah!

2. Thou rushing wind that art so strong,
   Ye clouds that sail in heaven along,
   O praise Him, hallelujah!
   Thou rising morn, in praise rejoice,
   Ye lights of evening, find a voice:
      O praise Him . . .

3. Thou flowing water, pure and clear,
   Make music for thy Lord to hear,
   Hallelujah, hallelujah!
   Thou fire so masterful and bright,
   That giveth man both warmth and light:
      O praise Him . . .

4. And all ye men of tender heart,
   Forgiving others, take your part,
   O sing ye, hallelujah!
   Ye who long pain and sorrow bear,
   Praise God and on Him cast your care:
      O praise Him . . .

5. Let all things their Creator bless,
   And worship Him in humbleness,
   O praise Him, hallelujah!
   Praise, praise the Father, praise the Son,
   And praise the Spirit, Three-in-One:
      O praise Him . . .

St Francis of Assisi (1182-1226)
Tr. William Henry Draper (1855-1933)

646.

All I once held dear
(Knowing You)

Phil 3:7-11

Graham Kendrick

Smoothly

1. All I once held dear, built my life up - on, all this world re - veres, and wars to own, all I once thought gain I have coun - ted___ loss; spent and worth-less now, com - pared to this. Know-ing You, Jesus, know - ing You, there is no great - er thing. You're my

all, You're the best,— You're my joy, my right-eous-ness, and I love You, Lord.—

2. Now my   love You, Lord,—   love, You, Lord._____

2. Now my heart's desire
   Is to know You more,
   To be found in You
   And known as Yours.
   To possess by faith
   What I could not earn,
   All-surpassing gift
   Of righteousness.

3. Oh, to know the power
   Of Your risen life,
   And to know You in
   Your sufferings.
   To become like You
   In Your death, my Lord,
   So with You to live
   And never die.

647.

All that I am

Rom 12:1; 2 Cor 12:10; Gal 2:20;
Phil 4:19

Capo 3 (D)

With feeling

James Wright

All that I am I lay be-fore You;
all I pos-sess, Lord I con-fess is no-thing with-out
You. Sa-viour and King, I now en-throne You;
take my life, my liv-ing sa-cri-fice to You. 1. Lord, be the

strength with-in my weak-ness; be the sup - ply in ev - 'ry need, that I may

prove Your prom - is-es to me, faith-ful and true in word and deed.

2. Into Your hands I place the future;
   The past is nailed to Calvary,
   That I may live in resurrection power,
   No longer I but Christ in me.

648.
All the ends of the earth
(Awaken the nations)

Ps 22: 27-28
Is 61:11; Rev 51:4

David Fellingham

Resolutely

All the ends of the earth will re-mem-ber, and
turn to the Lord of gl-ory; all the fam-ilies of the na-tions will bow
down to the Lord, as His right-eous acts of pow'r are dis-played. And
we will a-wak-en the na-tions, to bring their wor-ship to
Je-sus. And right-eous-ness and praise shall spring forth

2. Who will not fear the Lord of glory,
   Or bring honour to His holy name?
   For God has spoken with integrity and truth,
   A word which cannot be revoked.

649.
All the riches of His grace
(Oh, the blood of Jesus)

Is 1:18; 1 Jn 1:7

Jan Harrington

With simplicity, flowing
(Two part song)

1. All the rich - es of His grace, all the ful - ness of His bless - ings, all the sweet - ness of His love___ He gives to you,_____ He gives to me. All the me.

2. 1. Oh, the blood of Je - sus, oh, the blood of Je - sus, oh, the blood of Je - sus, it wash - es white as snow.

2. Oh, the word of Jesus, . . . it cleanses white as snow.

3. Oh, the love of Jesus, . . . it makes His Body whole.

*Then I heard what sounded
like a great multitude, like the roar
of rushing waters and like loud peals
of thunder, shouting: "Hallelujah!
For our Lord God Almighty reigns."*

REVELATION 19:6

650.

All you people

Ps 113:3-4; Rev 7:9

John Gibson

Bright & rhythmic

Chorus

(Leader) All you peo - ple, (All) sing un-to the Lord.— (Leader) All you_ na - tions,—

(All) sing un - to_ the Lord.— Come with_ dan - cing, come and

raise your_ voice_ to the King,— come and sing un-to_ the Lord._

(Fine)

Verse From the_ sun's ris - ing_ to the_ sun's set - ting,—

Middle section (over first two bars)

(Leader) People of Africa,
(All)   Sing unto the Lord. *(After each line)*

(Leader) Europe and Asia, . . .
          All of Australasia, . . .
          And all across America, . . .
          The rich and the poor will . . .
          The weak and the strong can . . .
          Every generation, . . .
          Every tribe and nation, . . .

651.

Almighty God
(I will only worship You)

Ps:19

Nathan Fellingham &
Adrian Watts

Yet a time is coming and has now come when the true worshippers will worship the Father in spirit and truth, for they are the kind of worshippers the Father seeks.

JOHN 4:23

652.

Almighty God, my Redeemer

Ps 32:7; 40:2-3; 62:5-7;
2 Cor 12:10

Darlene Zschech

With energy

Al- migh-ty God,— my Re- deem- er,— my hid- ing place,
My feet— are plant- ed on— this— rock,— and I— will not—

— my safe— re- fuge;— no oth- er name— like Je- sus,—
— be sha- ken;— my hope— it comes— from You— a- lone,—

1. — no pow'r— can stand— a- gainst— You.—
2. — my Lord— and my— — sal- va- tion.—

Your praise— is al- ways on— my— lips,— Your word— is liv-
You fill— my life— with great- er— joy;— yes I— de- light—

— ing in— my— heart,— and I— will praise— You with a new song:—
— my- self— in— You,— { and I— will praise— You with a new song:—

653.

Among the gods
(You alone are God)

Ps 86:5, 8-11

Carol Owen

With strength

1. A-mong the gods there is none like You,— O Lord, O Lord.— There are no deeds to com-pare with Yours, O Lord. All the na-tions You have made will come;— they'll wor-ship— be-fore You,— O Lord, O Lord.— For You are great and do mar-vel-lous deeds.—

Yes, You are great and do mar-vel-lous deeds.

You a-lone are God, You a-lone are God.

1.
2.3. (Fine)

Teach me Your ways,— O Lord, and I'll walk in Your

truth. Give me an un - di-vi-ded heart,— that I may fear Your

D.S. al Fine

name. For

2. You are so good and forgiving,
O Lord, O Lord.
You're rich in love to all who call to You.
All the nations You have made will come;
They'll glorify Your name, O Lord,
O Lord.

654.
And from Your fulness
(Grace upon grace)

Ps 103:4; Jn 1:16; 2 Cor 8:9;
Phil 4:6; Jas 1:17

Mark Altrogge

With energy

2. Lord, You're the Author
Of every good gift;
You give us all
We need to live.
Lord, You became poor
To make us rich,
You crown our lives with Your compassion.

655.

And He shall reign

Graham Kendrick

With energy

And

He shall reign for ev - er, His throne and crown shall ev - er en - dure. And He shall reign for ev - er, and we shall reign with Him.

2. He was given sovereign power,
   Glory and authority.
   Every nation, tribe and tongue
   Worshipped Him on bended knee.

3. On the throne forever,
   See the Lamb who once was slain.
   Wounds of sacrificial love
   Forever shall remain.

656.

Anointing, fall on me

Acts 10:44; 11:15

Donn Thomas

With a 'gospel' feel

A - noint-ing,— fall on me; a - noint-ing,—

fall on me.— Let the pow-er of— the Ho - ly Ghost— fall on me,— a-

noint-ing fall— on me. *Fine* *Verse* Touch my hands,— my

mouth, and my heart;— fill my life,— Lord, ev-'ry part.— Let the

pow-er of_ the Ho - ly Ghost___ fall on me,___ a - noint-ing, fall_ on

D.C. al Fine

me.   A -

657.
Are we the people?
(Last generation)

Is 9:2; Mt 9:2; Lk 10:2; Jn 8:12;
2 Pet 3:9; Rev 5:9; 14:6

Noel & Tricia Richards

With a driving rhythm

Are we the peo - ple who_ will see_ God's king-dom come,_ when He is known_ in ev - 'ry na - tion? One thing is cer - tain, we_ are clo - ser than_ be - fore;_ keep mov-ing on,_ last ge - ne - ra - tion.

1. These are the days— for har - vest,
to ga-ther in— the lost;— let
those who live— in dark - ness
hear the mes - sage of— the cross.—

2. We'll go where God is sending,
We'll do what He commands;
These years that He has waited
Could be coming to an end.

658.

As the deer pants
(Your waves of love)

Ps 42:1-2,7; 84:2

Richard Lewis

As the deer_____ pants for the wa - ter,_____ so my soul,_____ it thirsts for You, for You, O___ God,_____ for You, O___ God._____ As the When can I come be-fore_____You___ and see Your face? My heart and my flesh cry

love are break-ing o - ver me. Your waves of love are break-ing o -

- ver me._____

(Fine)

As the

D.S.

"'As surely as I live,' says the Lord, 'Every knee will bow before me; every tongue will confess to God.'"

ROMANS 14:11

659.
As water to the thirsty

Jn 4:14; Rev 21:6

Tune: OASIS

Brian Coleman

1. As wa - ter to the thirs-ty, as beau - ty to the eyes, as
strength that fol-lows weak-ness, as truth in-stead of lies; as
song-time and spring-time and sum - mer-time to be, so
is my Lord, my liv-ing Lord, so is my Lord to me.

2. Like calm in place of clamour,
   Like peace that follows pain,
   Like meeting after parting,
   Like sunshine after rain;
   Like moonlight and starlight
   And sunlight on the sea,
   So is my Lord, my living Lord,
   So is my Lord to me.

3. As sleep that follows fever,
   As gold instead of grey,
   As freedom after bondage,
   As sunrise to the day;
   As home to the traveller
   And all he longs to see,
   So is my Lord, my living Lord,
   So is my Lord to me.

Timothy Dudley-Smith

660.

As we behold You

2 Cor 3:18

David Baroni

Smoothly

As we be - hold You, as we be - hold You, we__ are
chan - ging in-to Your im-age. As we be - from glo-ry to
glo - ry. As we be - hold__ You__ in all of Your glo - ry.__
im - age__ from glo-ry to glo - ry,__
__ Lord, by Your Spi - rit__ we__ are chan-ging in-to Your
__ as we be - hold You,
__ liv - ing God. As we be -

661.

As we see the world
(Every place)

Rom 11:5,11-12; Rev 5:9; 13:7

Strong, slow 4

Lex Loizides

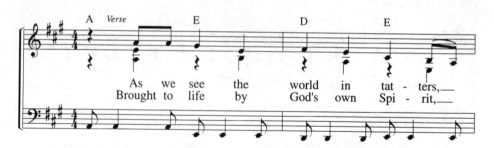

As we see the world in tat - ters,___
Brought to life by God's own Spi - rit,___

as we watch their dreams break down,
joined to - geth - er in His Son,

we can hear their qui - et an - guish:___ "come___ and
now the church with strength a - ri - ses___ like___ an

help___ us!" Ev - 'ry place, ev - 'ry___ place
ar - my.

where our feet shall— tread,_____ ev - 'ry tribe,

ev- 'ry— race_____ God has giv-en us.

2. In the midst of boastful darkness
   Shines a Light that cannot fail,
   And the blind behold His glory,
   Jesus! Jesus!
   Not content with restoration
   Of the remnant in the land,
   He has filled us with His power
   For the nations.

662.
At the foot of the cross

Rom 5:8; 1 Cor 15:3;
Heb 9:15; 1 Pet 3:18

With a gentle rhythm

Derek Bond

At the foot of the cross, I can hard-ly take it in, that the King of all cre-a-tion was dy-ing for my sin. And the pain and a-gon-y, and the thorns that pierced Your head, and the hard-ness of my sin-ful heart that left You there for dead.

663.

Baby Jesus in the manger
(Noël)

Is 7:14; 40:2; Mt 1:23; 2:11; 27:29,41; 28:6;
Lk 2:7; 24:6; 23:11,36; Mk 15:20,31; 16:6; 1 Pet 3:18

Smoothly

Gill Broomhall

1. Ba- by Je- sus in the man- ger, to the world He's still a
2. Gen- tle Je- sus, meek and low- ly, full of love so pure and

stran- ger. Wise men bring their gifts of_____ gold and myrrh, ba- by
ho- ly. He will teach and pray, show man- kind the way, gen- tle

Je- sus in the man- ger. No- el, No- el, No- el,
Je- sus, meek and low- ly.

hail the Im- man- u- el.____ 3. Lov- ing Je- sus, mocked and

664. Beauty for brokenness

(God of the poor)

Ps 140:12

Graham Kendrick

Thoughtfully

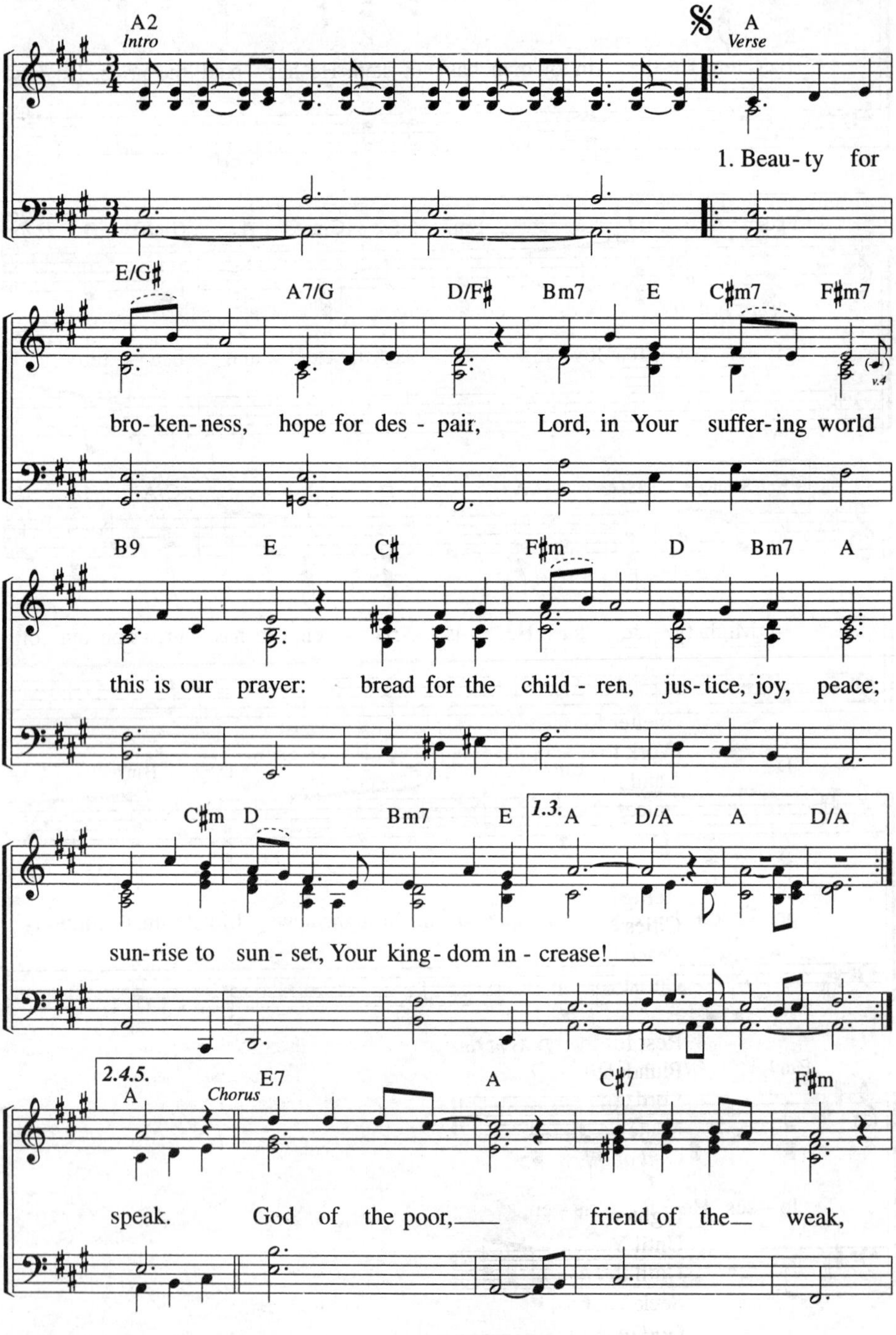

A2
Intro
A
Verse
1. Beau-ty for
E/G♯ A7/G D/F♯ Bm7 E C♯m7 F♯m7
v.4
bro-ken-ness, hope for des - pair, Lord, in Your suffer-ing world
B9 E C♯ F♯m D Bm7 A
this is our prayer: bread for the child - ren, jus-tice, joy, peace;
C♯m D Bm7 E
1.3.
A D/A A D/A
sun-rise to sun - set, Your king-dom in - crease!
2.4.5.
A
Chorus
E7 A C♯7 F♯m
speak. God of the poor, friend of the weak,

give us com-pas - sion we pray: melt our cold hearts, let
tears fall like— rain; come, change our love—— from a spark——
— to a— flame.——

2. Shelter for fragile lives, cures for their ills,
Work for the craftsmen, trade for their skills;
Land for the dispossessed, rights for the weak,
Voices to plead the cause of those who can't speak.
God of the poor . . .

3. Refuge from cruel wars, havens from fear,
Cities for sanctuary, freedoms to share;
Peace to the killing-fields, scorched earth to green,
Christ for the bitterness, His cross for the pain.

4. Rest for the ravaged earth, oceans and streams
Plundered and poisoned - our future, our dreams.
Lord, end our madness, carelessness, greed;
Make us content with the things that we need.
God of the poor . . .

5. Lighten our darkness, breathe on this flame
Until Your justice burns brightly again;
Until the nations learn of Your ways,
Seek Your salvation and bring You their praise.
God of the poor . . .

665.

Be free

2 Cor 3:17; Phil 1:6; 2:3

Dave Bilbrough

Joyfully

Be free in the love of God, let His Spi-rit flow with-in you. Be free in the love of God, let it fill your soul. Be free in the love of God, cel-e-brate His name with dan-cing. Be free in the love of God, He has made us whole.

2. God is gracious, He will lead us
   Through His power at work within us.
   Spirit, guide us, and unite us
   In the Father's love.

666.

Be glorified

Capo 3(D)

Majestically

Billy Funk

1. Be glo - ri - fied,___ be glo - ri - fied.
2. Wor - ship the Lord,___ wor - ship the Lord.___

Be glo - ri - fied,___
Wor - ship the Lord,___

be glo - ri - fied.___ Be glo - ri - fied___ in the heav-
wor - ship the Lord.___ Wor-ship the Lord___ in the heav-

- ens, be glo - ri - fied___ in the earth;___
- ens, wor-ship the Lord___ in the earth;___

667.

Behold the Lord

Rev 1:14-15,17-18; 4:8

Gerald Coates & Noel Richards

With strength

1. Be-hold the Lord up-on His throne; His face is shin-ing like the sun. With eyes blaz-ing fire, and feet glow-ing bronze, His voice like migh-ty wa-ters roars. Ho - ly, ho - ly, Lord God Al-migh - ty. Ho - ly, ho - ly, we stand in awe of You.

2. The First, the Last, the living One
   Laid down His life for all the world;
   Behold He now lives forever more,
   And holds the keys of death and hell.
   Holy, holy, Lord God Almighty;
   Holy, holy, we bow before Your throne.

3. So let our praises ever ring
   To Jesus Christ, our glorious King.
   All heaven and earth resound as we cry:
   "Worthy is the Son of God!"
   Holy, holy, Lord God Almighty.
   Holy, holy, we fall down at Your feet.

668. Behold the servant of the Lord

MOZART

W.A. Mozart

Be-hold— the ser-vant of— the Lord:— I wait— Thy guid-ing eye— to feel,— to hear— and keep— Thy ev-'ry word,— to prove and do Thy per-fect will; joy-ful— from my own works— to— cease, glad to— ful-fill all right-eous-ness.

2. Me if Thy grace vouchsafe to use,
   Meanest of all Thy creatures, me.
   The deed, the time, the manner choose:
   Let all my fruit be found of Thee.
   Let all my works in Thee be wrought,
   By Thee to full perfection brought.

3. My every weak though good design
   O'errule or change, as seems Thee meet:
   Jesus, let all my work be Thine -
   Thy work, O Lord, is all complete,
   And pleasing in Thy father's sight;
   Thou only hast done all things right.

4. Here then to Thee Thine own I leave;
   Mould as Thou wilt Thy passive clay;
   But let me all Thy stamp receive,
   But let me all Thy words obey,
   Serve with a single heart and eye,
   And in Thy glory live and die.

Charles Wesley (1707-88)

669. Be known to us in breaking bread

Mt 26:26; Mk 14:22; Lk 24:30;
Jn 6:54; 1 Cor 11:23; Rev 3:20

Tune: MANOAH

From Rossini (1792-1868)
(Greatorex Collection 1851)

With feeling

2. There sup with us in love divine;
   Thy body and Thy blood,
   That living bread, that heavenly wine,
   Be our immortal food.

3. We would not live by bread alone,
   But by Thy word of grace,
   In strength of which we travel on
   To our abiding place

James Montgomery (1771-1854)

Submit yourselves, then, to God. Resist the devil, and he will flee from you.

JAMES 4:7

670.
Bells they are ringing
(Name over all)

Phil 2:9

With energy

Jim Bailey

Verse

Bells— they are ring - ing, chil - dren are sing-ing, and we are ex-alt - ing the Name o - ver all. Flags— they are danc-ing, the church is ad-vanc - ing, as we are ro-manc - ing the Name o - ver all.

671.

Be still and know

Ps 46:4,10; Mt 16:18

Rocky, with energy

Lex Loizides

1. Be still and know that I am God:
I will be glo-ri-fied_ and praised_ in all_ the_ earth.
For My great name I will be found, and I can
nev-er be_ re-sis - ted, nev-er be_ un-done;_ I'm
nev-er lack - ing pow - er to glo-ri-fy_ My Son._ The

2. Be still and know that I am God;
   I have poured out
   My Holy Spirit like a flood.
   The land that cries for holy rain
   Shall be inheriting her promises
   And dancing like a child;
   A holy monsoon deluge shall
   Bless the barren heights,
   And those who sat in silence
   Shall speak up and shall be heard:
   My name will be exalted in the earth.

3. Be still and know that I am God;
   My Son has asked me
   For the nations of the world.
   His sprinkled blood has made a way
   For all the multitudes
   Of India and Africa to come;
   The Middle East will find its peace
   Through Jesus Christ My Son.
   From London down to Cape Town,
   From L.A. to Beijing,
   My Son shall reign the undisputed King!

672.   Be still and know that I am God

Ps 46:10

Meditatively

John L. Bell
Graham Maule

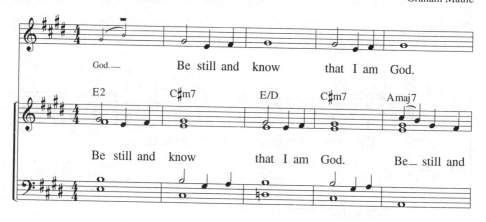

Trust in Him at all times, O people; pour out your hearts to Him, for God is our refuge.;

PSALM 62:8

673.

Blessèd be the name of the Lord
(The name of the Lord)

Neh 9:5; Job 1:21;
Prov 18:10

Capo 3 (D)

Clinton Utterbach

1. Bles-sèd be the name of the Lord,_____ bles-sèd be the name of the Lord._

_____ Bles-sèd be the name of the Lord_____ most_ high!_

_____ most_ high!_____

The name of the Lord_____ is_____ a strong tow-

The righteous run into it and they are saved. The name of the Lord and they are saved.

2. Glory to the name of the Lord,
   Glory to the name of the Lord.
   Glory to the name of the Lord,
   Most High.

   (Repeat)

3. Holy is the name of the Lord,
   Holy is the name of the Lord,
   Holy is the name of the Lord,
   Most High.
   (Repeat)

674.

Blessèd Jesus

Jn 4:14; Rev 5:12

Joey Holder

With a steady rhythm

1. Bles-sèd Je-sus, come to me, soothe my soul with songs of__ peace.

As I look to You a - lone, fill me with Your love.

Chorus

Glo - ri-ous, mar- vell-ous grace that res - cued____ me;

ho - ly, wor - thy is the Lamb who died for me.

2. Mountains high and valleys low,
You will never let me go;
By Your fountain let me drink,
Fill my thirsty soul.

Dear friends, let us love one another, for love comes from God. Everyone who loves has been born of God and knows God.

1 JOHN 4:7

675.

Blessing and honour
(Ancient of Days)

Is 9:7; Dan 6:26; 7:9; Lk 1:3
Phil 2:10-11; Rev 4:9; 5:12

Gary Sadler & Jamie Harvill

Bright & rhythmic

Verse Bless-ing and hon-our, glo-ry and pow-er be un-to the An-cient of Days; from ev-'ry na-tion, all of cre-a-tion bow be-fore the An-cient of Days.

Chorus Ev-'ry tongue in heav-en and earth shall de-clare Your glo-ry,

676.
Bless the Lord, my soul

Ps 103: 1;3-4;8;10;13-14

Jacques Berthier

Bless the Lord, my soul, and bless God's ho-ly name. Bless the Lord, my soul, who leads me in - to life.

1. It is God who for-gives all your guilt, who heals ev-'ry one of your ills, who re-deems your life from the grave, who crowns you with love and com - pas-sion.

2. The Lord is com - pas - sion and love, the Lord is pa-tient and rich in mer - cy. God does not treat us ac - cord - ing to our sins, nor re-pay us ac-cord-ing to our faults.

3. As a fa-ther has com-pas-sion on his child - ren, the Lord has mer-cy on those who re - vere Him;— for God knows of what we are made, and re - mem - bers that we are dust.

677.

Breathe on me

Jn 20:22

Tina Pownall

2. Fill me again, Spirit of Jesus.
   Fill me again, Holy Spirit of God.

3. Change my heart, Spirit of Jesus.
   Change my heart, Holy Spirit of God.

4. Bring peace to the world, Spirit of Jesus.
   Bring peace to the world, Holy Spirit of God.

678.

Breathe on me, breath of God

Gen 2:7; Job 3:4
Is 42:5; Ezek 37:5; Jn 20:22

Edwin Hatch 1835-89)
Adaptd. David Fellingham

Gently

1. Breathe on me, breath of God, and fill my life a - new;_____ that I may love as You love, and do the works_ that You_ do._____ _ Ho-ly Spi-rit,_ breathe on_____ me._____

And let__ ev - 'ry part__ of me__

glow with fire__ di- vine;__ with pas-sion in__ my life,__ Je-sus

let Your glo - ry shine.__ (And)

2. Breathe on me, breath of God,
   Until my heart is pure;
   Until my will is one with Yours
   Let holiness and love endure.
   Holy Spirit, breathe on me.

679.

Capo 1 (A)

With feeling

Burn it deep

Jn 2:17; 1 Cor 3:13

Kent & Carla Henry

Chorus

Burn it deep_ with-in my_ soul,_ new_ strength and fi - re, O Lord.

_ Burn it deep_ with-in my_ soul,_ new_ zeal and fi - re, O Lord._ Burn it deep_ with-in my_ soul,_ new strength and fi - re, it makes me whole._ Burn it deep,_ deep with-in_ my soul.

(Fine)

680.

By Your blood

Ps 27: 4; Heb 4:16; 10:19

David Fellingham

1. By Your blood I can en-ter the ho-li-est place, to the throne of my Fa-ther and King. There I find Your ac-cep-tance,— mer-cy and grace, and my life is re-newed a-gain. 2. Far a-You. I see the King up-on the throne, Je-sus, full of ma-jes-ty. I will fall down at Your

Last time to Coda

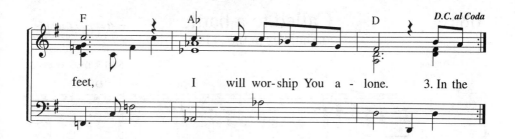

feet,   I   will wor-ship You a - lone.   3. In the

for,   You're the   one   my heart longs   for.

2. Far away from the stress and the turmoil of life,
   I now come to seek Your face.
   In the house of the Lord where Your presence is found,
   I now come to worship You.

3. In the light of Your presence I find deepest joy,
   There is no other place I would be.
   To behold Your beauty is all my desire,
   You're the one my heart longs for,
   You're the one my heart longs for.

681.

Called to a battle
(Thunder in the skies)

Mt 28:19; 1 Cor 15:54;
Eph 6:12; Rev 12:10-11

Noel & Tricia Richards

Driving
Verse

1. Called to a bat - tle, heav - en-ly war; though— — we may strug - gle,— vic-tor-y— is sure.— Death will not tri - umph,— though— —we may die; Je - sus has prom - ised— our e - ter - nal life.

Chorus

By the

2. Standing together, moving as one;
   We are God's army, called to overcome.
   We are commissioned, Jesus says go;
   In every nation, let His love be known.

682.
Can a nation be changed?

With awe

Matt Redman

1. Can a na-tion be changed?___ Can a na-tion be saved?___

Can a na-tion be turned___ back to You?___

We're on our knees,___ we're on our

knees a-gain.___ We're on our knees,___ we're on our

knees___ a - gain.

D.C. to verse 2.

To end

2. Let this nation be changed,
   Let this nation be saved,
   Let this nation be turned back to You.
   (Repeat)

At the name of Jesus every knee should bow, in heaven and on earth and under the earth, and every tongue confess that Jesus Christ is Lord, to the glory of God the Father.

PHILIPPIANS 2:10-11

683.

Can I ascend?
(I'm coming up the mountain)

Ex 3:5; 24:15; Ps 24:3-4

Matt Redman

Can I as-cend___ the hill of the Lord?___ Can I stand in that

ho - ly place?___ There to ap-proach___ the glo-ry of my

God; come to-wards_ to seek Your face.__ Pu-ri-fy_ my heart,__

__ and pu-ri-fy_my hands,___ for I know_it is_

__ on ho-lyground_I'll__ stand.___ I'm com-ing up the
I'm long-ing for Your

684.

Catch the fire
(Hear the beat of my heart)

Song 4:9; Is 40:31; Lk 15:4,20

Chris Bowater

Shep-herd, search-ing for the one that's lost; as the

Sa-viour, weep-ing for the world. Hear the

685.

Christ's is the world
(A touching place)

Tune: DREAM ANGUS

Scottish trad.

Rom 12:15

Tenderly

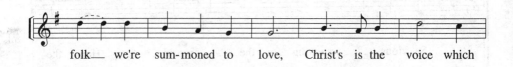

1. Christ's is the world in which we move, Christ's are the

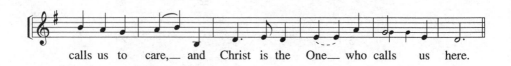

folk— we're sum-moned to love, Christ's is the voice which

calls us to care,— and Christ is the One— who calls us here.

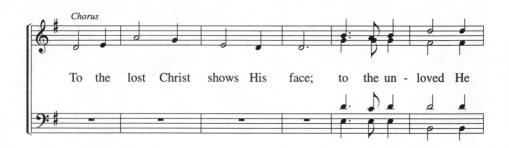

To the lost Christ shows His face; to the un - loved He

gives His em - brace: to those who cry in pain or dis-

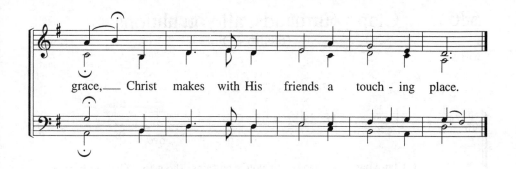

grace,— Christ makes with His friends a touch - ing place.

2. Feel for the people we most avoid,
   Strange or bereaved or never employed;
   Feel for the women, and feel for the men
   Who fear that their living is all in vain.

3. Feel for the parents who've lost their child,
   Feel for the women whom men have defiled,
   Feel for the baby for whom there's no breast,
   And feel for the weary who find no rest.

4. Feel for the lives by life confused,
   Riddled with doubt, in loving abused;
   Feel for the lonely heart, conscious of sin,
   Which longs to be pure but fears to begin.

John L. Bell and Graham Maule

686. Clap your hands, all you nations
(Psalm 47)

Ian White

Joyfully

1. Clap your hands, all you na-tions, shout to God with cries of

joy, O how awe-some is— the Lord most high, the

King ov-er all the earth! 2. He sub- Sing

praise to God,— sing prais-es to the King,— sing prais-es to the King.—

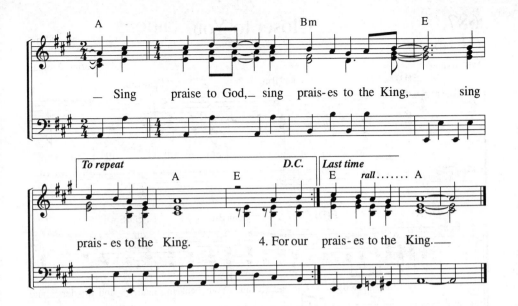

2. He subdued nations under us,
   The peoples under our feet,
   And He chose our inheritance for us,
   The pride of Jacob, whom He loved.

3. Now our God has ascended
   In the midst of shouts of joy,
   And the Lord is in among the trumpet sound,
   Among the trumpet sound.

   Sing praise to God,
   Sing praises to the King,
   Sing praises to the King.
   (Repeat)

4. For our God is King of all the earth,
   Sing Him a psalm of praise,
   For He rules above the nations on His throne,
   On His holy throne.

5. All the people are gathered
   Of the God of Abraham,
   For the kings of all the earth belong to God,
   And He is lifted high!

687.

Closer to You

Capo 2 (D)

Jas 4:7

With feeling

Patricia Morgan

Clo-ser to You,— Lord and clo-ser still,— till I am whol-ly in Your will.— Clo-ser to hear Your beat-ing heart,— and un-der-stand what You im-part.— O Breath of Life, come pu-ri-fy this heart of mine and sa-tis-fy.— My deep de-sire is to wor-ship You, Lord of my life,— come clo-ser still.—

688.   Come and join the celebration

Mt 1:23; 2:2,11;
Lk 2:16

Moderately

Valerie Collison

Come and join the ce‑le‑bra‑tion, it's a ve‑ry spe‑cial day; come and share our ju‑bi‑la‑tion, there's a new King born to‑day!

1. See the shep‑herds hur‑ry down to Beth‑le‑hem; gaze in won‑der at the Son of God who lay be‑fore them.

2. Wise men journey, led to worship by a star,
   Kneel in homage, bringing precious gifts from lands afar, so -

3. God is with us, 'round the world the message bring;
   He is with us, 'Welcome!' all the bells on earth are pealing.

689.

Come, Holy Spirit

Loralee Thiessen

Come, Ho - ly Spi - rit,___ come, Ho - ly Spi - rit,___ come to___ this place,___
Come, sof - ten our___ hearts,___ come, sof - ten our___ hearts,___ that we may___ o - bey,___

we will___ em - brace___ Your pre - sence.___
teach us___ Your way,___ come lead us.___

Come, Ho - ly Spi - rit.___

Come, Ho - ly Spi - rit.___

Bring an offering and come
before Him: worship the Lord in the
splendour of His holiness.

1 CHRONICLES 16:29

690.

Come into the heavenlies

Rev 5:12

Capo 3 (D)

Billy Funk

Building, with strength

Come in-to the heav-en-lies and sing the song the an-gels sing, Wor - thy, wor - thy. wor - thy. Wor - thy is the Lamb. Wor - thy is the Lamb.

691. Come, let us return

Deut 11:13-14; Jas 5:7

Capo 2(A)

Thoughtfully

Kevin Prosch

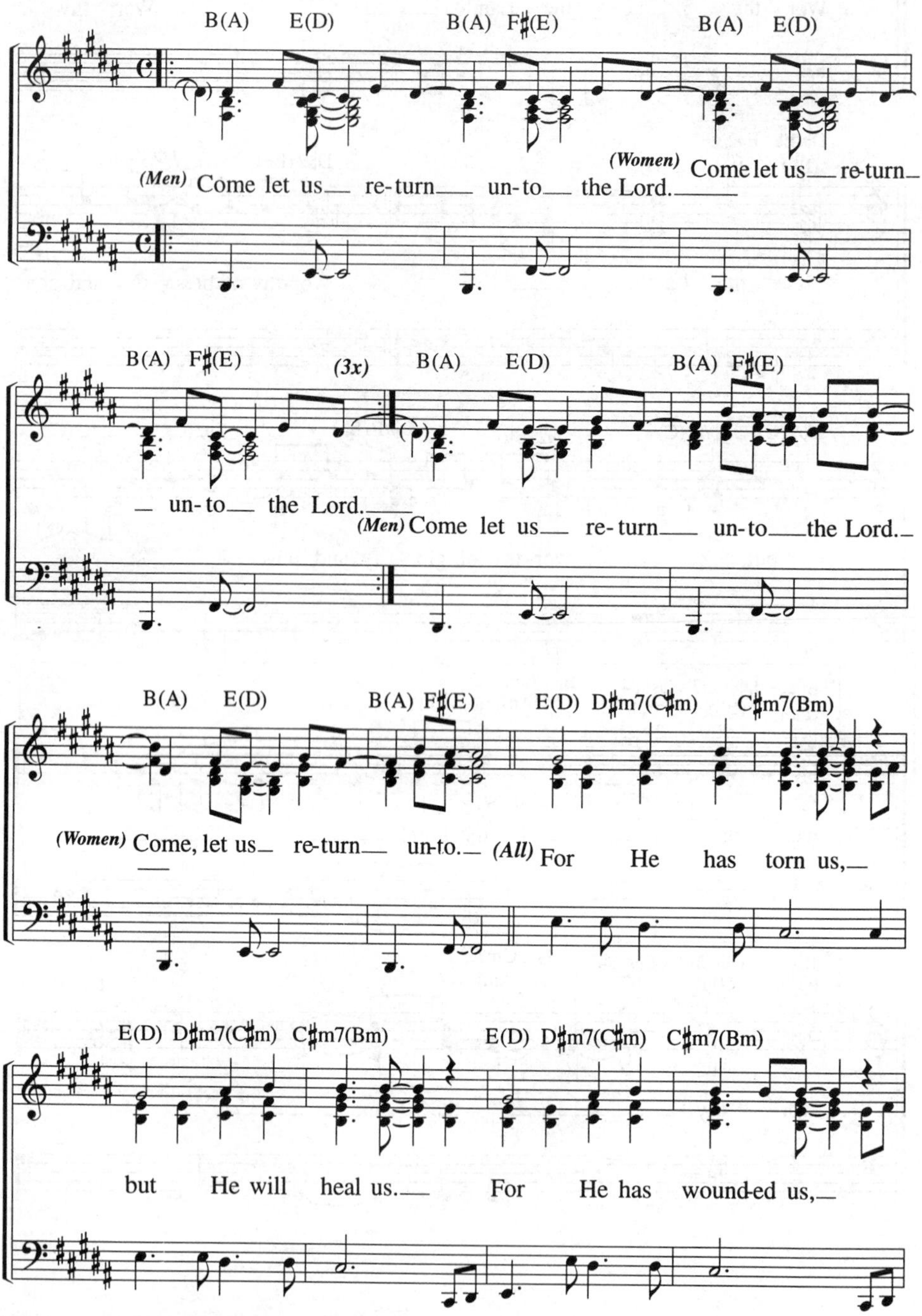

B(A) E(D) B(A) F♯(E) B(A) E(D)
(Men) Come let us re-turn un-to the Lord.
(Women) Come let us re-turn
B(A) F♯(E) (3x) B(A) E(D) B(A) F♯(E)
un-to the Lord.
(Men) Come let us re-turn un-to the Lord.
B(A) E(D) B(A) F♯(E) E(D) D♯m7(C♯m) C♯m7(Bm)
(Women) Come, let us re-turn un-to. (All) For He has torn us,
E(D) D♯m7(C♯m) C♯m7(Bm) E(D) D♯m7(C♯m) C♯m7(Bm)
but He will heal us. For He has wound-ed us,

692.
Come, let us worship Jesus
(King of the nations)

Rev 15:4,8

Graham Kendrick

With strength

1. Come, let us wor-ship Je - sus, King of na - tions,

Lord of_ all. Mag - ni - fi - cent and glor-i-ous, just and mer-ci-

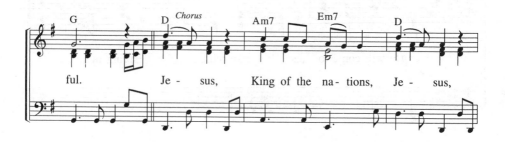

ful. Je - sus, King of the na-tions, Je - sus,

Lord of_ all. Je - sus, King of the na - tions, Lord of__

all. Lord of— all. 5. Fear God and give Him glo- ry, for His hour— of judge-ment— comes. Cre - a- tor, Lord Al - migh - ty, wor - ship Him a - lone.

2. Lavish our hearts' affection,
Deepest love and highest praise.
Voice, race and language blending,
All the world amazed.

3. Bring tributes from the nations,
Come in joyful cavalcades,
One thunderous acclamation,
One banner raised.

4. Come, Lord, and fill Your temple,
Glorify Your dwelling place,
'Till nations see Your splendour
And seek Your face.

5. Fear God and give Him glory,
For His hour of judgement comes.
Creator, Lord Almighty,
Worship Him alone.

693.   Come, my soul, and praise the Lord.

Mt 10:31; Lk 12:7

Flowing

John Pantry

2. *(Men)* Holy, holy is the Lord, *(Women echo)*
   (Men) Who may stand before His word? *(Women echo)*
   (Men) He knows my life so well, *(Women echo)*
   (Men) Yet loves me still. *(Women echo)*

694.
Come out of darkness

Joel 2:32; Mt 9:37; 13:39;
Rom 10:13; Acts 2:21 1 Pet 2:9;
1 Jn 1:7; Rev 7:14

Noel Richards & Doug Horley

Steady rock rhythm

Come out of dark-ness in-to the light; come out of dark-ness in-to the light. Come out of dark-ness in-to the arms of love,

Last time to Coda

in-to the arms of love. 1. To a world in dark-ness, to a world in pain, at this time You've called us, Your love to pro-claim; through Your wil-ling peo-ple

2. Do not be discouraged, see what God has done;
   He is working through us, this world shall be won.
   There will be a harvest when the nations hear.
   What are they going to hear?

695.

Capo 1 (Em)

Come to the power
(A mighty fortress)

Ps 48:3; Is 40:22; Phil 2:9

Richard Lewis

Rhythmic, with a reggae feel in chorus

Come to the pow-er,— the pow-er of the liv-ing God;—

His name is high-er,— high-er than an-y oth-er name.—

Migh-ty Je-ho-vah,— awe-some De-li-ver-er;—

His pow'r is great-er,— great-er than a-ny prin-ci-pa-li-ty.

A migh-ty for-tress is our God,

696. Confidence, we have confidence

Heb 4:16

Gently, building in strength

Chris Bowater

Con - fi - dence,___ we have con - fi - dence___ to come,___ to ask___ for mer - cy.___ Mer - ci - ful God, we cry: "Don't pass us by."___ Mer - ci - ful God, we pray: "Don't turn a - way;"___ in Your love___ re - mem - ber mer - cy. In Your love___ re - mem - ber mer - cy.

This is how we know what love is: Jesus Christ laid down His life for us.

1 JOHN 3:16

697.

Day by day
(I am carried)

Deut 33:27; Ps 23 :2; Is 43:19; Eph 2:9

Gently

Geoff Bullock

Verse

1. Day by day and hour by hour, Your love for me from hea-ven flows; like

streams of wa-ter in the de-sert, liv-ing wa-ters flow._____ You

walk be-side me, gent-ly guid-ing, lead-ing me through ev-'ry storm.

Ev-er-las-ting, ne-ver chang-ing grace and love di-vine.

-vine.   I am car-ried

2. Mercy's healing grace, relieving
   Every spot and every stain.
   Forgiven freely, no more guilty,
   Love has conquered shame.
   The broken mended, night has ended,
   Lost and lonely lost no more;
   For I am carried in the arms of
   Grace and love divine.

3. Never worthy, never earning,
   All my works now left behind.
   Ever onwards, ever upwards,
   You've called me on to rise
   Above my darkness, all my failure,
   Every fear and every pain.
   Always carried, always covered by
   Grace and love divine.

698.

Day of favour

Lev 25:10; Ps 23:5; Is 61:1-2
Mt 10:19-20; Mk 13:11; Lk 12:11-12
2 Cor 6:2; Rev 20:1

David Fellingham

Rhythmically

1. Day of fa - vour, day of grace; this is the day of ju - bi - lee.

The Spi - rit of the sov - 'reign Lord

is fal - ling now on me.

Let the oil from heav - en flow from the pre - sence of the

King. Je - sus, let Your pow - er flow

G   A   D   C/D   D

as we wor-ship, as we sing.   Set us free to make— You

G   D   C/D

known   to a world that's full of   shame.

D   A   G   A

Je-sus, let— Your glo-ry fall,   give us pow'r to speak Your

D   C/D   G/D   D   *2nd time D.C.*   **Last time**

(name.)

2. Day of favour, day of grace,
   This is the day of jubilee.
   The Spirit of the sovereign Lord
   Is falling now on me.
   Open wide the prison doors,
   Where satan's held the key.
   Bring deliverence to the bound,
   And set the captives free.
   Bring the good news to the poor,
   And cause the blind to see.
   The Spirit of the Lord
   Is falling now on me.

699. Days of heaven
(Lord, send the rain)

Lev 26:4; Deut 11:14; 28:12
2 Chron 6:27; Acts 4:31; Eph 6:17

David Fellingham

Quite slowly

Days_ of hea-ven here on the earth;
By_ Your word, and by Your Spi-rit

touched____ by pow-er, touched by love.
You send Your bless-ing here on us.

Lord, send the rain, let Your Spi-rit come and glo-ri-fy Je-sus.

Lord, send the rain, let Your Spi-rit come like a pent up flood,

driv-en by the breath of God.

2. We bring our worship, we see Your face;
We stand in wonder of Your grace.
Your kingdom presence, Your majesty;
Jesus, You're here now, hear our plea.

700. Did you feel the mountains tremble?

Lev 25:10; Ps 24:7,9; Is 40:3;
Mt 3:3; Mk 1:3; Lk 3:4; Rev 14:2;19:1,16

With anticipation

Martin Smith

1. Did you feel the mountains tremble?__ Did you hear the
   Did you feel the people tremble?__ Did you hear the

o-ceans roar, when the peo-ple rose to sing of__
sin-gers roar, when the lost be-gan to sing of__

Je-sus Christ, the ri-sen One?__
Je-sus Christ, the sav-ing One?__

Bridge

And we can see that God, You're mov-

2. Do you feel the darkness tremble,
When all the saints join in one song,
And all the streams flow as one river,
To wash away our brokeness?

701.

Capo 2 (G)

Don't be lazy

Heb 6:12

With pace

Ian Smale

Don't be la - zy, la - zy, la - zy, la - zy, but co - py those— who through faith and pa - tience re - ceive what God has pro - mised.

*Worship the Lord your God,
and serve Him only..*

MATTHEW 4:10

702.

Don't let my love grow cold
(Light the fire again)

Ps 139:23; Rev 3:18; 7:9

Capo 3 (D)

Strong & rhythmic

Brian Doerksen

Don't let__ my love__ grow cold;__ I'm call-ing out,__
You know_ my heart,__ my deeds;__ I'm call-ing out,__

"light the fire_ a-gain."___ Don't let__ my vi - sion die;__ I'm
"light the fire_ a-gain."___ I need_ Your dis - ci-pline;__ I'm

call - ing out,_____ "light the fire__ a-gain."__
call - ing out,_____ "light the fire__ a-gain."

I am here to buy gold,__

703.

Down the mountain the river flows
(The river is here)

Ps 46:4
Is 2:3; Rev 22:1

With joy

Andy Park

Fine

1. Down the moun-tain the ri-ver flows, and it brings re-fresh-ing wher-ev-er it goes. Through the val-leys and ov-er the fields, the ri-ver is rush-ing and the ri-ver is here. The ri-ver of God sets our feet a-dan-cing, the ri-ver of God fills our heart with cheer; the

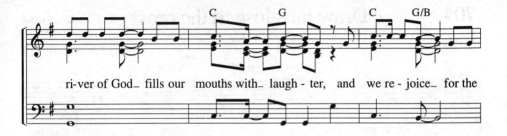

ri-ver of God_ fills our mouths with_ laugh - ter, and we re - joice_ for the

ri- ver is here.__

2. The river of God is teeming with life,
   And all who touch it can be revived.
   And those who linger on this river's shore
   Will come back thirsting for more of the Lord.

3. Up to the mountain we love to go
   To find the presence of the Lord.
   Along the banks of the river we run,
   We dance with laughter, giving praise to the Son.

704.
Draw me close to the cross

Jn 6:44; 19:34;
Rev 4:10; 22:1

Geoff & Judith Roberts

Meditatively

Draw me close to the cross, to the place of Your love, to the

place where You poured out Your mer - cy; where the

ri - ver of life that flows from Your wound - ed side brings re -

fresh-ing to those who draw near. Draw me close to Your

throne, where Your ma - jes - ty is shown, where the crown of my

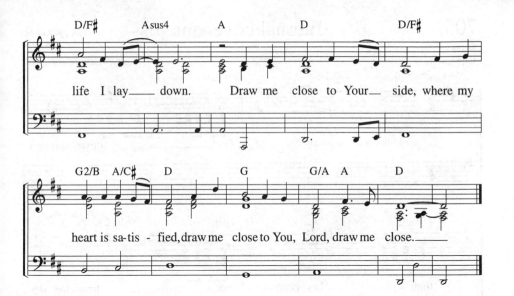

705.

Eternal covenant

Capo 3 (Em)

Eph 1:6-7,12,14;
Col 1:14; Heb 13:20

David Fellingham

With movement

E-ter-nal cov-en-ant of God down through time has been de-clared; draw-ing the heart of man in-to re-demp-tion's plan, mer-cy and grace re-vealed, by the blood and Spi-rit sealed. All our sins have been for - giv'n,

706.

Faithful and true

Ps 23:4; Rom 8:39
Heb 13:5,8; Rev 15:3; 19:11

Dave Bilbrough

Steadily

Faith - ful and true___ are all Your ways;___
Al - ways the same___ You ne - ver change;___

___ Your love for me___ will ne - ver fade a - way.___

___ ___ E - ven in my hour of deep-est need,___

___ You are al - ways there to walk with me.___

You know my words be-fore___ I speak;

Lord, I know that You will ne-ver for-sake___ me.

✛ *Coda*

___ ne-ver fade a - way.

707.

Faithful God

Ps 36:5

Capo 3(D)

Chris Bowater

Worshipfully and unhurried

Faith-ful God,_____ faith-ful God,_____

_ all suf-fi-cient One, I wor-ship You._____

_ Sha-lom my peace,_____ my strong De-liv-er-

er, I lift You up, faith-ful God._____

The twenty-four elders and the four living creatures fell down and worshipped God, who was seated on the throne. And they cried: "Amen, Hallelujah!"

REVELATION 19:4

708. Far above all other loves

1 Jn 2:28

David Fellingham

With strength

1. Far a-bove all oth-er loves,___ far be-yond all oth-er joys,___ hea-ven's bles-sings poured on me,___ by the Ho-ly Spi-rit's pow'r.___

Love's com-pel-ling pow-er draws my heart in-to Yours;___ Je-sus, how___ I love You, You're my Friend and my Lord.___ You have died___ and ri-sen so what

else can I say?— How I love You, Lord,

love You, Lord.

2. All ambition now has gone,
   Pleasing You my only goal;
   Motivated by Your grace,
   Living for eternity.

3. Looking with the eye of faith
   For the day of Your return;
   In that day I want to stand
   Unashamed before Your throne.

709.

Far and near
(Say it loud)

*1 Chron 16:24,28,31-33;
Ps 96:3,7,11,13; Ps 97:1*

Resolutely, with a gospel feel

Graham Kendrick

1. Far and near hear the call, wor-ship Him, Lord of
2. Deep and wide is the love hea-ven sent from a-

all; fa-mi-lies of na-tions come, ce-le-
bove; God's own Son for sin-ners died, rose a-

brate what God has done. Say it loud, say it
gain, He is a-live.

strong, tell the world what God has

done; say it loud, praise His

3. At His name let praise begin,
Oceans roar, nature sing.
For He comes to judge the earth
In righteousness and in His truth.

710.

Father God

Dave Bilbrough

Worshipfully

1. Father God, fill this place with Your love, with Your grace. As we call on Your name, visit us in pow'r again. Lord, we worship You. Lord, we worship You.

2. Spirit come with Your peace;
Heal our wounds, bring release.
Lord we long for Your touch,
Fill our hearts with Your love.

To Him who is able to keep you from falling and to present you before His glorious presence without fault and with great joy – to the only God our Saviour be glory, majesty, power and authority, through Jesus Christ our Lord, before all ages, now and for evermore! Amen.

JUDE: 24-25

711.

Father, I come to You
(Unending love)

Rom 5:2

Capo 2 (D)

John Barnett

Gently

1. Fa-ther, I come to_ You, lift-ing up my_ hands

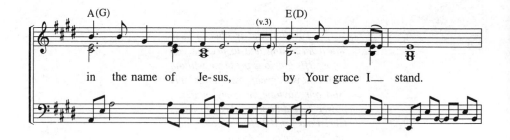

in the name of Je-sus, by Your grace I_ stand.

Just be-cause_You love_ me and I love Your_

Son, I know_ Your fa-vour, un-end-ing_

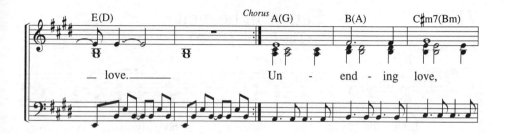

2. I receive Your favour, Your unending love,
   Not because I've earned it, not for what I've done;
   Just because You love me and I love Your Son,
   I know Your favour, unending love.

3. It's the presence of Your kingdom as Your glory fills this place,
   And I see how much You love me as I look into Your face.
   Nothing could be better, there's nothing I would trade
   For Your favour, unending love.

712.

Father in heaven
(The Lord's prayer)

Mt 6:9-13; Lk 11:2-4

Jim Bailey

With a latin feel

1. Fa - ther in hea - ven, ho - ly is Your name. Your king - dom come, Your will be done, let it be the same. On earth as it is in hea - ven, on earth as it is in hea - ven. On

3. For Yours is___ the king - dom, the
pow-er and___ the glo - ry, for - ev-er___ and ev - er and
ev - er___ a - men.___ For ___

2. Give us today all our daily bread;
   As we forgive our debtors,
   So You forgive our debts.
   (Repeat)
   And lead us not into temptation;
   Deliver us from evil.
   (Repeat)

713.
Father, like rain from the skies
(Come and satisfy)

Ex 16:4; Deut 11:14
Ps 119:105; Is 55 :2

Gently

Paul McWilliams & William Thompson

1. Fa-ther, like rain from the skies, send Your word in-to our
2. When will our hearts un-der-stand, You have our lives in Your

lives. We cry out: "Show us Your way,
hand? We cry out: "Come to us, Lord,

come to us, Fa-ther, we pray." Come and sa-tis-fy,—
guide us we pray with Your word."

Chorus

come and sa-tis-fy— my soul.— Come and sa-tis-fy,—

come and sa-tis-fy— my soul— and make— me whole.—

D.C.

I am the Alpha and Omega, the Beginning and the End. To him who is thirsty I will give to drink without cost from the spring of the water of life.

REVELATION 21:6

714.

Father of creation
(Let Your glory fall)

Mt 6:10; Lk 11:12
Rom 8:19; 2 Cor 2:14

David Ruis

With strength

Verse

1. Fa-ther of cre-a - tion, un-fold Your sov - 'reign plan.
   All of cre-a-tion is long - ing for Your un-veil-ing of pow'r.

Raise up a cho - sen ge-ne-ra - - tion
Would You re - lease Your a - noint - ing;

that will march through the land.
O God, let this be the hour. Let Your

Chorus

glo-ry fall in this room, let it go forth from here to the

2. Ruler of the nations,
   The world has yet to see
   The full release of Your promise,
   The church in victory.
   Turn to us, Lord, and touch us,
   Make us strong in Your might.
   Overcome our weakness,
   That we could stand up and fight.

715.

Father, You have given
(Not to us)

Is 9:7; Mt 6:1; Rom 12:1;
2 Cor 4:6-7; 2 Cor 5:18-19
Eph 4:8; Heb 2:4 1 Pet 2:9

With feeling, building in strength

Robert Critchley

1. Fa - ther You_ have gi - ven_ pre-cious gifts_ from hea - ven, e-
- quip-ping us_ to serve_ You as You move up-on_ the earth.__ You've pre-
- pared us for_ this hour,__ and a - noin-ted us_ with pow - er for
hum-ble acts_ of right - eous-ness,_ we free-ly vo - lun-teer_ to do_ Your work._

Bridge

Am - bas-sa-dors_ of re-con-ci-li-a - tion,__

2. Father, You have chosen the weak and the broken,
   These ones are the vessels
   Through whom You command Your strength.
   We offer up our lives as living sacrifices,
   Fill us with Your Spirit now,
   And send us out to bring the harvest in.

   Ambassadors of reconciliation . . .

Therefore, there is now no condemnation for those who are in Christ Jesus.

ROMANS 8:1

716. Filled with compassion
(For all the people who live on the earth)

Lk 19:10; 1 Tim 1:15
Heb 12:2; Rev 5:9; 7:9

Noel & Tricia Richards

Gently

1. Filled with compassion for all creation, Jesus came

into a world that was lost. There was but one way

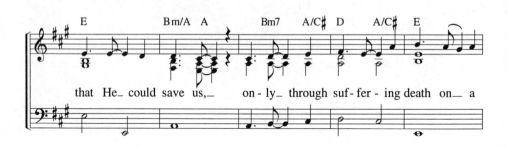

that He could save us, only through suffering death on a

cross. God, You are waiting, Your heart is

break-ing__ for all__ the__ peo-ple__ who live on__ the earth.

Stir us__ to__ ac-tion,__ filled with__ Your pas-sion__ for all__ the__

peo-ple__ who__ live on__ the earth.

To end

2. Great is Your passion for all the people
   Living and dying without knowing You.
   Having no Saviour, they're lost forever,
   If we don't speak out and lead them to You.

3. From every nation we shall be gathered,
   Millions redeemed shall be Jesus' reward.
   Then He will turn and say to His Father:
   "Truly my suffering was worth it all."

717.

Fill your hearts with joy

Tune: REGENT SQUARE

H T Smart (1813-79)

Capo 3 (G)

1. Fill your hearts with joy and glad-ness, sing and praise your God and mine! Great the Lord in love and wis-dom, might and ma-jes-ty di-vine! He who framed the star-ry hea-vens knows and names them as they shine.

2. Praise the Lord, His people, praise Him!
   Wounded souls His comfort know;
   Those who fear Him find His mercies,
   Peace for pain and joy for woe;
   Humble hearts are high exalted,
   Human pride and power laid low.

3. Praise the Lord for times and seasons,
   Cloud and sunshine, wind and rain;
   Spring to melt the snows of winter
   Till the waters flow again;
   Grass upon the mountain pastures,
   Golden valleys thick with grain.

4. Fill your hearts with joy and gladness,
   Peace and plenty crown your days;
   Love His laws, declare His judgements,
   Walk in all His words and ways;
   He the Lord and we His children –
   Praise the Lord, all people, praise!

Timothy Dudley-Smith

718.

Fire

Capo 3(D)

Jer 20:9; Acts 2:2-3; Rom 12:1

Paul Oakley

Fi-re, there's a fi-re, sweet fire burning in my heart.

Fi-re, there's a fi-re, sweet fire burning in my heart.

1. And I will run with all of the pas - sion You've put in me.
2. And I can feel the pow-er of Your hand up-on me.

I will spread the seed of the gos - pel ev-er-y-where.

Now I know I'll ne-ver be the same a-gain.

3. Let me feel Your tongues of fire resting upon me,
Let me hear the sound of Your mighty rushing wind.
Let my life be like an offering of worship,
Let me be a living sacrifice of praise.

719.

5000 + hungry folk

Mt 14:16-21; Mk 6:37-44;
Lk 9:13-17; Jn 6:5-13

Ian Smale

1. 5 0 0 0 + hun-gry folk,— 5 0 0 0 + hun-gry folk,— 5 0 0 0 + hun-gry folk came— 4 2 lis-ten 2 Je - sus.

1 2 3 4 5 6 7 8 9 10 11 12 bas-ket-fuls left ov-er.

2. The 6 x 2 said O O O,
The 6 x 2 said O O O,
The 6 x 2 said O O O,
Where can I get some food from?

3. Just 1 had 1 2 3 4 5,
Just 1 had 1 2 3 4 5,
Just 1 had 1 2 3 4 5
Loaves and 1 2 fishes.

4. When Jesus blessed the 5 + 2,
When Jesus blessed the 5 + 2,
When Jesus blessed the 5 + 2
They were increased many x over.

5. 5 0 0 0 + 8 it up,
5 0 0 0 + 8 it up,
5 0 0 0 + 8 it up,
With 1 2 3 4 5 6 7 8 9 10 11 12 basketfuls left over.

720.

Focus my eyes

Jn 4:23-24

Ian White

Gently

1. Fo-cus my eyes on You, O Lord, fo-cus my eyes on You; to

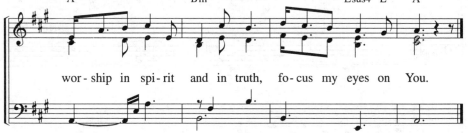

wor-ship in spi-rit and in truth, fo-cus my eyes on You.

2. Turn round my life to You, O Lord,
   Turn round my life to You;
   To know from this night You've made me new,
   Turn round my life to You.

3. Fill up my heart with praise, O Lord,
   Fill up my heart with praise;
   To speak of Your love in every place,
   Fill up my heart with praise.

721.
For the joys and for the sorrows
(For this I have Jesus)

Graham Kendrick

truth of what I am: for this I have
Je-sus, for this I have Je-sus, for this I have
Je-sus, I have Je-sus. For

2. For the tears that flow in secret,
In the broken times,
For the moments of elation,
Or the troubled mind;
For all the disappointments,
Or the sting of old regrets,
All my prayers and longings
That seem unanswered yet:

3. For the weakness of my body,
The burdens of each day,
For the nights of doubt and worry,
When sleep has fled away;
Needing reassurance,
And the will to start again,
A steely-eyed endurance,
The strength to fight and win:

722.

Friend of sinners

Joel 2:32; Mt11:19; Lk 7:34;
Acts 2:21; 4:12; Rom 10:13

Capo 2 (D)

Matt Redman

Gently

1. Friend of sin - ners, Lord of truth, I am fal - ling in— love with You. Friend of sin - ners, Lord of truth, I have fal - len in— love with You. Je - sus, I love— Your— name, the— name by which— we're— saved. Je - sus, I love— Your— name, the— name by which— we're— saved.

2. Friend of sinners, Lord of truth,
   I am giving my life to You.
   Friend of sinners, Lord of truth,
   I have given my life to You.

"You are worthy, our Lord and God, to receive glory and honour and power, for You created all things, and by Your will they were created and have their being."

REVELATION 4:11

723.

From every tongue
(We'll be set free)

Is 11:12; 26:8; 55:12
1 Thess 5:18; Rev 4:11; 5:12; 7:9

Wayne Drain

Rhythmically

1. From ev-'ry tongue, tribe and na-tion, shout-ed out from all cre-a-tion, all the earth sings forth Your praise. Ev-en the trees clap their hands, as the peo-ple of God take their stand, Je-sus Christ our ban-ner we raise. You're our God, our heart's de-

2. In every circumstance or situation
We give thanks and adoration,
Jesus Christ is worthy of praise.
Whenever our minds give in to fear and doubting,
Feeling alone or left out,
We lift our hands and we start to sing.

724.

From the sleep of ages
(Season of singing)

Ps 94:14; Song 1:3; 2:8-12; 3:2;
Mic 7:18; Acts 10:34; Rom 2:11;
1 Cor 12:9,28; 13:12; Eph 4:8; 6:9

Capo 2 (D)

Stuart Townend

With a half time feel

La la_ la la_ la la,— la la_ la la_ la la,— la la_ la la_
_ la la,— la la_ la la___ la la.___

Verse

1. From the sleep of a-ges,_ I am stirred by the kiss of love,
by the fra-grant per-fume_ when His name is men-tioned.
I have learned to wait for Him, to re-ceive His pre-sence_

2. There is no preferring
   In the Lover's loving;
   We are all His treasure,
   His desired inheritance.
   He has come with blessings
   From the Father's throne-room;
   Gifts of power and healing,
   For a needy people.
   The wonder, the pleasure
   Of knowing, of being known!

725.

From Your throne, O Lord

Lively

Chris Cartwright

1. From Your throne, O Lord, let Your fire fall upon us; let us feel the touch of the Spirit in our hearts, to equip us and empow'r us, send us out to heal the land, in Your name to shine the light of Christ.

2. From the Father's heart send us waves of Your compassion;
   Move us, Lord, to pray for Your will to come on earth.
   Interceding for a nation that is dying, lost and blind,
   Let us see them with the eyes of Christ.

3. Lord, we lift one voice in a song of joy and triumph;
   Let Your word rise up from our lips, that in our lives
   We will let the world know Jesus is the Victor and the King,
   Let our anthem ring throughout the land.

726.
Give me a heart of compassion
(Enable Your servants)

Mk 16:15; Acts 14:7; Rom 1:15,16; 2 Cor 1:3-4; Col 3:12

Driving, building with each verse

Jim Bailey

1. Give me a heart of compassion,
give me a hope for the lost.
Give me a passion for those who are broken and down.

Lord, I am ready and willing
to serve the weak and the young;
help me to put into action the words of this song.

Chorus
And enable Your servants, enable Your servants to preach good news,

to preach good news.___   And en -

2. I'll sing the songs of salvation,
   Boldly I'll speak out Your word.
   I'll let them know by my life,
   I will show You are Lord.
   I'll tell them all about Jesus,
   I'll tell them all about You;
   I'm not ashamed of the gospel
   Or what it can do.

3. We're moving forward together,
   As one voice boldly proclaim
   The old and the young will be strong,
   And we'll lift up Your name
   On to the streets to the people,
   Every man, woman and child,
   And as we go You are with us,
   You've given Your power.

   You've enabled Your servants . . .

727.   Give me, Lord, a dream from heaven

Capo 3 (D)

Eph 6:17; 2 Pet 3:12; Rev 21:2

Brightly

Dave Bilbrough

1. Give me, Lord, a dream from heav - en, let me
   set my face to serve You, to do the

see the things You see; give me pur-pose and di-rec-
things You'd have me do; stir with - in my heart a vi-

tion, Ho - ly Spi - rit, move on me. I would
sion, Lord, I will fol - low You.

Chorus

By Your Spi - rit and Your word, we would

hast - en   Your re - turn.

2. Give to me a holy passion,
   With every breath I will proclaim
   The message of Your kingdom,
   The glory of Your name.
   Lead me into action,
   Let me do the things You say;
   Send me to the nations,
   When You speak I will obey.

3. I believe that faith is rising,
   I can see a tidal wave
   Of Your Spirit that is moving
   To end this final age.
   There'll be shouts of acclamation
   When You come back for Your Bride;
   History's consummation
   Is here before our eyes.

728.
Give me oil in my lamp
(Sing hosanna)

Ps 18:28; Mt 25:4; 21:9;
Mk 11:9-10; Jn 12:13

Author unknown
Arr. Stuart Townend

Verse

1. Give me oil in my lamp, keep me burn-ing. Give me oil in my lamp, I pray. Give me oil in my lamp, keep me burn-ing, keep me burn-ing till the break of day.

Chorus

Sing ho - san - na, sing ho - san - na,

2. Give me joy in my heart, keep me praising . . .

3. Give me peace in my heart, keep me resting . . .

4. Give me love in my heart, keep me serving . . .

729. Give your thanks to the risen Son

Brightly

Dave Bilbrough

(Leader)
Give your thanks to the ris-en Son. (All) Give your thanks to the ris-en Son. To the (Leader)
Turn to Him, don't be a-fraid. Turn to Him, don't be a-fraid.

ho - ly and a - noin-ted one. (All) To the ho - ly and a - noin-ted one. (Leader) Who
Give Him hon-our, give Him praise. Give Him ho-nour, give Him praise.

fills our hearts_ with a joy-ful song._ Who (All) fills our hearts_ with a joy-ful song.__
Lift Him up_ to the high-est place._ Lift Him up__ to the high-est place.__

1.
(Leader) Je-sus. (All) Je-sus.

2.
Je-sus. Wor - ship

730.
God is great

Ps 104: 1-4, 19, 25-28

Capo 1 (G)

Graham Kendrick
& Steve Thompson

God is—great, a-maz-ing! Come, let His prais-es ring.

God is—great, a-stound-ing! The whole cre-a-tion sings.

sings.

sings.

1. His

Verse

cloth-ing is splen-dour and ma-jes-ty bright, for

He wraps Him-self in a gar-ment of light. He

spreads out   the   hea - vens, His   pa - lace   of   stars,   and

rides   on   the   wings   of   the   wind.

sings.

2. What marvellous wisdom the Maker displays,
   The sea vast and spacious, the dolphins and whales,
   The earth full of creatures, the great and the small,
   He watches and cares for them all.

3. The rain forest canopies darken the skies,
   Cathedrals of mist that resound with the choirs,
   Of creatures discordant, outrageous, ablaze
   In colourful pageants of praise.

4. Above His creation the Father presides:
   The pulse of the planets, the rhythm of tides,
   The moon makes the seasons, the day follows night,
   Yet He knows every beat of my heart.

5. Let cannons of thunder salute their acclaim,
   The sunsets fly glorious banners of flame,
   The angels shout 'holy' again and again
   As they soar in the arch of the heavens.

731.
God is raising up an army
(Children of the cross)

Joel 2 :28;
Acts 2:17-18,39; 1 Cor 1:27

With conviction

Jim Bailey

God is rais - ing up an ar - my made of those who are still young. God is lift - ing up their voi - ces, through the weak He'll shame the strong. It's been pro-phe-sied they will pro-phe-sy, God's sal - va - tion they will show; for the pro - mise is to the chil - dren, to our

732.

God is so good
(He's so good to me)

2 Cor 5:21; Heb 9:15

Author unknown
Arr. Stuart Townend

Brightly

God is so good, God is so good,
God is so good, He's so good to me.

2. He took my sin,
   He took my sin,
   He took my sin,
   He's so good to me.

3. Now I am free,
   Now I am free,
   Now I am free,
   He's so good to me.

4. God is so good,
   He took my sin,
   Now I am free,
   He's so good to me.

Let us then approach the throne of grace with confidence, so that we may receive mercy and find grace to help us in our time of need

HEBREWS 4:16

733.

God is so good

Ps 68:5; 104:3-4; Rom 1:20

Steadily, with awe

Kevin Prosch

(And) God_____ is so good._____

(And) God_____ is so good._____

1. 2. He rides____ up - on____ the wings____ of the
3. You reign____ on high____ in ma - jes-

wind, He is____ ex - alt - ed____ by His____ name Jah.____
ty, (and) the wi - dow's heart____ cau-ses____ to sing.____

He walks____ in the midst____ of the stones____ of fire,____
You hear____ the____ cry____ of the fa - ther-less,____

734.

God of heaven
(Heart of a lover)

Capo 2 (D)

Steadily

Deut 29:12; Song 2:16;
Is 49:15; 53:3; 66:13;
Rev 1:8; 17:14; 16:16

Stuart Townend

1. God of heav'n,— with the heart— of a lov-er;— conqu'-ring King,— with com-pas-sion in— His voice.. Sov'-reign Lord,— with the care of a mo-ther;— to You we bring— our—lives,— know-ing You will take— us— in.— So let's be pure and ho-

1st time to next verse
2nd time Chorus

2. Jesus Christ, You're the Alpha and Omega:
   King of kings, who laid aside His crown.
   Man of woes, but a Friend to the friendless:
   To You we bring our fears, knowing You will set us free.

735.

God, our God, blesses us

Ps 65:5-7

Rosie Fellingham

736.

God sent His Son
(Because He lives)

William J. Gaither

God sent His Son, they called Him Je-sus;
He came to love, heal, and for-give;
He lived and died to buy my par-don, an emp-ty
grave is there to prove my Sav - iour lives.

Chorus
Be - cause He lives I can face to - mor - row;

be-cause He lives _____ all fear is gone; _____ be-cause I know _____ He holds the fu-ture, _____ and life is worth the liv-ing just be-cause He lives. _____

2. How sweet to hold a new-born baby,
And feel the pride and joy he gives;
But greater still the calm assurance,
This child can face uncertain days because He lives.

3. And then one day I'll cross the river;
I'll fight life's final war with pain;
And then as death gives way to victory,
I'll see the lights of glory and I'll know He lives.

Gloria & William J Gaither

737.
God, You are an awesome God
(Awesome God)

Charlotte Exon
& Andy Thorpe

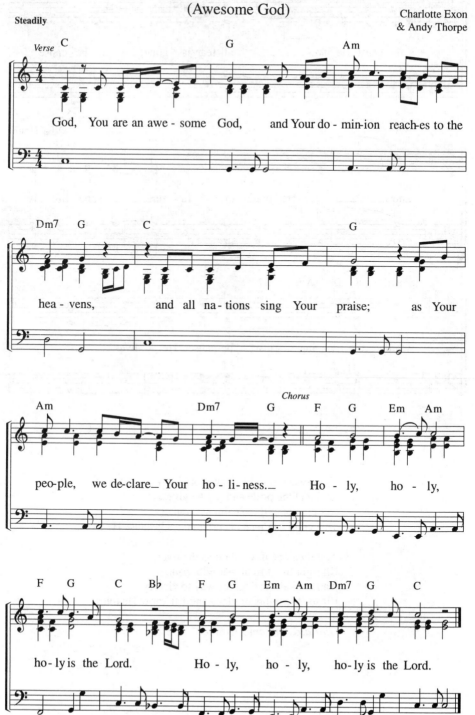

738.

Go forth and tell

Mt 28:19; Jn 12:46;
Rom 10: 13-15

Tune: GO FORTH
Capo 3 (D)

Michael Baughen

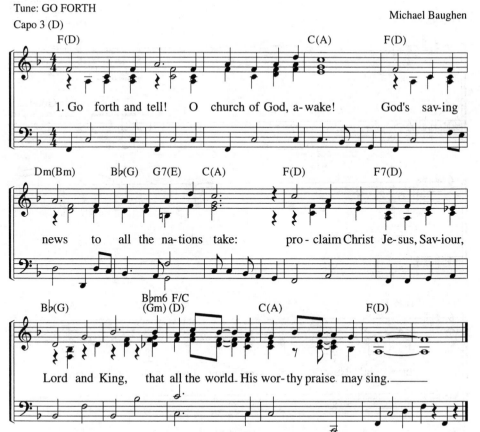

1. Go forth and tell! O church of God, a-wake! God's sav-ing news to all the na-tions take: pro-claim Christ Je-sus, Sav-iour, Lord and King, that all the world His wor-thy praise may sing.

2. Go forth and tell! God's love embraces all;
   He will in grace respond to all who call:
   How shall they call if they have never heard
   The gracious invitation of His word?

3. Go forth and tell where still the darkness lies,
   In wealth or want, the sinner surely dies:
   Give us, O Lord, concern of heart and mind,
   A love like Yours, compassionate and kind.

4. Go forth and tell! The doors are open wide:
   Share God's good gifts - let no one be denied;
   Live out your life as Christ your Lord shall choose,
   Your ransomed powers for His sole glory use.

5. Go forth and tell! O church of God, arise!
   Go in the strength which Christ your Lord supplies:
   Go till all nations His great name adore
   And serve Him, Lord and King forever more.

James E Seddon (1915-1983)

739. Good news, good news to you bring

Is 7:14; Mt 1:23;
Lk 2:10; Jn 3:16

Brightly, with strength

Graham Kendrick

1. Good news, good news to you we bring, al - le - lu - ia! News of great joy that an - gels sing, al - le - lu - ia! Tender mer-cy He has shown us, joy to all the world; for

us God sends His on-ly—Son, al - le - lu - ia!

2. Let earth's dark shadows fly away,
   Alleluia!
   In Christ has dawned an endless day,
   Alleluia!

3. Now God with us on earth resides,
   Alleluia!
   And heaven's door is open wide,
   Alleluia!

740.

Go to all nations

Mt 28:18-20; Rev 22:20

Joyfully

Bryn Haworth

Go to all nations, making disciples, baptising them in My name. Go to all nations, making disciples, baptising them in My name. I am coming soon. I am coming soon. I'm waiting at the gates for the Father's call. I am coming soon.

741. Great, great, brill, brill

Doug Horley

Oh, it's great, great, brill, brill, wick-ed, wick-ed, skill, skill, to have a friend like Je - sus.— Great, great, brill, brill, wick-ed, wick-ed, skill, skill, to have a friend like Him. Oh, it's Him. He's al-ways there, He al - ways listens,— He al - ways hears me when I talk to Him.— He loves me now and will for - ev-er,— I'll choose for Him ev-'ry day, day,— day.— Oh, it's

Look to the Lord and His strength; seek His face always.

1 CHRONICLES 16:11

742.
Great is the darkness
(Come, Lord Jesus)

Is 65:19; Joel 2:29; Mt 28:19;
Acts 2:18; 2 Pet 3:12; Rev 22:20

Growing in strength

Gerald Coates & Noel Richards

1. Great is_ the dark-ness_ that cov-ers_ the earth, op - pres-sion,_ in-jus-tice_ and pain. Na-tions_ are slip-ping_ in hope-less_ des-pair, though ma-ny_ have come in_ Your name. Watch-ing_ while sa-ni - ty dies, touched by_ the mad - ness_ and lies.___

Come, Lord Je-sus, come, Lord Je-sus, pour out— Your Spi-rit— we pray.

Come, Lord Je-sus, come, Lord Je-sus, pour out— Your Spi-rit on us to-day.

2. May now Your church rise with power and love,
   This glorious gospel proclaim.
   In every nation salvation will come
   To those who believe in Your name.
   Help us bring light to this world,
   That we might speed Your return.

3. Great celebrations on that final day
   When out of the heavens You come.
   Darkness will vanish, all sorrow will end,
   And rulers will bow at Your throne.
   Our great commission complete,
   Then face to face we shall meet.

743.

Great is the Lord

Eph 2:8-9

Rhythmically with an 'African' feel

David & Nathan Fellingham

Great_____ is the Lord;_____ Sov-'reign King,_____ we give You__ praise._____ 1. You spoke Your__ word and You res-cued__ me, You poured

2. And by the power of Jesus' name
   You have raised me up from my sin and shame.
   You've anointed me with the Spirit's power,
   And You've set my heart on fire.

3. By grace I'm saved through faith in God,
   Not by works alone but by Jesus' blood.
   Now I'm filled with strength by the Spirit's power,
   And You've set my heart on fire.

744.

Hallelujah! Jesus is alive

Capo 1 (D)

1 Cor 15:54-55; Gal 5:1;
Rev 1:8; 21:6; 22:13
Ron Kenoly

Hal-le-lu - jah!___ Je-sus is__ a - live,___ death has lost__ its vic - t'ry__ and the grave__ has been__ de - nied; Je - sus lives__ for - ev - er,__ He's a - live,___ He's a - live!___ He's the Al - pha and__ O - me- ga,__ the First and Last__ is He;__ the curse of sin__ is bro-

745.   Hands, hands, fingers, thumbs

Capo 3 (Em)

2 Sam 6:14; Ps 134:2

Lively

Doug Horley

Hands, hands, fin-gers, thumbs, we can lift to praise You.

Hands, hands, fin-gers, thumbs, we can lift to praise.

Hands, hands, fin-gers, thumbs, we can lift to praise You.

Jump front, jump back, yeah!_____ We were made to praise._

Last time to Coda

746.

Have you got an appetite?

Ps 34:8; Jn 6:57;
Heb 5:13-14

Mick Gisbey

Steadily

Verse

1. Have you got an ap-pe - tite? Do you eat what is right? Are you feed-ing on the word of God? Are you fat or are you thin? Are you real - ly full with-in? Do you find your strength in Him or are you star - ving?

Chorus

You and me all should be ex - er - cis - ing

re-gu-lar-ly, stand-ing strong all day long, giv-ing God the glo - ry. Feed-ing on the liv-ing Bread, not eat-ing crumbs but loaves in-stead; stand - ing strong - er, liv-ing long - er,

To repeat giv - ing God the glo - ry. **Last time** giv - ing God the glo - ry.

2. If it's milk or meat you need,
Why not have a slap-up feed,
And stop looking like a weed and start to grow?
Take the full of fitness food,
Taste and see that God is good,
Come on, feed on what you should and be healthy.

747.

Have you heard the good news?

Jn 1:5; 8:12; 12:46;
Rom 8:24-25; Titus 1:2;
Heb 6:19-20; 10:23; 1 Pet 1:3-4

Stuart Garrard

Have you___ heard the good___ news?___ Have you___ heard the good___ news?___ We can___ live___ in___ hope___ be-cause of___ what the___ Lord___ has___ done.___ Have you___

1. There is a___ way___ when there___ seems___
2. A hope for___ jus - tice

___ to___ be___ no___ way,___ there is a___ light___
and a___ hope___ for___ peace,___ a hope for___ those___

748.

Have You not said?
(Fill us up and send us out)

Is 43:1-2, 5-6, 10-12; Acts 1:8

Matt Redman

Rhythmically

1. Have You not said as we pass through water,
You will be with us? And You have said as we
walk through fire, we will not be burned.
We are not afraid, for You are with us; we will testify to the
honour of Your name. We are witnesses, You have shown us

Mid 8 *(optional)*

2. Bring them from the west, sons and daughters,
   Call them for Your praise.
   Gather from the east all Your children,
   Coming home again.
   Bring them from afar, all the nations,
   From the north and south,
   Drawing all the peoples in.
   Corners of the earth, come to see there's
   Only one Saviour and King.

749. Hear these praises from a grateful heart

(Love You so much)

Ps 84:11

Steadily

Russell Fragar

Hear these prais-es from a grate-ful heart,___
Lord, I love You,___ my soul sings,___

each time I think of You___ the prais-es start:___
in your pre-sence,_ car-ried on Your wings:{ love You

so much,_ Je-sus,_ love You so much.___

How my soul___ longs for You, longs to
hands,___ lift my heart, lift my

wor - ship You___ for ev - er in Your pow - er___ and
voice to - wards___ the hea- vens, for You are___ my

ma - jes - ty._____ Lift my shield.
sun and

750. He brought me to His banqueting table

(His banner over me)

Song of songs 2:4, 16; 6:3

With a steady rhythm

Kevin Prosch

The eyes of the Lord are on the righteous and His ears are attentive to their cry;

PSALM 34:15

751.

He has been given

Phil 2:9-10; Col 1:15-17

David Fellingham

With a steady rhythm

He has been giv-en a Name a-bove all names,— in earth and heav-en, let all cre-a-tion claim— that Je-sus Christ is King,— and Lord of all.— He is the Vic-tor ov-er sa-tan's reign,— His blood has tri-umphed ov-er sin and shame,— Je-sus Christ is King— and Lord of all.

752. He has clothed us with His righteousness
(We rejoice in the grace of God)

Steve & Vikki Cook

1. He has clothed us with His right-eous-ness, cov-ered us with His great love. He has show-ered us with mer-cy, and we de-light to know the glo-rious fa-vour, won-drous fa-vour of God.

2. He's brought us in-to His fa-mi-ly, made us heirs with His own Son. All good things He free-ly gives us, and we can-not con-ceive what God's pre-par-ing, God's pre-par-ing for us.

753.

He has risen

Ps 16:10; Mt 28:6; Mk 16:6
Lk 24:6; Acts 2:27
1 Cor 13 :12; 15:13-20; 1 Thess 4:16

Capo 2 (D)

Brightly

Gerald Coates,
Noel and Tricia Richards

He has— ri - sen, He has— ri - sen,

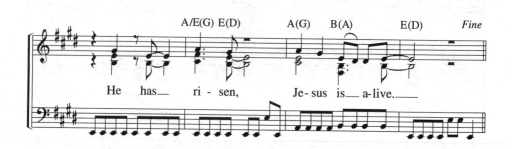

He has— ri - sen, Je - sus is— a-live.—

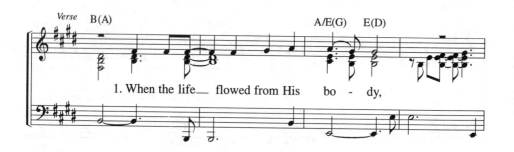

1. When the life— flowed from His bo - dy,

seemed like Je-sus' mis - sion failed.—

But His sa - cri - fice ac - com - plished,

vic - t'ry ov - er sin and hell.___

2. In the grave God did not leave Him,
   For His body to decay;
   Raised to life, the great awakening,
   Satan's power He overcame.

3. If there were no resurrection,
   We ourselves could not be raised;
   But the Son of God is living,
   So our hope is not in vain.

4. When the Lord rides out of heaven,
   Mighty angels at His side,
   They will sound the final trumpet,
   From the grave we shall arise.

5. He has given life immortal,
   We shall see Him face to face;
   Through eternity we'll praise Him,
   Christ, the Champion of our faith.

754.

He is lovely

Bob Fitts

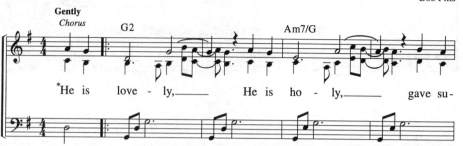

*He is love-ly,___ He is ho-ly,___ gave su-

preme-ly,___ that all men may see.___ He is gen-tle,___

— ten-der-heart-ed,___ ris-en Sav-iour,___ He is God.___

— Mas-ter, Ma-ker, Life__ Cre-a-tor, come and dwell__

(or "You are lovely")*

755.

He is the Lord

(Show Your power)

Gen 1:3; Ex 15:11; Is 43:13
Joel 2:32; Rom 10:13

Kevin Prosch

1. He is the Lord, and He reigns on high: He is the Lord. Spoke into the darkness, created the light. He is the Lord. Who is like unto Him, never ending in days? He is the Lord. And

2. Your gospel, O Lord, is the hope for our nation:
   You are the Lord.
   It's the power of God for our salvation:
   You are the Lord.
   We ask not for riches, but look to the cross:
   You are the Lord.
   And for our inheritance give us the lost:
   You are the Lord.

756.

He made the earth
(Our God)

Ps 8:3-5

Gill Broomhall

Brightly

1. He made the earth,_____ He made the sky,_____ He made the moon and stars, Ju-pi-ter and Mars. He made the sun_____ for ev-'ry- one, our God made them all._____ Our God is pow-er-ful,

2. He made the fish, He made the birds,
   Elephants and worms, creeping things that squirm.
   Mice so small, giraffes so tall;
   Our God made them all.
   Our God is wonderful, wonderful,
   Our God is great.
   Our God is wonderful, wonderful,
   Our God is great.

3. He made the boys, He made the girls,
   He made our mums and dads, to teach us good from bad.
   He cares for me, He cares for you;
   Our God loves us all.
   Our God is beautiful, beautiful,
   Our God is great.
   Our God is beautiful, beautiful,
   Our God is great.

757.
He picked me up
(I'm in love with the King)

Capo 2 (D)

Ps 40:2; Lk 15:6,9,24,32

Dave Bilbrough

Brightly

Chorus
He picked me up and He dus-ted me down, put my feet back on so-lid ground. He wel-comed me home and He caused me to sing, I'm in love, I'm in love with the King. He with the King.

Verse
1. For all my days I'll
2. Once I was lost, but

sing His praise, I'm so grate - ful.
now I'm found, yes, He saved me.

Yes,
He

I will - give my ev - 'ry - thing to the
called my name and my life was changed by the

One who sets me free. He
pow - er of His love.

758.

Here I am
(I will always love Your name)

Ps 107:14; 132:9; Is 61:10; Mt 26:42;
Jn 14:12; 15:13; 18:11; Rom 3:22;
2 Cor 5:21; Eph 2:8-9;
Phil 3:9; Rev 5:9

Rhythmically

Verse

Paul Oakley

1. Here I am,— and I have come— to thank You,— Lord,— for
   paid the price— at Cal-va-ry,— You shed Your— blood,— You

all You've done;_____ thank— You,
set me free;_____

Lord._____ You thank— You,

Lord._____ No great-er— love— was

e-ver— shown,— no bet-ter— life— e-ver was laid down._____

2. You took my sin, You took my shame,
   You drank my cup, You bore my pain;
   Thank You, Lord.
   You broke the curse, You broke the chains,
   In victory from death You rose again;
   Thank You, Lord.
   And not by works, but by Your grace
   You clothe me now in Your righteousness.

3. You bid me come, You make me whole,
   You give me peace, You restore my soul;
   Thank You, Lord.
   You fill me up, and when I'm full
   You give me more 'till I overflow;
   Thank You, Lord.
   You're making me to be like You,
   To do the works of the Father, too.

759.

Here I am once again
(Pour out my heart)

Ps 34:17; 69:33

Craig Musseau

Steadily

Here I am once a-gain, I pour out my heart for I know that You hear ev-'ry cry; You are lis-ten-ing, no mat-ter what state my heart is in. You are faith - ful to an-swer with words that are true and a hope that is real. As I feel Your touch, You bring a free - dom to

760.

He reigns

Mt 28:9; Mk 11:9; Lk10:18 Col 2:15

Capo 3 (D)

Rick Ridings

Driving

Chorus

He reigns, He reigns, Je-sus reigns,___ He reigns en-throned___ in ma-jes-ty.___ Shout your praise,___ His ban-ners raise,___ for

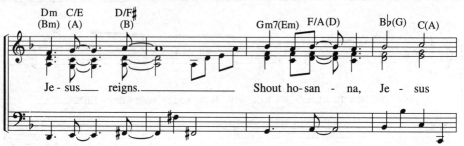

Je - sus___ reigns.___ Shout ho-san - na, Je - sus

reigns.___ 1. Our high-est praise___ we bring___

to our great e-ter - nal King._____ His glo-ry fills__ the skies,_

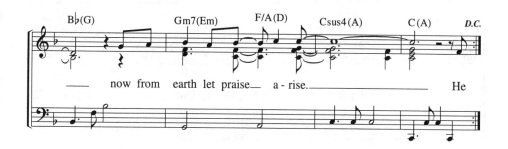

_____ now from earth let praise__ a - rise._____ He

2. He spoiled the hosts of hell,
   And like blazing stars, they fell.
   He led them forth in chains
   Now our mighty Victor reigns!

761.

Here in the presence
(I stand in the presence of the Lord)

1 Kings 19:11; Neh 1:5; Ps 47:2

Steadily

Chris Bowater

1. Here in the pre - sence of the great and awe - some God.

Here in the pre - sence of the Ho - ly One, the on - ly One.

Know-ing not how best to bring a-dor - ing love, to

bow, to weep, to fall, and yet You whis-per, "Child, draw near

and stand in the pre - sence of the Lord, and

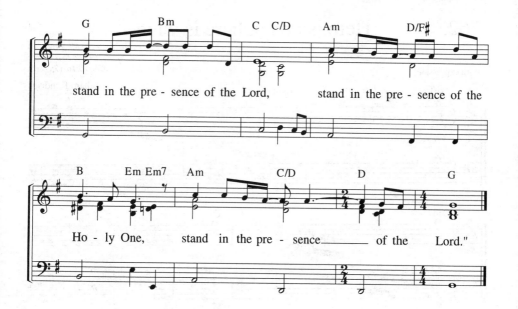

stand in the pre - sence of the Lord, stand in the pre - sence of the Ho - ly One, stand in the pre - sence_____ of the Lord."

2. Here in the presence of the great and awesome God,
   Majestic in His power yet full of grace:
   I seek His face.
   The passion in His eyes
   Searches deep inside:
   Such shining love intensifies,
   Yet melts away my fears.

762.

Here is bread, here is wine

Mt 26:26-27; Mk 14:22-23;
Lk 22:19-20; Jn 6:54-56;
1 Cor 10:16-17; 11:26

Graham Kendrick

With expression

In this bread there is heal - ing, in this cup there's life for - e - ver; in this mo - ment, by the Spi - rit Christ is with us here.

2. Here is grace, here is peace,
   Christ is with us – He is with us;
   Know His grace, find His peace –
   Feast on Jesus here.

3. Here we are, joined in one,
   Christ is with us – He is with us;
   We'll proclaim, till He comes –
   Jesus crucified.

763.

Here is the risen Son

Ezek 33:7; Phil 2:10-11
Rev 17:14; 19:16

Michael Sandeman

Strong and majestic

Here is the ri-sen Son___ rid-ing out in glo-ry,

ra-di-at-ing light all a-round.___ Here is the

Ho-ly Spi-rit, poured out for the na - tions,___ glo-ri-fy-ing

Je - sus___the Lamb.___ We will stand as a

1. (Fine) *2.3.*

peo - ple___ who are up-right and ho - ly, we will wor-ship___ the

764.

Here we are, Lord

(Dangerous people)

Esther 4:14; Phil 3:12,14
Heb 11:34,39;12:1

Gerald Coates,
Noel & Tricia Richards

Rhythmically

1. Here we are, Lord, more weak than strong; still be-lie-ving, still pres-sing on. Make us rea-dy with hearts that are brave. We will si-lence the lies of this age.

2. All God's heroes failed as we do,
   Sometimes doubting all that is true.
   Yet He calls us great people of faith,
   Working through us as history is made.

Peacemakers who sow in peace raise a harvest of righteousness.

JAMES 3:18

765. Here we stand in total surrender

Capo 2 (D)

With drive

2 Chron 7:14;
Joel 2:29; Acts 2 :18; Phil 1:6

Charlie Groves & Andy Piercy

1. Here we stand in to-tal sur - ren-der, lift-ing our voic - es, a-ban-doned to Your cause. Here we stand, pray-ing in the glo - ry of the one and on - ly Je - sus Christ, the Lord.

Chorus This time re - vi - val! Lord, come and heal our land; bring to com-

766.

His love

Ps 19:10; 107:9; 119:103;
Lk 6:21; Rom 8:38-39

David Ruis

Tenderly

1. His love___ is high-er than___ the high - est of moun-tains. His love goes deep-er than___ the deep - est of seas.___ His love,___ it stretch-es to___ the farth - est ho-ri - zon, and His___ love,_____ it reach-es to___

me.

3. His love is stronger than the angels and demons.
   His love, it keeps me in my life's darkest hour.
   His love secures me on the pathway to heaven,
   And His love is my strength and power.

3. His love is sweeter than the sweetest of honey.
   His love is better than the choicest of wine.
   His love, it satisfies the deepest of hunger,
   And His love, in Jesus it's mine.

4. Your love . . .

767.

Hold me closer to You
(May I never lose sight of You)

Tenderly

Noel & Tricia Richards

Hold me clos-er to You___ each day;___ may my love for You ne - ver fade.___ Keep my fo-cus on all___ — that's true;___ may I ne-ver lose sight___ of You.___ 1. In my fail-ure, in my suc-cess,___ if in sad-ness or hap-

pi - ness,— be the hope I am cling - ing to,— for my

heart be-longs— to You.—

2. You are only a breath away,
   Watching over me every day;
   In my heart I am filled with peace
   When I hear You speak to me.

3. No one loves me the way You do,
   No one cares for me like You do.
   Feels like heaven has broken through;
   God, You know how I love You.

768. Holiness is Your life in me
(Only the blood)

Rom 3:25; 1 Jn 1:7

Brian Doerksen

Ho-li-ness___ is Your life in me,___ mak-ing me clean through Your blood.___

___ Ho-li-ness___ is Your fire in me,___

purg-ing my heart___ like a flood.___ I know___

You are___ per - fect in ho - li-ness.___

Your life___ in me,___ set-ting me free,___

769.

Holy Child

Mt 2:11; Lk 2:16; 4:15; 19:10;
1 Cor 15:56; 2 Cor 1:20

Michael Baughen
Arr. Phil Burt

Tenderly

1. Ho-ly Child,____ how still You lie! Safe the man-ger, soft the hay; faint up-on____ the east-ern sky breaks the dawn of Christ-mas Day.

2. Ho-ly Child,____ whose birth-day brings shep-herds from their field and fold, an-gel

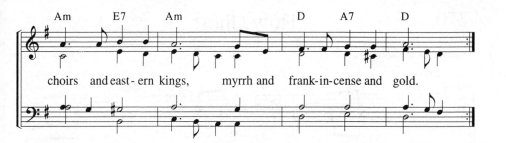

choirs and east-ern kings, myrrh and frank-in-cense and gold.

3. Holy Child, what gift of grace
   From the Father freely willed!
   In Your infant form we trace
   All God's promises fulfilled.

4. Holy Child, whose human years
   Span like ours delight and pain;
   One in human joys and tears,
   One in all but sin and stain:

5. Holy Child, so far from home,
   All the lost to seek and save:
   To what dreadful death You come,
   To what dark and silent grave!

6. Holy Child, before whose name
   Powers of darkness faint and fall;
   Conquered death and sin and shame-
   Jesus Christ is Lord of all!

7. Holy Child, how still You lie!
   Safe the manger, soft the hay;
   Clear upon the eastern sky
   Breaks the dawn of Christmas Day.

   Timothy Dudley-Smith

770.

Holy Ghost

Joel 2:30; Jn 3:8; Acts 2:2,19

Steadily, but with anticipation

Bjorn Aslakson

Ho - ly Ghost,___ You won-der-ful Ho - ly Ghost,___ ___ a wind blow-ing strong,___ blow-ing from hea - ven.___ We have de-ci - ded to go___ all the way___ with our God.___

(Final chorus)
Blood and fire, we call upon blood and fire,
A wind blowing strong, blowing from heaven.
Blood and fire, we call upon blood and fire,
A wind blowing strong, blowing from heaven.

771.

Holy, holy

Rev 4:8; 5:12

Capo 2 (D)

Nathan Fellingham

Worshipfully

Ho - ly, ho - ly, ho-ly is the Lord God Al - migh - ty. Who was and is and is to come, who was and is and is to come. Lift up His name with the sound of sing - ing, lift up His name

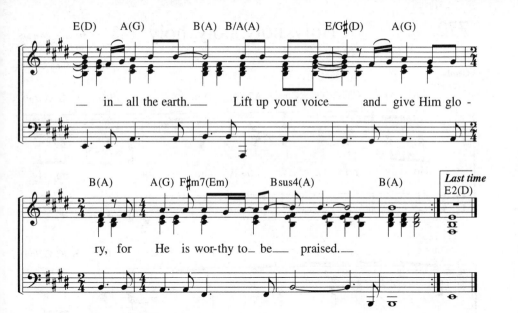

772.

Holy, holy, holy, holy

Mt 23:9; Rom 5:5;
Gal 3:13; Rev 4:8

Jimmy Collins-Owens

2. Gracious Father, gracious Father,
   We're so glad to be Your children,
   Gracious Father;
   And we lift our heads before You
   As a token of our love,
   Gracious Father, gracious Father.

3. Precious Jesus, precious Jesus,
   We're so glad that You've redeemed us,
   Precious Jesus;
   And we lift our hands before You
   As a token of our love,
   Precious Jesus, precious Jesus.

4. Holy Spirit, Holy Spirit,
   Come and fill our hearts anew,
   Holy Spirit! –
   And we lift our voice before You
   As a token of our love,
   Holy Spirit, Holy Spirit.

5. Hallelujah, hallelujah,
   Hallelujah, hallelujah –
   And we lift our hearts before You
   As a token of our love,
   Hallelujah, hallelujah.

773. Holy, holy, holy is the Lord

Rev 4:8; 5:12

(In His eyes)

Bryn Haworth

pre - cious   in   God's   sight,   so

pre - cious   in   His   eyes.

2. Worthy, worthy, worthy is the Lamb.
   Worthy, worthy, worthy is the Lamb.

3. Glory, I give glory to the Lamb of God.
   Glory, I give glory to the Lamb of God.

774. Holy, holy, Lord God Almighty

Rev 4:8

Capo 2 (D)

Richard Lewis

With awe

775.
Holy is Your name

Capo 5(Am)

Ps 16:5; 18:30; Gal 2:20;
Phil 4:19; Rev 15:3

John Paculabo

1.3. Ho - ly is Your name, Ye - shu - a, my De -
2. Per - fect are Your ways, Je - ho - vah, my

liv-er- er. Wor - thy of all praise, You ev - er - liv-ing
Fa - ther. Faith - ful is Your love, You gave Your-self for

God. me. In You I have se - cur-i-ty; in

You I put my trust. In You I have con-fi-dence, You

meet my ev - 'ry need.

D.C. al Fine

Be patient, then, brothers,
until the Lord's coming.

JAMES 5:7

776.

Holy One

Ps 16:5; 1 Cor 6:11; Ps 103:17; Jer 31:3

Steadily, building to the chorus

Mick Gisbey

Ho-ly One,___ my life is in Your

hand; my song an off-'ring of my heart, re-

deemed, washed clean, by faith I stand se-cure. In You

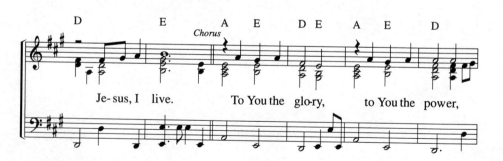

Je-sus, I live. To You the glo-ry, to You the power,

777.

Holy Spirit, move within me

Mt 6:6; Rom 8:18,26-27

Charlotte Exon

With feeling

Ho - ly Spi - rit, move with-in me, Ho - ly Spi - rit, come upon me now. Ho - ly Spi - rit, lead me to the
se - cret place of prayer, Ma - ni - fest the glo - ry of God.
Ho - ly Spi - rit, You are wel - come, Ho - ly Spi - rit, we de - sire___ You.
Ho - ly Spi - rit, wor - ship through us, Let us see the glo - ry of God.

Trust in the Lord for ever, for the Lord, the Lord, is the Rock eternal.

ISAIAH 26:4

778.
Hope of the world

Capo 1 (A)

Steadily

Ps 40:11; Jn 1:5; 12:24; 2 Cor 4:6
Eph 2:12; 5:8; Heb 10:20; 2 Jn 3

Robert Newey

1. Hope of the world,— You stepped in-to our time, and yet— they spurned You and— then turned a-way.— To a dy-ing world— You reached— out, but they did-n't want to hear — the words— You had to say.— But may the light—

779.

How can I be free from sin?
(Lead me to the cross)

Mt 7:13-14; Jn 14:16,27; Acts 4:12; Rom 3:21-22; 5:17;
Rom 6:22; Gal 6:14; Phil 3:9; Col 1:20; 2 Thess 3:16

Moderately

Graham Kendrick & Steve Thompson

1. How can I be free from sin? Lead me to the cross of Je - sus. From the guilt, the pow'r, the pain? Lead me to the cross of Je - sus. There's no oth - er way, no price that I could pay; sim - ply to the cross I cling.

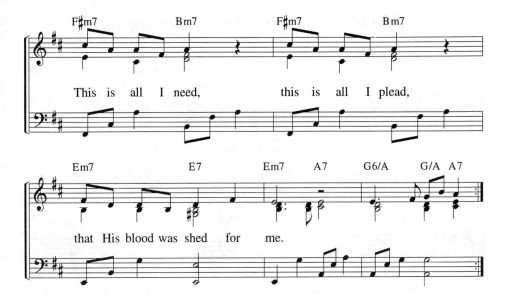

This is all I need, this is all I plead, that His blood was shed for me.

2. How can I know peace within?
   Lead me to the cross of Jesus.
   Sing a song of joy again!
   Lead me to the cross of Jesus.
   Flowing from above,
   All forgiving love
   From the Father's heart to me!
   What a gift of grace -
   His own righteousness,
   Clothing me in purity!

3. How can I live day by day -
   Lead me to the cross of Jesus,
   Following His narrow way?
   Lead me to the cross of Jesus.

780. How deep the Father's love for us

Capo 2 (D)

Thoughtfully

Ps 22:1; Mt 20:28
Mt 27:46; Mk 10:45; 15:34; Lk 23:35
Jn 3:16; 19:20; Gal 6:14; 1 Tim 2:6

Stuart Townend

1. How deep the Father's love for us, how vast be-yond all mea - sure, that He should give His on - ly Son to make a wretch His trea - sure. How great the pain of sear-ing loss, the Fa - ther turns His face a-way, as wounds which mar the Cho - sen One bring

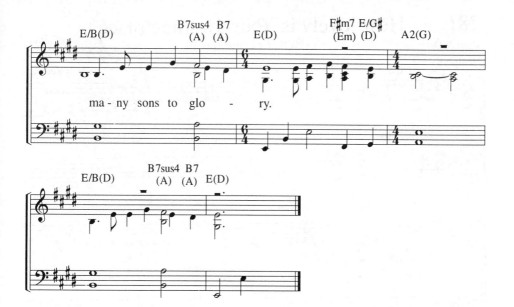

ma - ny sons to glo - ry.

2. Behold the man upon a cross,
   My sin upon His shoulders;
   Ashamed, I hear my mocking voice
   Call out among the scoffers.
   It was my sin that held Him there
   Until it was accomplished;
   His dying breath has brought me life -
   I know that it is finished.

3. I will not boast in anything,
   No gifts, no power, no wisdom;
   But I will boast in Jesus Christ,
   His death and resurrection.
   Why should I gain from His reward?
   I cannot give an answer,
   But this I know with all my heart,
   His wounds have paid my ransom.

781. How lovely is Your dwelling place
(Better is one day)

Capo 2 (D)

Ps 27:4; 34:8; 63:1,7;
Ps 84:1-2,10; Jas 4:8

Slowly, with awe

Matt Redman

1. How love-ly is Your dwel-ling place, O Lord Al-migh-ty. My soul longs and ev-en faints for You. For here my heart is sat-is-fied, with-in Your pre - sence. I sing be-neath the sha-dow of Your wings. Bet-ter is

And I heard a loud voice from the throne saying, "Now the dwelling of God is with men, and He will live with them. They will be His people, and God Himself will be with them and be their God.

REVELATION 21:3

782. How sweet the name of Jesus sounds

Ex 6:15; Is 65:19; Joel 2:32; Jn 6:58;
Acts 4:12; Rom 10:13; Heb 12:2

Chris Bowater

Smoothly

1. How sweet the name_ of Je - sus sounds_ in a be-lie-ver's ear;_____ it soothes his sor-rows, heals_____ his wounds,_ and drives a-way his fear. It makes the woun-ded spi-rit_ whole,

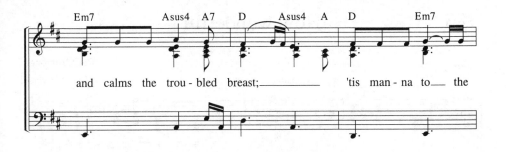

and calms the trou - bled breast;＿＿＿ 'tis man - na to＿ the

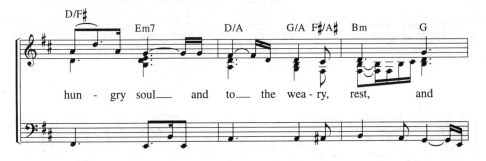

hun - gry soul＿ and to＿ the wea - ry, rest, and

to＿ the wea - ry, rest.

3. Dear name, the Rock on which I build,
My shield, and hiding place;
My never-failing treasury, filled
With boundless stores of grace.
Jesus, my Shepherd, Saviour, Friend,
My Prophet, Priest, and King;
My Lord, my Life, my Way, my End,
Accept the praise I bring,
Accept the praise I bring.

5. Weak is the effort of my heart,
And cold my warmest thought;
But when I see You as You are,
I'll praise You as I ought.
I would Your boundless love proclaim
With every fleeting breath;
So shall the music of Your name
Refresh my soul in death,
Refresh my soul in death.

John Newton (1725-1807)
Adpt. Chris Bowater

783. How wonderful

Rom 5:5; 2 Cor 5:19

Dave Bilbrough

As a jig

How— won-der-ful,— how— glori-ous—
is— the love of— God,— bring-ing— heal-ing,— for-
give-ness,— won-der-ful love. 1. Let cel-e-bra-
-tion ech-o through— this— land;— we bring re-con-ci-li-a-

- tion,___ we bring hope_____ to ev-'ry man._____ How___

2. We proclaim the kingdom
   Of our God is here;
   Come and join the heavenly anthem
   Ringing loud and ringing clear:

3. Listen to the music
   As His praises fill the air;
   With joy and with gladness
   Tell the people everywhere:

784. Humble yourselves

Capo 3 (Em)

1 Pet 5:6-7

Dave Bilbrough

1. Hum-ble your-selves un-der God's migh-ty hand, so that He will lift you up.

Cast all an-xi-e-ty on Him, be-cause He cares for You.

I bow down

be-fore You,   my

Lord.

2. Open your hearts
   To the Lord your God,
   And know His love for you.

785.
I am the apple of God's eye
(Spiritual fruit)

With a latin rhythm

Ps17:8; 33:2; 91:11; 150:4
Song 2:4; Ezek 34:26

Jim Bailey

1. I am the AP - PLE of__ God's eye, His BA-
NA - NA o - ver me is love.

2. For where - ev - er this__ MAN - GOES,__ a
3. SU - MA or la - ter you__ will see__ there is
He O - RAN - GES His__ an - gels__ to look af - ter me,__ as His

bles-sings__ PLUM-met from__ a-bove.__ The

To next verse

GREAT FRUIT_ of God,__ the GREAT FRUIT_ of God,_ the

GREAT FRUIT_ of God_ it o - ver- flows.__ The

GREAT FRUIT_ of God,__ the GREAT FRUIT_ of God,__ the

GREAT FRUIT_ of God_ it o - ver- flows.__

2. Never have to play the GOOSEBERRY,
   Feel like a LEMON, no not me,
   For wherever this MAN-GOES,
   A RASPBERRY it never blows.

3. I will praise Him on the TANGERINE,
   Praise Him on the MANDARIN;
   SATSUMA or later you will see
   There is always a CLEMENTINE for praising Him.

786.

I am Yours
(Pure like You)

David Gate

Gently

Verse

1. I am Yours and You are mine,

friend to me for all of time.

Chorus

And all I have___ now___ I give to You;___

and all I want___ now___ is to___ be___ pure,___ pure like

You.

D.C. *Last time*

2. I'm not afraid
   Of earthly things,
   For I am safe
   With You my King.

Before they call I will answer; while they are still speaking I will hear.

ISAIAH 65:24

Here I am! stand at the door and knock. If anyone hears My voice and opens the door, I will come in and eat with him, and he with Me.

REVELATION 3:20

787. I believe in God the Father

Steadily

Is 7:14; Mt 1:23; Mk 16:19;
Acts 1:9,11; 10:42; Rom 6:9; 2Tim 4:1;
Heb 1:3; 8:1; 10:12; 12:2; 1Pet 3:18-19; 4:5

Wayne Drain

Chorus

I be-lieve in God___ the Fa - ther, I be-lieve in Je-sus_ the Son:_
- lieve! *(Tacet.)*

I be-lieve in God the Ho - ly Spi - rit,

I be-lieve_ in the Three in One.___

Verse

I be-lieve He was born___ of___ a vir - gin, was

cru - ci - fied___ and bu - ried in___ the ground.___ De-

788.   I believe there is a God in heaven

Is 53:5; Jn 3:14; 19:30;
Col 1:20; Heb 7:27

Dave Bilbrough

I be-lieve there is a God in heav'n who paid the price for all my
sin; shed His blood to o-pen up the way for me to walk with
Him. Gave His life up-on a cross, took the pun-ish-ment for
us, of-fered up Him-self in love, Je- sus,

789.

I bow down

Heb 7:17,25; 1 Jn 1:7

With feeling

David Fellingham

I bow down____ in hum-ble a-dor - a - tion,____ speak Your name____ ____ with love and de - vo - tion,____ Je - sus, the Lamb sa-cri-ficed for me. I see Your face,___ Your ten-der hands____ scarred for me. I fall at Your feet____ with songs of prais - es sing - ing;____ my joy is com-plete.____ You ful-fil my long - ing.__ Pro - phet of

God, my Priest_ and my King, I wor-ship___ and a - dore. Be-
fore the Fa - ther's throne___ You ev - er in - ter - cede;___ You
al-ways hear my prayer,___ what - ev-er I may plead.___ You wipe a-way my
tears,_ You give me_ vic-tor - y; by Your blood_ I am cleansed,_ I am
free.

790.
I could sing unending songs
(The happy song)

Rom 8:31

Joyfully

Martin Smith

(Oh,) I could sing un-end-ing songs of how You saved my soul. Well, I could dance a thou-sand miles be-cause of Your great love. My heart is burst-ing, Lord, to tell of all You've done. Of how You changed my life and wiped a-way the past. I wan-na shout it out, from ev-'ry roof top sing.

2nd time to bridge

791.

I cry out
(Good to me)

Josh 21:45; Ps 28 :1-2

Craig Musseau

Steadily

I cry out for Your hand of mer-cy to heal me. I am
weak, I need Your love to free me. O Lord, my
Rock, my strength in weak-ness, come res-cue me, O
Lord. You are my hope, Your pro-mise ne-ver
fails me. And my de-sire is to fol-low You for e-

ver. For You are good, for You are good, for You are good to____

me. For You are good, for You are good, for You are good to____

D.C.

(Fine)

me.

792.
I don't want to be a Pharisee
(Matthew 23)

Mt 23:24

With life

Ian Smale

"If you believe, you will receive whatever you ask for in prayer."

MATTHEW 21:22

793.

I dream
(Believer)

Ps 57:5,11; 82:3; 108:5; Is 64:1; Joel 2:28;
Lk 15:20; Acts 2:3,17; Rev 22:2

Matt Redman

With energy

1. I dream of tongues of fi-re rest-ing on Your peo-ple,
I dream of all the mi-ra-cles___ to come.

I hope to see the com-ing heal-ing of the na-tions,
I long to see the pro-di-gals___ re-turn.

So ma-ny hopes___ and long-ings in You;___

when will all the dreams come true? I'm a believ-er in Your king-dom, I am a seek - er of the new things, I am a dream - er with some old dreams, let them now come. (will You now come?)

2. I hope to see You come down,
   Rend the mighty heavens,
   And let Your glory cover all the earth;
   To see Your sons and daughters
   Come to know and love You,
   And find a purer passion in the church.
   These are the things my heart will pursue:
   When will all the dreams come true?

3. May Your church now reach out,
   Sowing truth and justice,
   Learn to love the poor and help the weak.
   When Your kingdom's coming
   It will touch the broken,
   Place the lonely in a family.
   So many hopes and longings in You:
   When will all the dreams come true?

794.

If My people

Capo 3 (Bm)

Graham Kendrick

795.
I have a Maker
(He knows my name)

Ps 28 :2; Mat 10 :30;
Lk 12:7; Eph 1:4

Tommy Walker

I have a Maker, He formed my heart;
I have a Father, He calls me His own;

be-fore even time be-gan my life was in His hand.
He'll never leave me, no mat-ter where I go.

He knows my name,

He knows my ev-'ry thought; He sees each tear

that falls and hears me when I call.

796.
I have come to love You

Gently, building to the chorus

Matt Redman

Verse

1. I have come to love You, I have come to love You to-day.___ I have come to love You, I have come to love You to-day.___

Chorus

And to-day___ and for-ev-er more___ I'll love your name.

And to-day___ and for-ev-er more___ I'll love Your

name.

2. I have come to worship,
   I have come to worship today.
   (Repeat)

3. I have come to thank You,
   I have come to thank You today.
   (Repeat)

797.

I have heard
(I won't let go)

Steadily, with rhythm

Gen 32:24,26; Mt 7:7
Lk 6:35; 11:9; 1 Cor 13:5

Stuart Townend

1. I have heard_ that You_ are swift___ to bless_ the seek-er,__
   As Ja-cob wres-tled so__ I'll wres-tle with_ Your an-gel,_

and I be-lieve_ that You_ will hear___ the con-stant cry;____
and though I'm wea-ry, I___ will not___ be o-ver-come,_

so I will call_ un-til_ I know___ I've had_ an an-swer,_
for You have giv-en me_ a pas-sion for_ Your king-dom,_

I need Your pow er,_ Lord!__
O let Your glo-ry_ fall!__

I won't let go,____

I won't let go____ un-til_ You bless_

You. 3. For a hun - ger that__ will o

2. I have heard that You show mercy to a nation,
   And I believe that You give power to Your church;
   So now I'm asking You to open up the heavens,
   Pour out Your mercy, Lord!
   For Your gospel to be lived among Your people,
   For Your miracle of healing on the streets;
   For the government to fear the Lord Almighty,
   We need Your power, Lord!

3. For a hunger that will overcome my weakness,
   For a love that will seek its own reward;
   For my life to make a difference in this nation,
   I need Your power, Lord!

*Delight yourself in the Lord
and He will give you the desires of
your heart.*

PSALM 37:4

798.

I have loved you

Jer 31:3 Acts 10:39-40;
Rom 8:37; 1 Pet 5:7

Kent Henry

Steadily

(And) I have loved you with an ev-er-last-ing love,____ and I have drawn____ you with my lov-ing kind - ness. And I have -ness.

1. Be-cause God loved____ you and____ to keep____
2. And cast-ing all____ of your cares____ on Him____

— His own,____ for He cares for you,____ He brought____
— there's a love____

799. I have made You too small in my eyes

(Be magnified)

Capo 3 (D)

With feeling

Lynn DeShazo

1. I have made You too small in my eyes; O Lord, forgive me. And I have believed in a lie that You were unable to heal me.
2. I have leaned on the wisdom of men; O God, forgive me. And I have responded to them instead of Your light and Your mercy.

But now, O Lord, I see my wrong; heal my heart, and show Yourself strong. And in my eyes and with my song, O Lord, be magnified, O

800. I just want to be where You are

Ps 23:5; 28:7; 84:

Tenderly, quite slow

Don Moen

I just want to be where You are, dwel-ling dail-y in Your
I just want to be where You are, in Your dwel-ling place for-

pre - sence. I don't want to wor-ship from a - far,
ev - er. Take me to the place where You are,

draw me near to where You are.
I just want to be with You.

I want to be where You are, dwel-ling in Your

pre - sence, feast-ing at Your ta-ble, sur-round-ed by your

801.

I know a place

Ps 46:1; Rom 5:9; 8:38-39
2 Cor 12:9; Phil 4:7; Rev 22:1

Nathan Fellingham

1. I know a place where bles- sings from heav'n are poured, mer-cy and grace___ a- bound- ing. Through Je- sus' blood we have now been set free in-to the Fa - ther's lov - ing.___ And I will trust___ in___ You___ a - lone, my___ re - fuge___ and___

strength._____ For all the trials__ that__ come__ my way, Your__ grace__ is suf - fi - cient__ for me._____

I can sing the won-drous sto-ry of the King who died for me.__

2. I know a place where there is no guilt or fear,
   As I come into His presence.
   I can now know a peace which surpasses all,
   Nothing shall separate us.

3. I know a place where a wonderful river flows,
   That fills me with His glory;
   Bringing us life, we're stirred to adore Him,
   A perfect joy everlasting.

802.
I know a place, a wonderful place
(At the cross)

Capo 2 (D)

1 Cor 15:3; Col 2:14; 1 Pet 3:18

Flowing

Randy & Terry Butler

I know a place, a won-der-ful place,

where ac-cused and con-demned find

mer-cy and grace. Where the wrongs we have done,

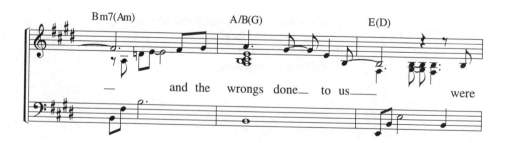

and the wrongs done to us were

803. I know You love to crown the humble
(Bowing down)

Ps 95:6; Micah 6:8; Mt 11:29

Matt Redman

Lyrics:

1. I know— You love— to crown— the hum- ble, pour - ing— out grace— for the bro - ken heart.— You— bless— the meek,— You meet— the low - ly; Lord,— as— I bow,— lift me— to You.— I

lie- ver— on—— their knees?—— And my Lord,—— will You— be pleased—

— to look up - on me, to look up - on me?—— (I)

2. I'd like to be one such believer,
Keeping my knees firmly on the ground.
I'd like to tread humbly before You;
Lord, as I bow, lift me to You.

804.   I lift my eyes to the quiet hills

Ps 121:1-2,6,8

Capo 3 (D)

Michael Baughen
& Elisabeth Crocker

Tenderly

1. I lift my eyes to the qui-et hills, in the press of a bu-sy day; as green hills stand in a dus-ty land, so God is my strength and stay.

2. I lift my eyes
To the quiet hills,
To a calm that is mine to share;
Secure and still
In the Father's will,
And kept by the Father's care.

3. I lift my eyes
To the quiet hills,
With a prayer as I turn to sleep;
By day, by night,
Through the dark and light,
My Shepherd will guard His sheep.

4. I lift my eyes
To the quiet hills,
And my heart to the Father's throne;
In all my ways,
To the end of days,
The Lord will preserve His own.

Timoth Dudley-Smith

805.

I long for You, O Lord

Job 19:27; Ps 84:2; Jn 6:3

With feeling

Steve & Vikki Cook

806.

I love the Lord
(Psalm 116)

Ps 116:1-7,12-14,16,18

Ian White

Brightly

1. I love the Lord for He has heard me, He has
   Lord for His com-pas - sion and His

heard my mer - cy plea. From
gra - cious, right - eous ways. He pro-

deep with - in my troub-led heart, I cried
tects the sim - ple heart- ed

— "O Lord, save me!" I love the ones, and

in my need, the Lord saw me, and

2. I love the Lord for all the goodness
    That I never can repay,
    But I lift the cup of salvation,
    And call upon His name.
    I will fulfil my vows before the Lord,
    In the presence of His saints,
    O, make me now Your servant, Lord,
    You have freed me from
    You have freed me from these chains.

807.
I love You, Lord, my strength
(Youre my stronghold)

Ps 18:1-2, 7, 15-17

Phil Lawson Johnston

Brightly

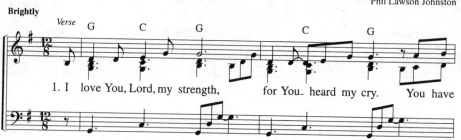

1. I love You, Lord, my strength, for You heard my cry. You have

been my help in trou- ble. I've put my trust in You,___ my

ref - uge___ and my hope, You're the Rock on which I

stand.___ *Chorus* You're my strong - hold,___ You're my

2. I love You, Lord, my strength,
   You reached down from on high,
   And You rescued me from trouble.
   You've taken hold of me,
   And set me on a rock,
   And now this is where I stand.

3. I love You, Lord, my strength,
   There is no other rock,
   And now I will not be shaken.
   The sea may roar and crash,
   The mountains quake and fall,
   Ah, but on this Rock I stand.

808.
I'm a friend of Jesus Christ
(Jesus is the Boss)

Capo 3 (Em)

Rom 6:23; 10:9

With energy

Verse

Doug Horley

I'm a friend of Je-sus Christ, (I'm a friend of Je-sus Christ,)

He's God's Son and He's a-live,— (He's God's Son and He's a-live,)—

I will trust in Him it's true, (I will trust in Him it's true,) He's

al-ways there to see me through. (He's al-ways there to see me through.)

Sound— off, *Je-sus*, sound— off, *is Lord*, sound— off, *Je-sus*,

(Rap)
I said, come on everybody and move your feet;
The rhythm is hot, it's a powerful beat.
The time is right to do some business,
Get on your feet and be a witness
To the Holy One,
The King of kings, God's only Son;
Jesus Christ, that's His name,
He died to take our sin and shame.

809. I'm looking up to Jesus

Heb 12:2

Ian Smale

I'm look-ing up to Je-sus,— His face is shin-ing beau-ty.—

I'm feel-ing so un-wor-thy,— yet His Spi-rit leads me on.

I'm look-ing up to Je-sus,— His ra-di-ance sur-rounds me.—

I feel so pure and clean, a taste of

heav-en on— earth. I'm look-ing up to Je-sus.—

Last time

810.
I'm standing here to testify
(Come to the light)

Joel 2:25; Ps 100:5; 106:1; 107:1;
118:1,29;135:3; 136:1; Mt 11:19;
Lk 7:34; Jn 15:15; Jas 2:23; 4:8

With a steady rhythm

Kevin Prosch

(Leader) I'm stand-ing here__ to tes - ti - fy, (All) O, the Lord is good. to (Leader)
did not think__ I could have peace,

sing of how__ He changed__ my heart. (All) O, the Lord is good.
trapped in - side__ by fear__ and shame. (Leader) He

(Leader) I was bound__ by hate and pride, (All) O, the Lord is good. (Leader)
wiped a - way__ all of my grief, when

nev - er know - ing of__ His light. (All) O, the Lord is good. I (Leader)
I be - lieved__ up - on__ His name.

2, 4. Chorus
(All) Come to the light,__ come as you are;__ you can be__

811.

I need You

Is 42:7

With feeling

Chris Bowater

I need You like dew in the de - sert, like re-
fresh-ing sum-mer rain,— come and pour Your love a-gain— on
me.— I'm find - ing that ev - 'ry time— I come and
ask for some - thing more You ne-ver fail— to pour Your love on
me.— And peace like a ri - ver flows, and waves of mer - cy

ev - er roll; take me deep - er, I want to know You more. Pour Your love,— pour Your love,— pour Your love— on me.

812.

In every circumstance

Neh 8:10; Eph 1:18-19

David Fellingham

With a 12/8 feel

In ev-'ry cir - cum-stance of life You are with me, glorious Fa - ther. And I have put my trust in You, that I may know the glor - i - ous hope to which I'm called.

813.

In God alone
(Mon âme se repose)

Mt 11:29

Music: Jacques Berthier

In God a-lone my soul can find rest and peace, in
Mon â-me se re-pose en paix sur Dieu seul: de

God my peace___ and joy. On-ly in God my
lui vient mon___ sa-lut. Oui, sur Dieu seul mon

soul can find its rest,___ find its rest___ and peace. In
â-me se re-po-se, se re-pose___ en paix. Mon

Grace, mercy and peace from God the Father and from Jesus Christ, the Father's Son, will be with us in truth and love.

2 JOHN: 3

814. In my life proclaim Your glory

(Lord of all mercy)

Phil 2:10; Rev 5:12

Geoff Bullock

1. In my life— pro-claim. Your glo—ry, in my heart— re-veal— Your ma—jes-ty; then my soul— shall speak the won-ders of— Your grace,— and this heart of mine— shall sing Your praise..

In my words— pro-claim. Your mer-cy, in my life— re-veal— Your pow—er; then my soul— shall be a mir-ror of— Your love,— and this heart of mine— shall sing Your praise..

Chorus

Lord of all mer-cy, God of all grace,— Lord of all right-eous-ness;— Lord of the hea-vens,

Lord of the earth,— en - throned in ma - jes - ty.—

Wor-thy of hon - our, wor-thy of praise,— all glo-ry and ma-jes-ty;— I

give you the hon - our, I give You the praise,— and pro-claim Your glo-ri-ous

pow'r. pow'r, and pro - claim Your glo-ri-ous pow'r.

2. In my soul unveil Your love, Lord,
   Deep within my heart renewing me.
   Day by day Your life trasnsforming all I am,
   As this heart of mine reflects Your praise.
   Lord of all, enthroned in glory,
   Grace and mercy, truth and righteousness,
   Every knee shall bow before this Christ, our Lord,
   As all creation sings Your praise.

815.

In mystery reigning

Ps 89:6; Heb 2:9; 13:8

John Pantry

2. A beauty that's timeless, who can compare?
   All earth stands in silence, when You appear.
   Your kingdom is boundless, Your love without end;
   Wonder of wonders, this King is my friend!

3. All power has been given into Your hands;
   Through blood and by suffering You now command.
   And no opposition can stand in Your light;
   Crowned King of heaven, we kneel at the sight.

816. In my weakness You are strong
(You are the Lord)

Mal 3:5; 1 Cor 3:13

Strong & rhythmic

Wayne Drain

Verse

1. In my weak-ness— You are strong,— when I fall short You carry me— a-long.— In-to my dark-ness— You shine Your light,— when I feel blind-ed, You re - store my sight.— You are the Lord, You ne-ver change, You still the storm when I call Your name.— You're all I want, You're al-ways— there, no mat-ter

so I'll serve You, Lord, serve You, Lord, serve You, Lord, for the rest, rest of my days. You are the

2. I'm inconsistent, but You are true;
   I don't trust myself, but I depend on You.
   Look through my selfishness, and see my heart;
   Bring out the precious from the worthless parts.

817.

In the Lord

Capo 3 (D)

Jacques Berthier

In the Lord I'll be ev-er thank-ful, in the Lord I will re-joice! Look to God, do not be a-fraid; lift up your voi-ces, the Lord is near, lift up your voi-ces, the Lord is near! In the

El Se-nyor és la me-va for-ça, el Se-nyor el me-u cant. Ell m'ha e-stat la sal-va-ci-ó. En ell con-fi-o, i no tinc por. En ell con-fi-o, i no tinc por. El se

818.
In the name of Jesus

Mk 5:12; Acts 8:7; 19:15;
1 Cor 15:57

Author unknown
Arr. David Ball

819.

In these days of darkness
(Carry the fire)

Is 6:8

With conviction

Sue Rinaldi & Steve Bassett

1. In these days of dark - ness, who will bear the light?— In

all of this— con-fu - sion, who will rage a-gainst— the night? And

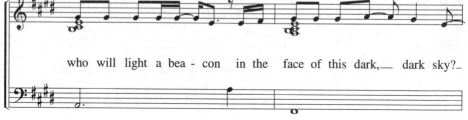

who will light a bea - con in the face of this dark,— dark sky?—

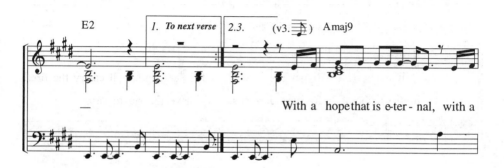

— With a hope that is e-ter - nal, with a

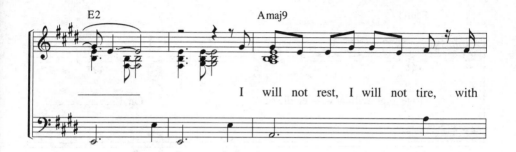

I will not rest, I will not tire, with

all my strength I'll car-ry the fire._____

2. Where there is oppression,
   Who will raise the flame?
   For the sake of all the children,
   Who will touch the fields of shame?
   And who will light a beacon
   In the face of this dark, dark sky,
   With a hope that is eternal,
   With a love that will never die?

3. Who will burn with passion,
   Blazing from the heart,
   To forge a new tomorrow?
   We must tell the world
   Of a hope that is eternal,
   Of a love that will never die.
   And we will light a beacon
   In the face of this dark, dark sky.

820.
In these days of refreshing

Jn 1:16; Phil 3:10

Slowly, with strength

David Fellingham

Lyrics:

In these days of re-fresh-ing, in these
tas-ted of Your ful-ness, one bles-sing

days of vi-si-ta-tion, there is a rea-son
af-ter a-no-ther, and that is the rea-son

why You've come. We have
we say "come."

It's not just to make us laugh or cry, to

shake or fall, but to glo-ri-fy Je-sus,

821.
Into the darkness
(Come, Lord Jesus, come)

*Is 7:14; 9:2; Mt 1:23;
Phil 2:9; Rev 22:20*

Maggi Dawn

1. In-to the dark - ness of this world,— in-to the sha - dows of the night; in-to this love - less place— You came,— light-ened our bur - dens, eased our pain,— and made these hearts Your home. In-to the dark - ness once— a-gain,— O come, Lord Je-sus, come.—

Come with Your love—

to make us whole, come with Your light to lead us on, driving the darkness far from our souls: O come, Lord Jesus, come.

2. Into the longing of our souls,
   Into these heavy hearts of stone,
   Shine on us now Your piercing light,
   Order our lives and souls aright,
   By grace and love unknown,
   Until in You our hearts unite,
   O come, Lord Jesus, come.

3. O Holy Child, Emmanuel,
   Hope of the ages, God with us,
   Visit again this broken place,
   Till all the earth declares Your praise
   And Your great mercies own.
   Now let Your love be born in us,
   O come, Lord Jesus, come.

(Last Chorus)

Come in Your glory, take Your place,
Jesus, the Name above all names,
We long to see You face to face,
O come, Lord Jesus, come.

822.   I once was frightened of spiders

Jn 14:27

Ian Smale

1. I once was frigh-tened of spi-ders, I once was frigh-tened of the dark; I once was frigh-tened by ma-ny, ma-ny things, e-spec-ial-ly things that barked. But now I'm ask-ing Je-sus to help these fears to go,— 'cause I don't want them to be part of me, no, no, no, no, no.

2. I once was frightened by thunder,
And frightened of lightning too;
I once was frightened by many, many things
That crashed and banged and blew.
But now I'm asking Jesus
To help these fears to go,
'Cause I don't want them to be part of me,
No, no, no, no, no.

"Worthy is the Lamb, who was slain, to receive power and wealth and wisdom and strength and honour and glory and praise!"

REVELATION 5:12

823.

Is anyone thirsty?

Jn 7:37-39

With strength

Graham Kendrick

Is an-y-one thirs-ty,____ an-y-one?____ Is an-y-one thirs-ty?____ Is Je-sus said:____ "Let them come____ to me____ and drink,____ let them come____ to me."____ O,____ let the liv-ing wa-ters flow,____ O,____

824.

I see the Lord

Is 6:1,3; Rev 4:8; 17:14; 19:16

Chris Falson

Capo 3 (D)

With awe

I see the Lord— seat-ed— on— the— throne,—— ex-

-alt-ed:— and the train of His— robe— fills the— tem-ple— with

glo - ry: the whole earth— is— filled,——

— the whole earth— is— filled,—— the

whole earth— is— filled—— with Your glo - ry.

825.

I sing a simple song of love

Deut 33:27; Lk 15:20

(Arms of love)

Craig Musseau

I sing a sim - ple song of love to my Sav-
iour, to my Je - sus. I'm grate-ful for the things You've done.
my lov-ing Sav - iour, O pre-cious Je - sus.
My heart is glad that You've called me Your own;

826.   I sing praises to Your name

1 Chron 16:25; Ps 48:1; 96:4; 145:3

Terry MacAlmon

2. I give glory to Your name...

827.

Is it true today?
(History maker)

Mk 16:17-18; Lk 15:20

With energy

Martin Smith

Verse

1. Is it true____ to-day that when peo - ple pray

cloud-less skies____ will break, kings and queens____

_ will shake? Yes, it's true,____ We'll see mi - _

and I be-lieve____ it,____ I'm liv-ing for You.____

1.2.4. To next section *3.*

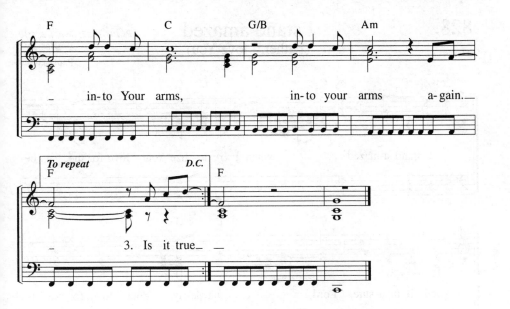

into Your arms, into your arms a-gain.

3. Is it true

2. Is it true today,
   That when people pray
   We'll see the dead men rise,
   And the blind set free?
   Yes, it's true . . .

3. Is it true today,
   That when people stand
   With the fire of God
   And the truth in hand,
   We'll see miracles,
   We'll see angels sing,
   We'll see broken hearts
   Making history?
   Yes, it's true . . .

828.

Slow 4

I stand amazed
(Father, I love You)

Ps 103:11-12; Song 1:2; 4:10
Rom 8:39

Paul Oakley

Verse

I stand a-mazed___ when I re-a-lize Your love for me___ is be-yond all mea-sure. Lord, I can't de-ny___ Your love for me is___ great.

Chorus

It's as___ high, high as___ the hea-vens___ a-bove,___ such is___ the depth of___ Your love___ to-ward those who fear___ You. O___ Lord, far as___ the east is___ from___

829.   I stand amazed in the presence

Is 6:5; Mt 26:39,42
Mk 14:36; Lk 5:8; 18:13; 22:42-44
1 Cor 13:12; 2 Cor 5:21; 1 Pet 2:24; Rev 22:4

Tune: MY SAVIOUR'S LOVE

Capo 1 (G)

Charles H. Gabriel (1856-1932)

1. I stand a-mazed in the pre-sence of Je-sus the Na-za-rene, and won-der how He could love me, a sin-ner, con-demned, un-clean.

How mar-vel-lous! How won-der-ful! And my song shall ev-er be:
(O how)   (O how)

How mar-vel-lous! How won-der-ful is my Sa-viour's love for me.
(O how)   (O how)

2. For me it was in the garden He prayed,
"Not My will, but Thine:"
He had no tears for His own griefs,
But sweat drops of blood for mine.

3. In pity angels beheld Him,
And came from the world of light
To comfort Him in the sorrows
He bore for my soul that night.

4. He took my sins and my sorrows,
He made them His very own;
He bore the burden of Calvary,
And suffered and died alone.

5. When with the ransomed in glory
His face I at last shall see,
'Twill be my joy through the ages
To sing of His love for me.

In the same way, let your light shine before men, that they may see your good deeds and praise your Father in heaven.

MATTHEW 5:16

830. I, the Lord of sea and sky

Is 6:8; Ezek 11:19; 36:26

Daniel L. Schutte

Triumphantly

1. I, the Lord of sea and sky, I have heard My
   I, who made the stars of night, I will make their

peo-ple cry; all who dwell in dark and sin
dark-ness bright. I will speak My word to them.

My hand will save.
Whom shall I

send?

Here I am, Lord. Is it I, Lord? I have heard You

call-ing in the night. I will go, Lord, if You

lead me;___ I will hold Your peo-ple in my heart.___

heart.___

2. I, the Lord of snow and rain,
   I have borne My people's pain;
   I have wept for love of them -
   They turn away.
   I will break their hearts of stone,
   Give them hearts for love alone;
   I will speak My word to them.
   Whom shall I send?

3. I, the Lord of wind and flame,
   I will tend the poor and lame,
   I will set a feast for them -
   My hand will save.
   Finest bread I will provide
   Till their hearts are satisfied;
   I will give My life to them.
   Whom shall I send?

831. It is good to give thanks to the Lord

Ps 106:1,6-7,14,43-44,48

John Bell & Graham Maule

1. It is good to give thanks to the Lord,— to re-mem-ber all He has done;— then God will re-mem-ber our prais-es when He looks— with love on His peo-ple.

Chorus

O give thanks to the Lord,— for His love en-dures for ev-er.— O give thanks to the Lord,— for the Lord a-lone is good.

2. Our sin is the sin of our fathers,
   We have done wrong, we all have been evil;
   Like those who once lived in bondage,
   We paid no heed to all You had done.

3. Our fathers forsook Your love,
   At the Red Sea they questioned their God;
   They fell from their faith in the desert,
   And put God to the test in the wilderness.

4. Time after time He would rescue them,
   Yet in malice they dared to defy Him;
   Despite this He came to their aid
   When He heard their cries of distress.

5. Save us, O Lord, in Your love;
   Bring us back from all that offends You.
   Look not alone at our sins,
   But remember Your promise of mercy.

6. Blessed be the Lord God of Israel
   Both now and through all eternity;
   Let nations and people cry out
   And sing Amen! Alleluia!

The Word became flesh and made His dwelling among us. We have seen His glory, the glory of the One and Only, who came from the Father, full of grace and truth.

JOHN 1:14

832.

It is the cry of my heart
(Cry of my heart)

Ps 86:11

Terry Butler

It is the cry of my heart to fol-low You. It is the cry of my heart to be close— to You. It is the cry of my heart to fol-low all of the days— of my life.——

1. Teach me Your ho-ly ways,— O Lord,—

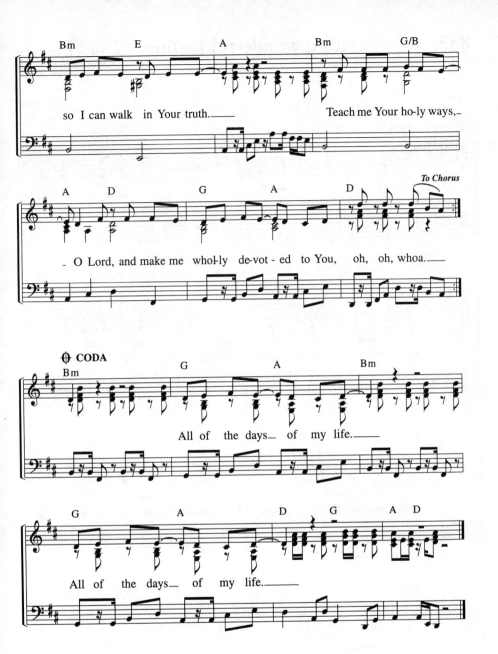

2. Open my eyes so I can see
   The wonderful things that You do.
   Open my heart up more and more
   And make it wholly devoted to You.

833.

It's a wonderful feeling

Mt 7:24,26; Lk 15:20,24,32
Jn 3:30; 10:28; 2 Cor 5:17

Brightly

Ian Smale

Capo 2 (D)

It's a won-der-ful, won-der-ful, won-der-ful feel - ing, it's a won-der-ful feel - ing to know you're saved.— It's a won-der-ful, won - der-ful, won - der-ful, WON - DER-FUL! won - der-ful feel - ing to know you're saved.— 1. My life is built on rock, not sand; it's a

won-der-ful feel - ing   to   know you're saved.__ And   none can steal me

D.C. al Fine

from God's hand; it's a   won-der-ful feel - ing   to   know you're saved.__

2. I once was lost but now I'm found;
   It's a wonderful feeling to know you're saved.
   In Father's arms I'm safe and sound;
   It's a wonderful feeling to know you're saved.

3. My old life's gone, I'm now brand new;
   It's a wonderful feeling to know you're saved.
   Much less of me, much more of You;
   It's a wonderful feeling to know you're saved.

834.

It's getting clearer
(You are my strength)

Brightly, with strength

Ps 28:7; Mt 6:10; Lk 11:12
Phil 3:13-14; Heb 12:1

Dave Bilbrough

1. It's get-ting clear-er, the light is dawn-ing,

I'm pres-sing on to a high-er place.

The past be-hind me, I'm mov-ing for-ward,

and I will fol-low af-ter You.

You are my strength, You are my shield,

2. There is a passion that burns within me,
I long to see Your kingdom come.
To know Your presence, to seek no other;
I hunger, Lord, for more of You.

835. It's rising up

Is 42:9-10; Hos 11:10; Amos 3:8; Rev 5:5

With expectation

Matt Redman & Martin Smith

1. It's ris-ing up__ from coast to coast,__ from north to south,__ and east to west;__ the cry of hearts__ that love Your name,__ which with one voice__ we will pro-claim.__

for-mer things__ have ta-ken place,__ can this be the__ new day__ of praise?__ A heav'n-ly song__ that comes to birth,__ and reach-es out__ to all__ the earth.__ Oh, let the cry__ to na-tions ring,__ that

2. The

Chorus E   F#m7   E

O what__ a song__ we'll sing and O what__ a tune__
O what__ a joy__ will rise and O what__ a sound__

A   B F#m7   G#m7

__ we'll bear;__ You de-serve__ an an-them__ of__ the
__ we'll make;__

A   A   D.C. To end E

1. high-est__ praise.__   *2.* high-est__ praise.__

2. Now we see a part of this,
   One day we shall see in full;
   All the nations with one voice,
   All the people with one love.
   No one else will share Your praise,
   Nothing else can take Your place;
   All the nations with one voice,
   All the people with one Lord.
   And what a song we'll sing upon that day.

3. Even now upon the earth
   There's a glimpse of all to come;
   Many people with one voice,
   Harmony of many tongues.
   We will all confess Your name,
   You will be our only praise;
   All the nations with one voice,
   All the people with one God.
   And what a song we'll sing upon that day.

836.   I've fallen in love

Heb 10:20; 12:2; 1 Jn 2:15

With energy

Pete Cant

1. I've fal - len in love,— (I've fal-len in love —) since the first time— we met, (since the first time— we met) there at— the cross where— You paid for— my sin, You op- ened— the way to— my heart and— came in, oh, I've fal- len in love,— — (I've fal-len in love,—) yes, I've fal- len in love.— (I've fal-len in love.— —)

2. I've fal-len in love,—   Je-sus— my Lord, on - ly You have— my heart, on - ly You can— know;— words don't— ex - press what— my heart tries— to say, that I— have fal-len— in love._____   3. I've fal - len in love,_

2. I've fallen in love (I've fallen in love)
   Since the first time we met, (since the first time we met)
   When I finally looked unto You,
   You broke my hardened heart in two,
   Oh, I've fallen in love, (I've fallen in love)
   Yes, I've fallen in love. (I've fallen in love.)

3. I've fallen in love (I've fallen in love)
   Since the first time we met, (since the first time we met)
   When You stole my love of the world
   And placed my heart's affection on You,
   Oh, I've fallen in love, (I've fallen in love)
   Yes, I've fallen in love. (I've fallen in love.)

837.
Capo 2 (A)

I've got a love song

Matt Redman

Gently, building with each verse

1. I've got a love— song in— my heart,— (I've got a love— song in— my heart,)—
2. I've got a pas - sion in— my heart,— (I've got a pas - sion in— my heart,)—

— it is for— You, Lord,— my God.— (It is for— You, Lord,— my God.)—
— it is for— You, Lord,— my God.— (It is for— You, Lord,— my God.)—

(x4)

Chorus

— La la la— la la— la la— la la la— la la— la la

— la la la— la la— la la.—

Double time

E(D)

3. I've got re-joic-ing in_ my heart,_ (I've got re-joic-ing in_ my heart,)_

_)

F#(E)

1.2.
B(A)

_ it is for_ You, Lord, _my God._ (It is for_ You, Lord, _my God.)_

Last time only
B(A)

4. And there is dancing in my heart, *(Echo)*
It is for You, Lord, my God.   *(Echo)*
And there is dancing in my heart, *(Echo)*
It is for You, Lord, my God.   *(Echo)*

5. I've never known a love like this, *(Echo)*
I've never known a love like this. *(Echo)*
I've never known a love like this, *(Echo)*
I've never known a love like this. *(Echo)*

838.

I waited patiently
(Many will see)

Capo 3 (D)

Ps 40: 1-5

Steadily

Ian White

1. I wait-ed pa-tient-ly for the Lord, — He turned and heard— my cry. He lift-ed me from the pit, — out from the mud and mire. He put my feet on a rock, and gave me a firm place to stand. He put a new— song in my— mouth, a hymn of praise to God, — a hymn of praise— to God. —

2. Blessed is the man who trusts the Lord,
   And turns from all the proud,
   From all those who have turned aside,
   To follow what is false.
   Many are the wonders that You have done,
   All the things You have planned;
   Were I to count they still would be
   Too many to declare,
   Too many to declare.

839.

I walk by faith

Is 54:17; Rom 8:31; 2 Cor 5:7

Rocky

Chris Falson

I_ walk by_ faith, each_ step by_ faith, to_ live by_ faith, I put my trust in_ You.

Last time to CODA

1. I_

2. Ev-'ry step I take_ is_ a step of faith;_ no wea-pon formed a-gainst_ me_ shall pros - per._ And ev-'ry prayer I make_ is_

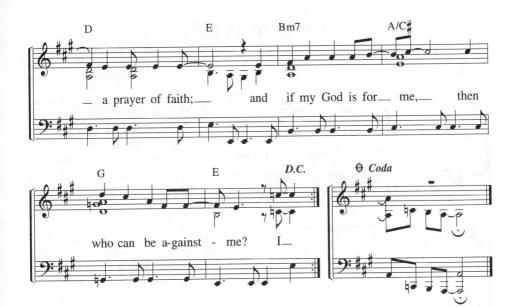

840. I want to be holy

Jn 8:12; Rom 12:1; 1 Cor 9:24; Eph 4:31; Phil 3:14; Heb 12:1-2

Paul Oakley & Alan Rose

Strongly

I want to be ho-ly, I want to be right-eous, I want to live my life the way— You want— me to.— I want to be blame-less, not walk-ing in dark-ness, I want to be a liv-ing sac-ri-fice— to You. I'm gon-na run the race,—I'm gon-na run to win,— throw off ev-'ry-thing— that hin-ders me,—

Last time to Coda ⊕

yeah, yeah.___ I'm gon-na fix my eyes up-on__ the King,__ and leave my sin be-hind.___ I want to be so___ much bet - ter, I want to be more__ like You.___ Keep tak-ing me fur- ther and deep - er, I want to right the wrong,___ I want to

*From the fulness of His grace
we have all received one blessing
after another.*

JOHN 1:16

841. I want to be out of my depth in Your love

Ps 42:7; Lk 42:7

Doug Horley & Noel Richards

Gently

I want to be out of my depth— in Your love,—
feel-ing Your arms— so strong—— a-round— me. Out of my depth— in Your love,—
— out of my depth— in You.— I want to be —

Learn-ing to let— You lead,— put-ting all trust—
Things I have held— so tight,— made my se-cu-

in You;⎯ deep - er in - to⎯ Your arms,⎯
- ri - ty;⎯ give me the strength⎯ I need⎯

sur - round- ed by You.
to sim - ply let go.⎯

842.

I want to know

Eph 1: 6,9,13,17-20; Col 3:5

Steadily

Evan Rogers

1. I want to know the glo-ri-ous in-he-
2. I want to know Your wis-dom and Your re-

-ri-tance that You have giv'n to me. And
-ve-la-tion, draw-ing me to You.

I want to know the hope that You have called
I want to know the pow-er of Your migh-

— me to, O Lord, I want to know Your truth.
-ty strength which raised Je-sus from the dead.

I want to know You bet-
Your mys-

Am7　　　**D**　　　**G**　**D/F♯**

- ter,___ the Spi - rit with - out mea - sure, to know_
- t'ry,___ the grace You've giv - en free - ly, I know_

Em　　**F**　　　　　**D**　　　**1.**

___ the ful - ness that's___ in You._____ I want to know_
___ my life is hidd'n___ in You._____

2.3.　　　*1st time D.C.*　**G**

___

843.

I was lost
(Like a child)

Mt 24:35; Mk 13:31; Lk 15:24,32; 21;33

Paul Oakley

Steadily

1. I was lost with-out a trace, all ex-cept for the eyes of hea-ven. Now my Sa-viour's love has found me, and His love has brought me home. and His per-fect love will con-quer all. I'm like a

2. I can sleep in peace tonight,
   I won't worry about tomorrow,
   Now I know my Daddy loves me,
   And His perfect love will conquer all.

3. Heaven and earth may pass away,
   And mountains fall into the ocean;
   But His word is everlasting,
   And His love goes on and on.

844.

I will be Yours
(Eternity)

Is 65:19

Gently flowing

Brian Doerksen

I will be Yours,___ You will be mine___ to-geth - er in e-ter-ni-ty.___

___ Our hearts of love___ will be en - twined,___ to- geth-

er in e-ter-ni-ty,___ for-ev - er in e-ter-ni-ty.___

No— more tears of pain— in our eyes;—

no— more fear or shame,— for we— will be— with You,—

— for we— will be—with You.—

845.

I will come and bow down

Ps 16:11; Acts 2:28

Martin J. Nystrom

Tenderly

I will come and bow down at Your feet, Lord Je-sus. In Your
pre-sence is ful-ness of joy.___ There is no-thing,___ there is
no one___ who com-pares with You; I take
plea-sure in wor-ship-ping You, Lord.___

*May the God of hope fill you
with all joy and peace as you trust in
Him, so that you may overflow with
hope by the power of the Holy Spirit.*

ROMANS 15:13

846.

I will cry mercy
(Cry mercy)

2 Chron 7:14; Amos 5:15
Zech 7:9; Mt 23:23

Sue Rinaldi & Steve Bassett

With feeling

847.
I will dance, I will sing
(Undignified)

2 Sam 6:14,22

With life and energy

Matt Redman

I will dance, I will sing, to be mad for my King.

No - thing, Lord, is hin - der - ing the pas - sion in my soul.___

pas - sion in my soul.___ And I'll be - come ev - en more un -

dig - ni - fied than this. (Some would say it's

fool - ish - ness but) I'll be - come ev - en more un - dig - ni - fied than

848.
Capo 2(A)

I will extol the Lord
(Holy and awesome)

Ps 145: 1-2; Prov 1:7; 9:10

Ian White

Steadily

849.
I will follow You to the cross
(Lay myself down)

Ps 42:7; Is 64:6;
Mt 16:24; Mk 8:34; Lk 9:23

With feeling

Sue Rinaldi

I will fol-low You to the cross___ and lay my-self down,___

lay my-self down.___ I will fol-low You to the cross___ and

lay my-self down,___ lay my-self down.___ 1. Rid me___ of___ these___ dir-

- ty___ clothes,___ cleanse me___ from all___ this pol-lu - tion.___ I choose___

___ to___ walk___ in___ pu - ri - ty,___ oh, pu-ri-fy me,___

2. Kiss me with Your healing touch,
   Take me to the heat of the fire;
   Bathe me in your liquid love,
   Oh, saturate me, saturate me.

850.
I will give thanks to the Lord
(O Most High)

Ps 7:17; 32:7; Heb 13:8

Mark Altrogge

I will give thanks to the Lord with all my heart,
I will be glad and exalt in You, my Lord,

I will sing glorious praises to Your
yesterday, today, forever, You're the

name;
same.

O Most High,

You who are my stronghold, when troubles come,

851.
I will offer up my life
(This thankful heart)

Ps 51:7; Lk 7:38
Jn 4:24; Phil 2:8

Matt Redman

Gently

Verse

1. I will of-fer up my life in spi-rit and truth,— pour-ing out the oil of love as my wor-ship to You.— In sur-ren-der I must give my ev - 'ry part;— — Lord, re - ceive the sac - ri - fice of a bro - ken heart.—

Chorus

— Je-sus, what can I give,— what can I bring— to so faith-ful a friend,— — to so lov - ing a King?— Sav - iour, what can be said,—

2. You deserve my every breath
   For You've paid the great cost;
   Giving up Your life to death,
   Even death on a cross.
   You took all my shame away,
   There defeated my sin,
   Opened up the gates of heaven,
   And have beckoned me in.

852.
I will praise You
(Psalm 138)

Ps 138: 1-3,8

Bryn Haworth

en-dures— for— ev - er,_____ and Your faith-ful - ness__

_____ is to the clouds._____ Do not for -

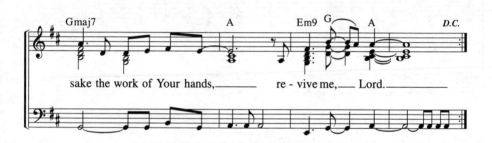

sake the work of Your hands,_____ re - vive me,__ Lord.____

2. You have exalted above all things
   Your name and Your word.
   You have exalted above all things
   Your name and Your word.
   I called to You, and You answered me.
   When I called to You, You made me strong.

Praise be to the God and Father of our Lord Jesus Christ, who has blessed us in the heavenly realms with every spiritual blessing in Christ.

EPHESIANS 1:3

853.

I will praise You with the harp
O Holy One of Israel

Ps 71:22-24

Capo 2 (D)

With energy

Ian White

1. I will praise You with the— harp for Your faith-ful-ness, O my God. I will sing my praise to— You with the lyre, with the lyre.

2. Those who want to harm me
   Are put to shame and confused.
   I will sing my praise to You
   With the lyre, with the lyre.

854.
I will rest in Christ

Mt 11:28; Lk 8:24; Jn 14:0;
2 Cor 4:8; Phil 4:7

Geoff Bullock

Steadily

1. I will rest— in Christ— like the calm with-in— the storm;— I can find— se-cu-ri-ty— in Him who leads— me on.— I will put my faith,_____ my trust and ev-'ry hope, for the peace of God— will touch my soul,— in Him I will— be whole.— Him I am— se-cure.— I will rest_____ in Christ; I will

2. I am not dismayed,
   I am not cast down;
   I will never be alone,
   I need never fear.
   I can always hope,
   I can always love,
   For the love of God has
   Touched my heart,
   In Him I am secure.

3. I will trust in Christ
   Like a rock in stormy seas;
   I have found a shelter in
   His life and peace in me.
   I have found the way,
   The truth, this perfect life;
   And the hope in me
   Is found in Him,
   The lover of my soul.

855.

I will sing, I will sing

Ps 126:5; Jn 8:36;
1 Cor 15:57; Phil 2:10-11

Max Dyer

Brightly

1. I will sing, I will sing a song—— un-to the Lord, I will
Chorus Al - le - lu, al - le - lu - ia, glo - ry to the Lord, al - le -

sing, I will sing a song—— un-to the Lord, I will sing, I will sing a song——
lu, al - le - lu - ia, glo - ry to the Lord, al - le - lu, al - le - lu - ia, glo -

—— un-to the Lord, al - le - lu - ia, glo - ry to the Lord.
- ry to the Lord, al - le - lu - ia, glor - ry to the Lord.

Repeat for chorus

2. We will come, we will come as one before the Lord, (*3 times*)
   Alleluia, glory to the Lord.
   Allelu, alleluia . . .

3. If the Son, if the Son shall make you free, (*3 times*)
   You shall be free indeed.
   Allelu, alleluia . . .

4. They that sow in tears shall reap in joy, (*3 times*)
   Alleluia, glory to the Lord!
   Allelu, alleluia . . .

5. Every knee shall bow and every tongue confess, (*3 times*)
   That Jesus Christ is Lord.
   Allelu, alleluia . . .

6. In His name, in His name we have the victory, (*3 times*)
   Alleluia, glory to the Lord.
   Allelu, alleluia . . .

"Holy, holy, holy is the Lord God Almighty; the whole earth is full of His glory."

ISAIAH 6:3

856.

I will sing of the Lamb

Ps 132:9; Prov 16:18
Is 61:10; Mt 9:36-38
14:14; Mk 6:34; Lk10:2
Jn 9:39; Rom 6:9; Gal 2:20
Eph 5:2; Phil 2:8; 1 Pet 2:24; Rev 5:9

Steadily

Stuart Townend

1. I will sing of the Lamb, of the price that was paid for me, pur - chased by God, giv - ing all He could give! Here now I stand in the gar - ments of right-eous-ness; death has no hold, for in Je - sus I live.

2. I will sing of His blood that flows for my wret - ched-ness, wounds that are bared, that I may be healed; pow'r and com - pas - sion, the marks of His mi - ni - stry: may they be mine as I har - vest His field.

Chorus

Oh, I will sing of the Lamb. Oh, I will

sing of the Lamb.___ My heart fills with won - der, my mouth fills with___ praise!___ Hal - le - lu - jah, hal - le - lu - jah.

2. Once I was blind, yet believed I saw everything,
   Proud in my ways, yet a fool in my part;
   Lost and alone in the company of multitudes,
   Life in my body, yet death in my heart.

   Oh, I will sing of the Lamb.
   Oh, I will sing of the Lamb.
   Oh, why should the King save a sinner like me?
   Hallelujah, hallelujah.

3. What shall I give to the Man who gave everything,
   Humbling Himself before all He had made?
   Dare I withold my own life from His sovereignty?
   I shall give all for the sake of His name!

   Oh, I will sing of the Lamb.
   Oh, I will sing of the Lamb.
   I'll sing of His love for the rest of my days!
   Hallelujah, hallelujah.

857. I will wait

Ps 22:2; 42:8; 59.16; 77:6; 91:5;
Is 8:17; Lam 3:24-26

Meditatively

Maggi Dawn

He gives strength to the weary and increases the power of the weak. Even youths grow tired and weary, and young men stumble and fall; but those who hope in the Lord will renew their strength. They will soar on wings like eagles; they will run and not grow weary, they will walk and not faint.

ISAIAH 40:29-31

858. I will wave my hands

Ian Smale

Lively

I will wave my hands in praise and a - dor-a - tion, I will
wave my hands in praise and a - dor-a - tion, I will wave my hands in
praise and a - dor-a - tion, praise and a - dor-a - tion to the
liv - ing God. For He's giv - en me hands that
just love clap - ping: one, two, one, two, three, and He's

859.

I will worship
(You alone are worthy of my praise)

Deut 6:5; 11:22; 19:9; Josh 24:15
Ps 27:4,8; 95:6
Ps 105:4; 123:1
Mk 12:30; Lk 10:27; Heb 12:2

Worshipfully, with strength

David Ruis

1. I will wor-ship__ (I will wor-ship) with all of__ my heart. (with
   I will seek You__ (I will seek You) all of__ my days.

all of__ my__ heart.) I will praise You__ (I will praise You) with
(all of__ my__ days.) I will fol-low__ (I will fol-low)

all of__ my____ strength. (all my strength.)____
all of__ Your__ ways. (all Your ways.)____ I will give You

all my__ wor-ship, I will give__ You all my praise.__

You a-lone— I long to— wor - ship, You a-lone— are

wor-thy— of— my——— praise.——

2. I will bow down, (I will bow down,)
   Hail You as King, (hail You as King,)
   I will serve You, (I will serve You,)
   Give You everything. (give You everything.)
   I will lift up (I will lift up)
   My eyes to Your throne, (my eyes to Your throne,)
   I will trust You, (I will trust You,)
   I will trust You alone. (trust You alone.)

860.
I worship You, Almighty King
(Extravagant praise)

Lev 19:2; 2 Sam 6:14;
Ps 34:8; Eph 1:11;
Col 3:12; Heb 12:14; 1 Jn 1:7

With a jazz funk feel

Nathan Fellingham, Luke Fellingham
& Louise Hunt

I wor-ship You,_ Al-migh - ty King,_ the Ho - ly_ One,_____ for You_____ a-lone_____ have filled me with_ new life._____ My great - est_ Friend,_____ You've re-deemed_ my soul;_____ You've won_ my heart

2. You've called me Lord to live for You in holiness,
I've been made clean and chosen as Your son.
Through Jesus Christ You've made me whole,
My heart is filled with love for You.

861.
I worship You, O Lord
(Lord over all)

Jn 4:24

Callie Gerbrandt

Flowing

I wor-ship You, O Lord in spi-rit and truth; I bow my face be-fore Your throne, I praise You, Lord. I glo-ri-fy Your name, I mag-ni-fy Your name; and I ex-alt You Lord ov-er all, I praise You, Lord.

862.

I would rather be
(Your presence)

Ps 84:10-12; 95: 6; Jn 1:14;
Rom 5:2; Phil 3:7-8

Evan Rogers

Smoothly

1. I would ra - ther be___ a door-keep - er in___ Your house___ than

have the ma - ny things___ this world could of - fer.

All that I___ have gained___ I now count___ as loss,___ there's

no-thing that___ com-pares___ to know-ing___ You. In Your

pre - sence is where I want___ to___ be,___ the

place where You— re-veal— Your grace— and glo - - - ry. Your
pre - sence brings me to— my— knees,— I
bow down and— de-clare—— that You— are ho - ly.

3. I would rather have one day in Your courts, O Lord,
Than have a thousand days somewhere else.
You are my sun and shield, no good thing will You withold,
For blessed are the ones who trust in You.

863.

Jesus

Phil 2:9-11

Andy Thorpe

Je - sus,___ (Je - sus,___) Je - sus,___ (Je - sus,__) it's the Name__

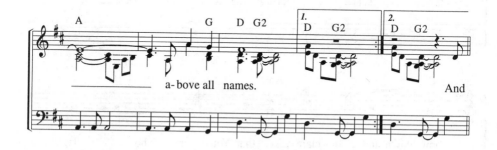

_____ a- bove all names. And

at the name of Je- sus ev-'ry knee shall bow,___ and ev-'ry

tongue con - fess He is Lord.

864.

Jesus at Your name
(You are the Christ)

Rom 8:15; Phil 2:10-11;
1 Jn 5:6

Chris Bowater

Steadily

Je-sus, at Your name___ we bow the knee.

Je-sus, at Your name__ we bow__ the knee, Je-sus, at Your name__ we

bow the knee. and ac - know-ledge You__ as Lord.

You are the Christ You are the Lord;

Through Your Spi-rit in our lives___ we know who__ You are.___

865.

Capo 1 (D)

Jesus Christ
(Once again)

Matt Redman

Thoughtfully, not too fast

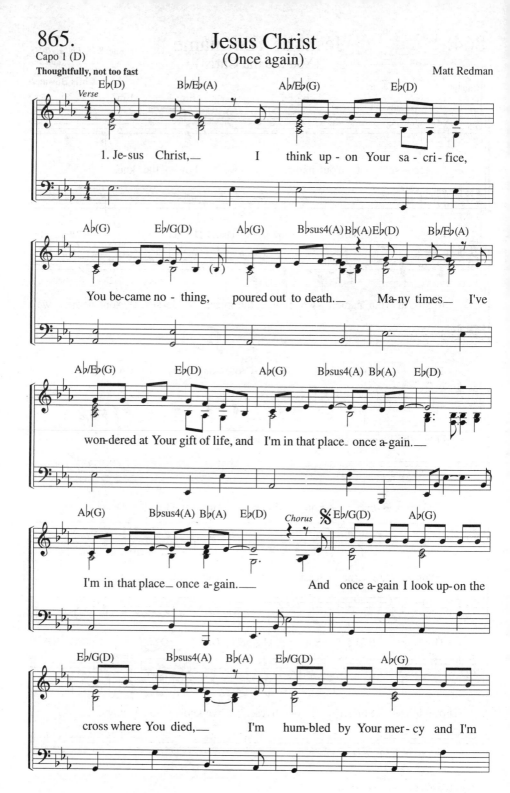

1. Je-sus Christ,— I think up-on Your sa-cri-fice, You be-came no - thing, poured out to death.— Ma-ny times— I've won-dered at Your gift of life, and I'm in that place— once a-gain.— I'm in that place— once a-gain.—

Chorus And once a-gain I look up-on the cross where You died,— I'm hum-bled by Your mer-cy and I'm

2. Now You are exalted to the highest place,
   King of the heavens, where one day I'll bow.
   But for now, I marvel at this saving grace,
   And I'm full of praise once again.
   I'm full of praise once again.

866. Jesus Christ is the Lord of all

Acts 4:12; 10:36

Steve Israel
& Gerrit Gustafson

Strongly, with a 'gospel' feel

Je-sus Christ— is the Lord of all, Lord of all— the— earth.—

Je-sus Christ— is the Lord of all, Lord of all— the— earth.—

Lord of all— the— earth.— On - ly One God—

o - ver the na - tions, on - ly one Lord— of all; in

no oth-er name— is there sal-va - tion,

1st time D.C.

Je-sus—is Lord of— all.   Je-sus Christ—is Lord of— all.

Je-sus Christ— is Lord of—— all.   Je-sus Christ— is Lord of——

D.C. al fine

all.   Je-sus Christ— is Lord of——— all.———

867.

Jesus, forgive me

Martin Lore

1. Je-sus, for-give me. Je-sus, free me. Je-sus, touch me. Je-sus, fill me. I lift my head,— lift my heart,— lift my soul— to— You. I give my life,— give my-self,— give it all— to—You.

2. Jesus, teach me.
   Jesus, lead me.
   Jesus, guide me.
   Jesus, use me.

Shout for joy to the Lord, all the earth. Worship the Lord with gladness; come before Him with joyful songs.

PSALM 100:1-2

868.

Jesus, I am thirsty
(More of You)

Jn 4:14

Capo 3 (D)

Don Harris & Martin J Nystrom

With feeling

Je-sus, I am thirs-ty, won't You come and fill___ me? Earth-ly things have left me dry,___ on-ly You can sa-tis-fy,___ all I want is more___ of You. All I want is more of You,___ all I want is more of You;___ no-thing I de-sire,___Lord,___

_ but more of You.____ All I want is

More of You.____

869.

Jesus, I love You

Is 6:1; Jer 31:3; Dan 7:9

Fairly slow

Judith Butler & Paul Hemingway

Chorus

Je - sus, I love__ You, I wor - ship and a - dore__ You.

Je - sus, I love__ You, Lord I glo - ri - fy Your name.

Verse

1. You are migh - ty, O Lord,____ the An - cient of Days.__ Your love stands for - ev - er,
2. You are reign - ing on high,____ ex - al - ted King.__ Your throne is e - ter - nal,

un - fail - ing Your ways.__

You are Lord ov - er all.__

D.C. al fine

"There is no-one holy like the Lord; there is no-one besides You; there is no Rock like our God."

1 SAMUEL 2:2

870.
Jesus is the name we honour
(Jesus is our God)

Phil 2:9-10; Heb 1:3; Rev 1:7

Phil Lawson Johnston

1. Je - sus is the name we ho - nour;
Je - sus is the name we praise. Ma - jes - tic
Name a - bove all oth - er names, the high - est heav'n and
earth pro - claim that Je - sus is our God. We will
glo - ri - fy, we will lift Him high, we will

give Him ho - nour and praise. We will glo - ri- fy, we will lift Him high, we will give Him ho - nour and praise.

2. Jesus is the name we worship;
   Jesus is the name we trust.
   He is the King above all other kings,
   Let all creation stand and sing
   That Jesus is our God.

3. Jesus is the Father's splendour;
   Jesus is the Father's joy.
   He will return to reign in majesty,
   And every eye at last will see
   That Jesus is our God.

871.

Jesus, Jesus
(Friend of sinners)

Mt 11:19; Lk 7:34; Jn 1:14; 4:8; Phil 2:9

Bryn Haworth

pre - sence— has filled this— place. We will

draw near— to—You, we come, Lord,—to seek Your face,

2. Jesus, Jesus,
   My heart aches, my soul waits,
   For Your healing, Lord, I pray.
   Jesus, Jesus,
   Mighty God, holy Child,
   Name above all names.

3. Jesus, Jesus,
   Son of God, Son of Man,
   My soul thirsts for You.

872.

Jesus, Lamb of God
(How I love You)

Is 53:12; 1 Cor 15:3;
Eph 1:7; 1 Pet 2:24; Rev 7:14
Alan Rose

Je - sus, Lamb of God, I stand re - deemed, washed
Je - sus, con - qu'ring King, You died for me, You

in Your blood. And in the ho - ly place I'll bow to
bore my sins. Your love has brought me to my knees to

1.
wor - ship and a - dore.
wor - ship and a -

2.
- dore, to

wor - ship and a - dore.

How I

love___ You, how I love___ You, how I

love— You, how I love You, how I love

You.

873.
Jesus, lover of my soul
(It's all about You)

Jn 6:68; Rev 1:8
14; 21:6; 22:13

Paul Oakley

Je - sus, lov-er of my soul,___ all con-su - ming fire___ is in Your___ gaze.___ Je - sus, I want You___ to know___ I will fol - low You___ all my___ days.___ For no-one else___ in his-to-ry___ is like___ You,___ and his-to-ry___ it-self___ be-longs___ to You.___ Al- pha and___ O-me-

874.
Jesus, lover of my soul

Ps 40:2

John Ezzy, Daniel Grul
& Stephen McPherson

Moderately

Verse
Je-sus,— lov-er of my soul,— Je-sus,— I will
ne-ver let You go:— You've tak-en me— from the mi-ry clay,—
You've set my feet up-on— the rock— and now I know:—

Chorus
I love You, I need You, though my world will fall,— I'll
nev-er let— You go;— my Sa-viour, my clos-est Friend,—

I will wor-ship You__ un - til the ve - ry end.__

til the ve - ry end.__

875. Jesus, remember me

Lk 23:42

Prayerfully ♩ = 69

Jacques Berthier

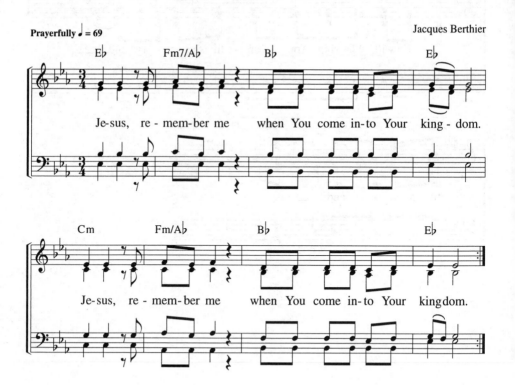

Je-sus, re-mem-ber me when You come in-to Your king-dom.

Je-sus, re-mem-ber me when You come in-to Your kingdom.

Surely God is my salvation; I will trust and not be afraid. The Lord, the Lord, is my strength and my song; He has become my salvation."

ISAIAH 12:2

876. Jesus, restore to us again

Mt 5:17; 17:4; Mk 9:5;
Lk 9:33; 24:44; Jn 1:14; 16:13;
Eph 6:17; 1 Thess 1:5; Rev 19:13

Graham Kendrick

Flowing

1. Je-sus, re - store to us a - gain the gos-pel of Your ho-ly name, that comes with pow'r, not words a - lone, owned, signed and sealed from heav-en's throne. Spi-rit and word in one a - greed; the pro-mise to the pow-er wed.___ The word is near, here in our mouths and

in our hearts, the word of faith; pro - claim it on the Spi - rit's breath: Je - sus!

2. Your word, O Lord, eternal stands,
   Fixed and unchanging in the heavens.
   The Word made flesh, to earth come down
   To heal our world with nail-pierced hands.
   Among us here You lived and breathed,
   You are the Message we received.

3. Spirit of truth, lead us, we pray
   Into all truth as we obey.
   And as God's will we gladly choose,
   Your ancient powers again will prove
   Christ's teaching truly comes from God,
   He is indeed the living Word.

4. Upon the heights of this great land
   With Moses and Elijah stand.
   Reveal Your glory once again,
   Show us Your face, declare Your name.
   Prophets and law, in You complete
   Where promises and power meet.

5. Grant us in this decisive hour
   To know the Scriptures and the power;
   The knowledge in experience proved,
   The power that moves and works by love.
   May word and works join hands as one,
   The word go forth, the Spirit come.

877. Jesus, what a beautiful name

Eph 1:7; Heb 2:14
1 Pet 2:24; Rev 5:12

Flowing

Tanya Riches

2. Jesus, what a beautiful name.
   Truth revealed, my future sealed,
   Healed my pain.
   Love and freedom, life and warmth,
   Grace that blows all fear away.
   Jesus, what a beautiful name.

3. Jesus, what a beautiful name.
   Rescued my soul, my stronghold,
   Lifts me from shame.
   Forgiveness, security, power and love,
   Grace that blows all fear away.
   Jesus, what a beautiful name.

Let the name of the Lord be praised, both now and for evermore.

PSALM 113:2

878. Just the mention of Your name

Chris Bowater

Just the men-tion of Your name causes me to fall be-
Just the men-tion of Your name re-af-firms the love that

fore You, tears____ flow as I a - dore You,
holds me, speaks once more of love that knows me,

at the men-tion of Your name, just the men-tion of Your

1. name.   2. name.   Je - sus,

Je - sus, Je - sus.

Je - sus,   at the men-tion of Your

name_____ I wor-ship._____

879.

Let all the world

Ps 66:4; 69:34; Rev 5:13

Tune: LUCKINGTON

Words: George Herbert (1593-1633)
Music: Basil Harwood (1859-1949)

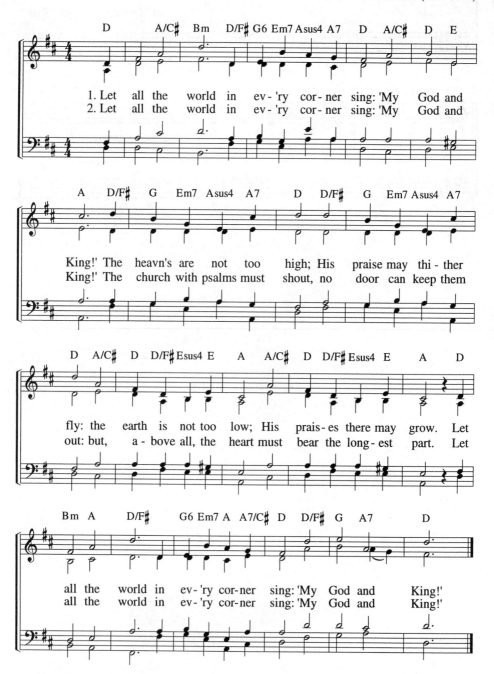

1. Let all the world in ev-'ry cor-ner sing: 'My God and King!' The heavn's are not too high; His praise may thi-ther fly: the earth is not too low; His prais-es there may grow. Let all the world in ev-'ry cor-ner sing: 'My God and King!'

2. Let all the world in ev-'ry cor-ner sing: 'My God and King!' The church with psalms must shout, no door can keep them out: but, a-bove all, the heart must bear the long-est part. Let all the world in ev-'ry cor-ner sing: 'My God and King!'

Clap your hands all you nations; shout to God with cries of joy.

PSALM 47:1

880.   Let everything that has breath

Matt Redman

2. Praise You in the heavens.
   Joining with the angels,
   Praising You forever and a day.
   Praise You on the earth now,
   Joining with creation,
   Calling all the nations to Your praise.

   If they could see . . .

881. Let every tribe and every tongue
(We give You praise)

Ex 3:14; Rev 5:9-10,12

With strength

Debbye Graafsma

Let ev-'ry tribe and ev-'ry tongue bring praise to the Lamb, for He has tri-umphed ov-er all,— He has tri-umphed. With His blood— He has re-deemed— us for ev-er to reign with Him in glo-ry,— a-men.

We sing glo-ry, glo-ry to the Lamb; Son of God, the Great I

Wor-thy, wor-thy is the Lamb; Ho-ly, re-sur-rect-ed

882.
Let the chimes of freedom ring
(Chimes of freedom)

With a lilting feel

Dave Bilbrough

1. Let the chimes of free-dom ring all a-cross the
2. O-pen wide your pri-son doors to greet the Lord of

earth; lift your voice in praise to Him and
life; songs of tri-umph fill the air, Christ

sing of all His worth, and sing of all His worth. live. Let
Je-sus is a-live, Christ Je-sus is a-

Chorus
all the peo-ple hear the news of the One who comes to

save: He's the Lord of all the u-ni-verse, and for-ev-er He shall

3. In every corner of the earth,
   To every tribe and tongue,
   Make known that God so loved this world
   That He gave His only Son,
   He gave His only Son.

4. Spread the news and make it plain
   He breaks the power of sin;
   Jesus died and rose again,
   His love will never end,
   His love will never end.
      Let all the people . . .

5. He will return in majesty
   To take His rightful place
   As King of all eternity,
   The Name above all names,
   The name above all names.
      Let all the people . . .

883.

Let the church arise

Ps 126:3; Is 2:3; Ezek 34:26-27
Mic 4:2; 1 Pet 2:24

With life

Phil Wilthew

1. Let the church a - rise,—— and let the dark-ness—— fall.——

Say to those in—— chains,—— "you are now set—— free".——

Sick-ness has died its—— death—— through the blood of—— Christ.——

To all the op-pressed,——

He now pro - mis - es life.————

Chorus

Je - sus, Lord of all,___ come to us___
Je - sus, Lord of all,___ come to us___

___ in a time of drought;___ send___ Your show -
___ in a time of need;___ send___ re - vi -

- ers, let us know the rich - es of Your mer - cy.___
- val, let our na - tion* see___ Your awe - some glo - ry.___

Last time to Coda
2nd time D.C.

(1st time tacet)

Come, let us go___ to the house___ of God,___

___ with His prai - ses in our hearts;___ For the Lord has done___

* *2nd time* the nations

great things for us,___ and His glo-ry's com-ing a-gain.___

2. Awake, O church, sing with all your might;
The Lord of all the earth is in your midst.
He is mending lives, He is winning hearts;
In these coming days let revival start.

"Great and marvellous are Your deeds, Lord God Almighty. Just and true are Your ways, King of the ages."

REVELATION 15:3

884.   Let the righteous sing

Ps 68:3-6

Capo 3 (D)

Bryn Haworth

Bright and rhythmic

Let the right - eous sing, come let the right - eous dance, re -
Shout for joy— to God who rides up - on— the clouds, how

joice be - fore— your God, be hap - py— and joy - ful,
awe - some are— His deeds, so great is— His pow - er.

Last time to Coda

give Him— your praise. We give You— our praise.

He gives the des - ol - ate— a— home,

He leads the pris-oners out__ with sing -

ing. Fa-ther to__ the fa - ther-less, de - fen-der of__ the wi-

dow is__ God in His ho - ly place._____ So

⊕ CODA

we give You__ our praise, we give You__ our praise.

885.

Let us draw near

Heb 10:22; Jas 4:8; Rev 7:14

David Fellingham

Let us draw near to God in full as-sur-ance of faith, know-ing that as we draw near to Him, He will draw near to us. In the ho-ly place we stand in con-fi-dence, know-ing our lives are cleansed in the blood of the Lamb, we will wor-ship and a-dore.

Come near to God and He will come near to you.

JAMES 4:8

886. Let us draw near with confidence
(Great High Priest)

With strength

Heb 2:14; 4:15-16; 10:19-22
1 Jn 3:8; Rev 13:8
Mark Altrogge

1. Let us draw near with con - fi - dence, we have a Great High Priest.

(v.2) There's mer-cy e-nough for all our sins, we have a Great High Priest. He was made weak and He was tried, we have a Great High Priest. He's a-ble to feel and sym - pa - thise,

2. Let us each come with conscience cleansed,
We have a Great High Priest.
It's by His shed blood we enter in,
We have a Great High Priest.
We trust in no merits of our own,
We have a Great High Priest.
But look to the power of the cross alone,
We have a Great High Priest.

887.

Let us go

Ps 24:3-4; Is 2:3; Mic 4:2 Mt 27:51
Mk 15:38; Lk 23:45; Heb 10:20,22
1 Jn 1:7; Rev 17:14; 19:16

Rocky

Paul Oakley

Let us go— up to the house— of God—

with a shout of praise,— with a song of ce-le-bra - tion.

Last time to CODA

We'll as-cend— the hill of— the Lord,— we can stand in the ho-

ly place. We can have— clean hands— and a pure heart;—

His blood can cleanse us— from all our— un-righ-teous - ness.

Praise the Lord. Praise, O servants of the Lord, praise the name of the Lord.

PSALM 113:1

888.
Let Your love come down

Driving

Noel & Tricia Richards

Chorus

Oh,_____ oh,_____ oh,_____ let Your love_ come down._

Verse

1. There is vio - lence in_ the air.

Fear_ touch - es all_ our lives._

How much pain_ can peo - ple bear?_

2. There is power in Your love,
   Bringing laughter out of tears.
   It can heal the wounded soul.
   In the streets where anger reigns,
   Love will wash away the pain.
   We are calling, heaven's love come down.

889.

Let Your word

David & Nathan Fellingham

Strong and rhythmic

Verse

1. Let Your word run free-ly through this na - tion,— strong De-
liv - 'rer, break the grip— of Sa - tan's pow'r. Let the cross—
— of Je - sus stand a - bove— the i - dols of this land, let a -
noin - ted lives— rise up and take— their stand. And we will

Chorus

glo - ri - fy the— Lamb, slain from e - ter - ni - ty.

Je-sus is Lord, we de - clare His— name, and stand in His vic-to-

ry, and stand in His vic-to - ry. ry.

Verses 2 & 3

2. With pro - phet-ic words of pow'r, ex-pose the dark - ness;— with
3. Let the Ho-ly Spi - rit's fi - re burn with-in us,— cleansed from

a - pos-tol - ic wis-dom build the church.— With zeal for the lost— let the
sin and pure with-in we stand up - right. Not yield-ing to wrong,— we will

sto - ry be told,— let the shep-herds feed the lambs with-in their folds. And we will
live in ho-li-ness, bring-ing glo - ry to the Sa - viour, we will shine. And we will

890.

Lift Him up
(Lift Him high)

Capo 3 (D)

Brightly

Mt 7:7; Lk 11:9; Jn 12:32

Dave Bilbrough

Lift Him up, lift Him high, let His prais-es fill the sky. Oh,
heav-en's gates are op-en wide_____ to those who hear the call.
call. 1. Through ev-'ry gen-er-a - tion this truth will al - ways shine, that
Christ came down a- mong____ us, now He is glo-ri - fied.____

2. The message of the kingdom
Stands unshakeable through time:
That man can be forgiven,
If you seek then you will find.

From the rising of the sun to the place where it sets, the name of the Lord is to be praised.

PSALM 113:3

891.

Like a candle flame
(The candle song)

Mt 1:21,23; Lk 2:13; Jn 1:4

Graham Kendrick

Softly, with awe

Verse

1. Like a can-dle flame, flick-'ring small in our dark-ness.
Un-cre-a-ted light shines through in-fant eyes.

Chorus

(Men) God is with us, al-le-lu-ia,
(Women) God is with us, al-le-

lu-ia,
(Men) come to save us, al-le-lu-ia,
(Women) come to save us,

(All)
al - le - lu - ia!_____ ia! ia!

2. Stars and angels sing,
   Yet the earth sleeps in the shadows;
   Can this tiny spark
   Set a world on fire?

3. Yet His light shall shine
   From our lives, Spirit blazing,
   As we touch the flame
   Of His holy fire.

892.

Lord, for the years

Mt 16:24; Mk 8:43; Lk 9:23; 19:10;
Eph 2:12; 1 Tim 2:1-2; 2 Tim 3:16

Tune: LORD OF THE YEARS

Michael Baughen

1. Lord, for the years Your love has kept and guid-ed, Urged and in-spired us, cheered us on__ our way,__ Sought us and saved us, par-doned and pro-vid-ed: Lord of the years,__ we bring our thanks to-day.

2. Lord, for that word, the word of life which fires us,
Speaks to our hearts and sets our souls ablaze,
Teaches and trains, rebukes us and inspires us:
Lord of the word, receive Your people's praise.

3. Lord, for our land in this our generation,
Spirits oppressed by pleasure, wealthand care:
For young and old, for commonwealth and nation,
Lord of our land, be pleased to hearour prayer.

4. Lord, for our world where men disown and doubt You,
Loveless in strength, and comfortlessin pain,
Hungry and helpless, lost indeedwithout You:
Lord of the world, we pray that Christ may reign.

5. Lord for ourselves; in living power remake us -
Self on the cross and Christ upon the throne,
Past put behind us, for the future take us:
Lord of our lives, to live for Christ alone.

Timothy Dudley-Smith

Lord, have mercy

2 Chron 7:14

Dave Bilbrough

With feeling

Lord, have mer - cy,___ Lord have mer - cy;___

___ move in pow - er on this land._____

Hear our prayer, hear our prayer, O__ Lord,

O_____ Lord. O__ Lord.

894. Lord, I come before Your throne of grace

Capo 2 (A)

(What a faithful God)

Building, with strength

Deut 7:9; 32:4; Ps 16:11;25: 33:4;
61:4; 145:13; 146:6; Mt 11:28; 1 Cor 1:9; 2 Cor 1:4

Robert & Dawn Critchley

1. Lord, I come be-fore Your throne of grace; I find rest in Your pre-sence, and ful-ness of joy. In (v.2)

(v.2) wor-ship and won-der I be-hold Your face, sing-ing what a faith-ful God have I. What a faith-ful God have I, what a faith-ful God.

2. Lord of mercy, You have heard my cry;
Through the storm You're the beacon, my song in the night.
In the shelter of Your wings, hear my heart's reply,
Singing what a faithful God have I.

895.
Capo 3 (G)

Lord, I come to You
(The power of Your love)

Is 40:31; Lk 15:20; Rom 12:2

Geoff Bullock

1. Lord, I come to You— let my heart be changed, re-newed,— flow-ing from the grace that I found in You. And Lord, I've come to know— the weak-ness-es I see— in me— will be stripped a-way— by the pow'r of Your love.—

2. Lord unveil my eyes, let me see You face to face,
   The knowledge of Your love as You live in me.
   Lord renew my mind
   As Your will unfolds in my life, in living every day
   By the power of Your love.

896.   Lord, I have heard of Your fame
(Remember mercy)

Hab 3:2

Capo 2 (D)

Brian Doerksen

Steadily

Lord, I have heard of— Your fame,

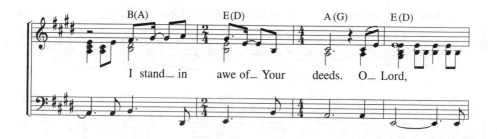

I stand— in awe of— Your deeds. O— Lord,

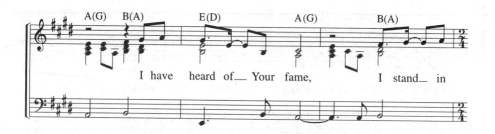

I have heard of— Your fame, I stand— in

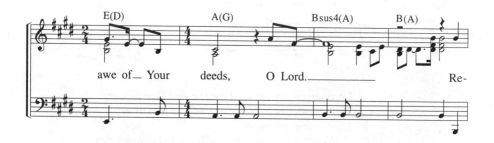

awe of— Your deeds, O Lord.———— Re-

897. Lord, I lift Your name on high
(You came from heaven to earth)

1 Cor 15:3-4

Rick Founds

Lord, I lift Your name on high; Lord I love to sing Your

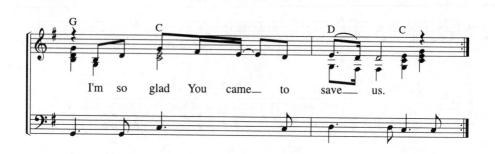

prais - es. I'm so glad You're in my life;

I'm so glad You came to save us.

You came from heav - en to earth to show the way,

898. Lord, I long to see You glorified
(Lord of all)

Num 14:21;
Ps 72:19; Hab 2:14; 3:3

Capo 3 (D)

Steadily

Steve McPherson

1. Lord, I long to see You glorified in ev-'ry-thing I do; all my heart-felt dreams I put a-side, to see Your Spi-rit move with pow-er in my life.

2. Je-sus, Lord of all e-ter-ni-ty, Your child-ren rise in faith; all the earth dis-plays Your glo-ry, and each word You speak brings life to all who hear. Lord of

899.
Lord, look upon my need
(I need You)

Ps 51:1,7; 139:3,16

Rick Founds

Lord, look up-on_ my need, I need_ You,_ I need_

_ You._ Lord, have mer-cy now_ on me, for-give_

_ me, O Lord, for-give me,_ and I will be_

_ clean._ O_ Lord, You are_ fa-mil - iar with_ my_ways,

there is noth-ing hid from_ You._____ O__ Lord, You know_ the num-

ber of_ my_ days, I want to live my life for_ You._____

900.
Lord, my heart cries out
(Glory to the King)

Ps 3:3; 68:5

Darlene Zschech

Verse

Lord, my heart cries out, 'Glo-ry to the King.' My great-est
O-pen my ears, let me hear Your voice, to know that

love in life, I hand You ev-'ry-thing:
sweet sound, oh, my soul re-joice:

'glo-ry, glo-ry,' I hear the an-gels sing.

an-gels sing. You're the

Chorus

Fa-ther to the fa-ther-less, the

901.   Lord of all creation

With strength

Joe King

1. Lord of all cre-a-tion, let this gen-e-ra-tion see a vis-it-a-tion of Your pow'r; put to flight all the pow'rs of dark-ness, O come, Lord Je-sus,— come.

Chorus

Lord of all cre-a-tion, let this gen-er-a-tion see a vis-it-a-tion of_ Your_ pow'r. Lord of all cre-a-tion, there's an ex-pec-ta-tion ris-ing in this na-tion ev-'ry_ hour.

2. Father God, forgive us,
Send Your cleansing rivers,
Wash us now and give us holy power;
Fill this land with Your awesome presence,
O come, Lord Jesus, come.

Sing to the Lord, for He has done glorious things; let this be known to all the world.

ISAIAH 12:5

902.

Lord of all hopefulness

Mt 13:55; Mk 6:3;
Lk 8:24; 15:20;
Jn 14:27; 2 Thes 3:16

Capo 1 (D)

Tune: SLANE

Irish Traditional Melody
Arr. David Ball

Lord of all hopefulness, Lord of all joy, whose trust ev-er child-like, no cares could de-stroy; be there at our wak-ing, and give us, we pray, Your bliss in our hearts, Lord, at the break of the day.

2. Lord of all eagerness, Lord of all faith,
   Whose strong hands were skilled
   At the plane and the lathe,
   Be there at our labours,
   And give us, we pray,
   Your strength in our hearts, Lord,
   At the noon of the day.

3. Lord of all kindliness, Lord of all grace,
   Your hands swift to welcome,
   Your arms to embrace,
   Be there at our homing,
   And give us, we pray,
   Your love in our hearts, Lord,
   At the eve of the day.

4. Lord of all gentleness, Lord of all calm,
   Whose voice is contentment,
   Whose presence is balm,
   Be there at our sleeping,
   And give us, we pray,
   Your peace in our hearts, Lord,
   At the end of the day.

Jan Struther (1901 – 1953)

903.

Lord of the dance

2 Sam 6:14; Ps 149:4

With life

Kevin Prosch

Lord of the dance,__ You're the dan - cing Lord.__

1.2.3. (Lord of the dance,__ You're the dan - cing Lord.)__ *4.*

Ev - 'ry - bo - dy dance, yeah!__

Well ev-'ry-bo-dy dance, now,__
stop me now,__

get in the Ho - ly Ghost.__
I'm gon-na give it ev-'ry-thing I've got.__

"From the lips of children and infants you have ordained praise'"

MATTHEW 21:16

904.

Lord, pour out Your Spirit
(Great awakening)

Ps 68:28; Is 13:13; 62:2; 66:18;
Joel 2:28,32; Hag 2:6; Acts 2:17,21;
Rom 8:19; 10:13; Heb 12:26

Ray Goudie, Dave Bankhead & Steve Bassett

With expectation

1. Lord, pour out Your Spi-rit on all the peo-ples of the

earth; let Your sons and daugh-ters

speak Your words of pro-phe-cy. Send us dreams and

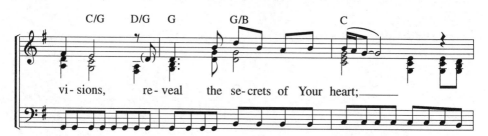

vi-sions, re-veal the se-crets of Your heart;

Lord, our faith is ris-ing, let all heav-en sound the com-

2. Lord, pour out Your Spirit
   On all the nations of the world;
   Let them see Your glory,
   Let them fall in reverent awe.
   Show Your mighty power,
   Shake the heavens and the earth;
   Lord, the world is waiting,
   Let creation see the coming of Your day.

905.
Lord, we come in adoration
(Go in Your name)

Mt 28:19; Phil 2:10;
Rev 17:14; 19:16

Dave Bilbrough

Bright and rhythmic

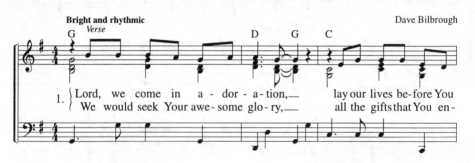

1. Lord, we come in a-dor-a-tion,— lay our lives be-fore You
   We would seek Your awe-some glo-ry,— all the gifts that You en-

now. We are here to reach the na-tions,— to
dow; called to reach this gen-e-ra-tion,— and

tell the world of Je - sus' pow'r.—
now is the ap - point- ed hour.—We will

Chorus

go in Your name; go and pro-claim Your king- dom. Go

in Your name, for we have been cho-sen to

tell all cre-a-tion that Je-sus is King of all kings.

2. We believe that You have spoken
   Through Your Son to all the earth;
   Given us this great commission
   To spread the news of all Your worth.
   Set apart to serve You only,
   Let our lives display Your love;
   Hearts infused that tell the story
   Of God come down from heaven above.

3. Grant to us a fresh anointing,
   Holy Spirit, be our guide;
   Satisfy our deepest longing -
   Jesus Christ be glorified.
   Every tribe and every people,
   Hear the message that we bring;
   Christ has triumphed over evil,
   Bow the knee and worship Him.

906.
Lord, we cry to You
(God, break through)

Ps 85:6; Acts 2:2-3

David Fellingham

2. Lord, we cry to You: God, break through!
   Move upon Your church in revival.
   Like a mighty wind and tongues of fire,
   Let Your Spirit come in revival.

3. Lord, we cry to You: God, break through!
   Sweep across this land in revival.
   Like the mighty rain, flood this land again;
   Let Your power come in revival.

907.   Lord, we long to see Your glory

Jn 17:24

Richard Lewis

With awe

stay__ in Your pre - sence,__ and wor- ship at Your feet for ev - er-

more._____ Ho - ly God._____

Ho - ly God._____

908.
Lord, we long to see Your glory
(Help us to sing)

Capo 3 (D)

2 Sam 6:14;
1 Cor 13:12; 2 Tim 2:12;
Rev 5:10; 21:2; 22:5

With strength, not too fast

Nathan Fellingham

Lord, we long_ to see_ Your glo-ry, Lord, we long to feel_ Your_ pow'r. In these times_ of re-fresh - ing, we long to know You_ more.___ To be-hold_ You in Your ma-jes-ty,_ our hearts are filled with_ joy; as we look_ to-wards_ the com - ing King,_ we cry

909.   Lord, we've come to worship You

Ian Smale

With a gentle rhythm

Lord, we come to wor-ship You,— Lord, we come to praise: Lord, we've come— to wor-ship You— in oh, so ma-ny ways.— Some of us shout, and some of us sing, and some of us whis-per the praise we bring; but Lord, we all— are ga-ther-ing— to give to You— our praise.

910. Lord, You are the Author of my life

Mt 6:10; Rom 8:29; Eph 1:12-12; Phil 1:6

Judy Pruett

Flowing

Lord, You are the Au - thor of__ my life,__ You have be - gun__
Lord, You are the Lord__ of all__ my days,__ You are the Lord__

__ a work__ in me,__ You have pre - des - tined me__ to
__ of all__ my nights,__ You__ have cho - sen me__ to

do Your per - fect will.__ And Lord, fin - ish in me__
car - ry forth__ Your word.__ So Lord, let__ me seek__

__ what You've__ be - gun,__ guide me by__ Your migh - ty hand,__
__ Your ho - ly face,__ may I al - ways walk__ with You,__

Lord; Let me trust_ in You.__ And Lord, and let Your

will be_ done.

911. Lord, You are worthy

Rev 4:8; 5:12

Capo 1 (E)

David Baroni

With a gospel feel

1. 2. Lord, You are wor - thy, Lord, You are wor - thy, Lord, You are wor - thy, we give You praise. praise.

3. Lord, You are ho - ly, Lord, You are ho - ly,

2. Lord, You are worthy....

3. Lord, You are holy...

4. Lord, we adore You...

5. Lord, You are worthy...

912.   Lord, You have my heart

Ps 27:8; Rom 12:1

Tenderly

Martin Smith

Lord, You have my heart, and I will search for Yours;

Je-sus, take my life and lead me on.
let me be to You a sa-cri-fice.

(Men) And I will praise You,

(Women) I will praise You, Lord.

Lord. And I will sing of love come down.

I will sing of love_ come_ down._ Show Your

Asus4   A   D   Dsus4   G   D/F# Asus4

—   And   as   You   show   Your   face,_____

Last time

face,   we'll   see   Your_   glo - ry   here.

A   G   D/F# Asus4 A   D   Dsus4   D   Dsus4

Last time

D

—   we'll   see   Your   glo - ry   here.

913.

Lost in the shuffle
(Dancing with the Father)

Eph 2:6; Heb 10:22

Lively

Wayne Drain

1. Lost in the shuf-fle, I was lost as a goose, the
de-vil had a rope out, and it looked just like a noose. But
just be-fore I went off of that deep end, my
Fa-ther threw me out a line, for-gave me of my sin. Now we're
(Last time)

2. He took me to the water and He cleaned me real good,
   Then He raised me up to be with Him, I feel just like I should.
   He filled me with His Spirit, I drank the whole cup,
   Now when He calls I hear it,
   Hey, turn that volume up!
   'Cause we're dancin' . . .

"My soul glorifies the Lord and my spirit rejoices in God my Saviour."

LUKE 1:46

914.
Love songs from heaven

Mt 5:16; Jn 1:5; 8:12

Building, with strength

Noel & Tricia Richards

1. Love songs_ from hea - ven_ are fil - ling_ the earth, bring-ing_ great hope to_ all na - - tions. E - vil_ has pros - pered,_ but truth is_ a - live; in this_ dark world the light still shines.

2. No - thing_ has si - lenced_ this gos - pel_ of Christ; it ech - oes down through_ the a - - ges. Blood of_ the mar - tyrs_ has made Your_ church strong; in this_ dark world the light still shines.

For You__ we live, and for You we__ may__ die;

through us__ may Je - sus__ be__ seen.

For You__ a - lone we will of - fer__ our__ lives;

in this__ dark world our__ light will shine.

3. Let every nation be filled with Your song:
   This is the cry of Your people.
   We will not settle for anything less,
   In this dark world our light must shine.

915. Magnificent Warrior

Josh 5:13-15
Ps 93:1; 45:3-5; 149:6-9

Graham Kendrick

1. Mag-ni-fi-cent War-ri-or ar-ray'd for bat - tle, we see You rea - dy to slay Your en - e-mies. O migh-ty Cap - tain of heav - en's arm - ies, we bow be - fore You, we wor-ship You. So take Your sword up-on Your side, O Migh-ty One, clothe Your-self with splen-dour

2. Magnificent Warrior,
   We hear Your strong command
   To join the ranks of light
   And march into the fight;
   By faith to overthrow
   Ten thousand Jerichos,
   To make Your judgements known
   In all the earth.

916.
Makes you wanna dance
(People just like us)

Acts 4:12; Rev 1:7; 7:9

Russell Fragar

With energy

917.

Make us a house of prayer

Is 56:7; Mt 21:13;
Mk 11:17; Lk 19;46

Daniel Brymer

Lyrics:

Make us a house of prayer, that we might
Lord, teach us to pray un-ceas-ing-ly

meet You there on be-half of the na - tion to a
night and day.

dy-ing ge-ne-ra - tion, make us a house of prayer.

And Make our in-ter-ces - sion for

You a migh - ty wea-pon. O Lord, teach us to pray.

918. May God be gracious to us
(May the peoples praise You)

Ps 67:1-7

Lyrics adapted by Ian White from NIV text
1973, 1978, 1984, International Bible Society
Music by Ian White

1. May God be gra-cious to us___ and bless___ us,___ make His face___ to shine___ up - on us.___ May Your ways_ be known___ ov-er the earth___ and Your sal-va - tion a - mong all na - tions.

2. May the nations be glad and sing for joy,
   For with justice You rule the people You guide.
   May Your ways be known over all the earth,
   And Your salvation among all nations.

3. Then the harvest will come to the land,
   And God, our God, will bless us.
   God will bless us, and all the ends
   Of earth will fear Him.

919. May I sing a song of love

(Draw me near)

Ex 3:5; Heb 10:22

Capo 2 (A)

David Gate

Building in strength

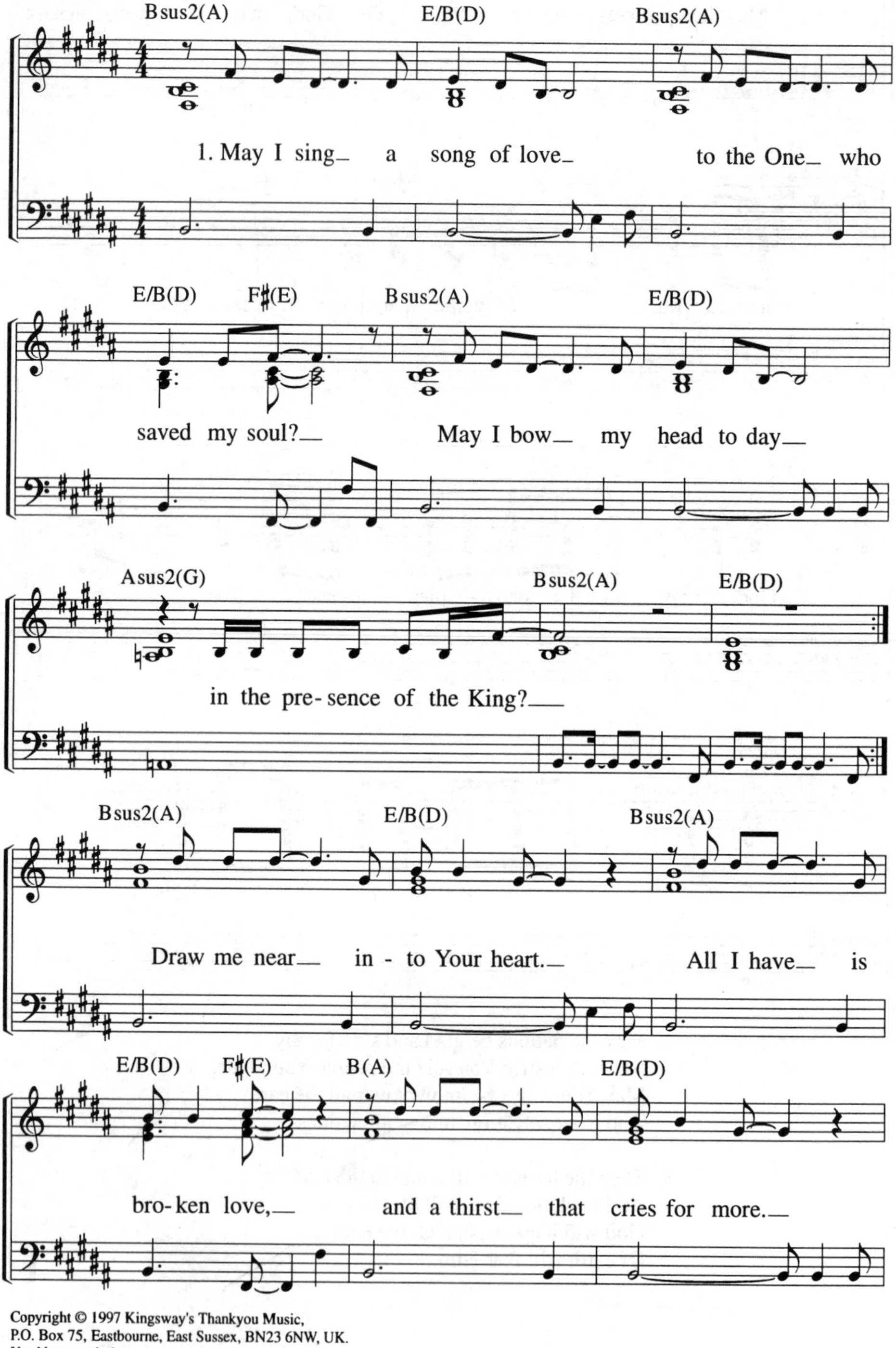

Bsus2(A) E/B(D) Bsus2(A)
1. May I sing a song of love to the One who
E/B(D) F♯(E) Bsus2(A) E/B(D)
saved my soul? May I bow my head to day
Asus2(G) Bsus2(A) E/B(D)
in the pre- sence of the King?
Bsus2(A) E/B(D) Bsus2(A)
Draw me near in - to Your heart. All I have is
E/B(D) F♯(E) B(A) E/B(D)
bro- ken love, and a thirst that cries for more.

Draw— me near to— You.——

Last time   *Fine*

2. You have called and I will come,
   Lift my hands up to Your throne;
   Worship You on holy ground -
   That's what I long to do.

920. May our worship be as fragrance
(A living sacrifice)

Rom 12:1; Rev 8:4; 12:11

Chris Bowater

May our wor- ship be as fra- grance, may our wor- ship be as in- cense_ poured forth. May our wor- ship be ac-

cep- ta- ble as a liv - ing sac- ri- fice,_ as a

liv - ing sac- ri- fice._ We are wil - ling_

921.

Men of faith
(Shout to the north)

Mt 28:18; Acts 10:36
2 Cor 12:10; Phil 2:10

Martin Smith

Strongly

1. Men of faith, rise up and sing of the
   wo - men of the truth, stand and
   church with bro - ken wings; fill this

great and glor - ious King; you are strong when you feel
sing to bro - ken hearts, who can know the heal - ing
place with songs a - gain, of our God who reigns on

weak, in your bro - ken - ness com - plete.
pow'r of our glor - ious King of love.
high: by His grace a - gain we'll fly.

Shout to the north and the south, sing to the

east and the west: Je - sus is Sa - viour to all,

922.

Merciful God and Father
(Healing grace)

Lk 18:13

Capo 1 (D)

John Chisum & Gary Sadler

Steadily

Mer-ci-ful God and Fa-ther, lov-ing us like no oth-er, hear our prayer,— the cry of our hearts,— as we come to You. We ack-now-ledge our— trans-gres - sions,— we con-fess to You— our sins;— show us mer-cy and— com-pas - sion,—

923.

Mighty God

Is 7:14; 9:2,6; Mt 1:23

Mark & Helen Johnson and Chris Bowater

In a lively half-time

Migh - ty God,____ ev - er-last - ing Fa - ther, won-der-ful

Coun - sel - lor,____ You're the Prince____ of Peace.____

____ 1. You are Lord of hea - ven, You are called Em-

man - u - el;____ God is now with us,____

ev - er pres - ent to de - li - ver. You are God e - ter-

nal, You are Lord of all the earth;___ love has

come to us,___ bring - ing us___ new birth._____

2. A light to those in darkness,
   And a guide to paths of peace;
   Love and mercy dawns,
   Grace, forgiveness and salvation.
   Light for revelation,
   Glory to Your people;
   Son of the Most High,
   God's love gift to all.

924. Mighty is our God

Jn 1:3; Phil 2:9;
Col 1:16; Rev 4:11

Capo 3 (G)
With life

Eugene Greco, Gerrit Gustafson
& Don Moen

Then a voice came from the throne, saying: "Praise our God, all you His servants, you who fear Him, both small and great!"

REVELATION 19:5

925.

Mighty is the Lord

1 Chron 16:25; Ps 61:1; 96:4;
145:3; Prov 18:10; Is 9:6

Capo 1 (A)

Lively

A.P. Douglas

1. Migh - ty is the Lord and most wor - thy of praise,—
Na - tions will rise__ and__ na - tions will fall,—

praise Him all you peo - ple.
praise Him all you peo - ple.

Look up - on Him,__ God a-
But there is One__ who is

lone__ who saves:__ praise the Lord of all.__
Lord__ of all:__ praise the Lord of all.__

He is Won - der - ful,__ Coun - sel - lor,__

glo-ri-ous Prince___ of Peace.___ He is Lord and King___ of

ev-'ry-thing,___ His prais-es nev-er cease.___ He is

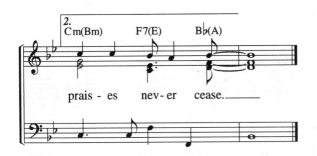

prais-es nev-er cease.___

2. Awesome and great, like the strongest tower:
Praise Him all you people.
He is the One with limitless power:
Praise the Lord of all.
Leaders may come and presidents fall:
Praise Him all you people.
But there is One who is Lord of all:
Praise the Lord of all.

926.

Mighty, mighty Lord

Mt 6:9; Lk 11:2; Rev 15:3

Carol Owen

Steadily

1. Migh-ty, migh-ty Lord. Pre-cious is Your name. Won-der-ful Your ways, wor-thy of all praise, Je-ho-vah. Je-ho-vah. Hal-lowed be Your name, Lord God Al-

2. Migh-ty, migh-ty Lord. Ho-ly is Your name. Glo-ri-ous and true, great in all You do, Je-ho-vah.

migh-ty,   for Yours is the king-dom,   the pow-er and the glo -

ry, for- ev- er   more._____

927.

More than oxygen

Heb 1:3

Brian Doerksen

Steadily

1. More than ox - y - gen,_____ I need your love;_____ more than life - giv - ing food_____ the hun - gry dream of._____ More than an el - o - quent word_____ de - pends on the tongue;_____

2. More than magnet and steel are drawn to unite.
   More that poets love words to rhyme as they write.
   More than comforting warmth of sun in spring.
   More than the eagle loves wind under its wings.

3. More than a blaz - ing fire____ on a win - ter's night,____

more than the tall e - ver-greens____

928.

Most holy Judge
(I'm justified)

Rom 3:22-26; 8:15-17

Capo 3 (D)

Steve & Vikki Cook

Driving

Verse

1. Most ho-ly Judge,_____ I stood be-fore__ You guil - ty,

when you sent Je-sus to_ the cross_____ for my sin.__ There Your__

love was re-vealed,_____ Your jus-tice vin - di-cat - ed,

one sac-ri-fice__ has paid_ the cost_____ for all__ who trust__ in Je-

2. I come to You,
And I can call you "Father",
There is no fear
There is no shame before You.
For by Your gift of grace
Now I am one of Your children,
An heir with those who bear Your name,
And share the hope of glory.

929.

Mukti Dil-aye
(He saves)

Lk 2:7; Acts 4:12; Rom 3:25

Author unknown
Arr. June George
& Martin J Smith

Steadily

Muk - ti dil-a-ye Ye-su naam,_____ Shan-ti dil-a-ye Ye-su
Peace comes to you in Je-sus' name,_____ sal-va-tion in no oth-er

naam.
name.

1. Ye - su da-ya____ ka be - h - ta____ sa-gar,____
2. Cha - r(e)-ni main too - ney jan - am-(e) li-ya Ye-su:
3. Ham-(e) sab-(e) key____ pa - pon____ ko mi-ta-ne:
4. Krus____ par-(e) ap-(e)-na khoon - (e) ba-haa kar:

Ye - su da-ya____ ka be - h - ta____ sa-gar,____
Cha - r(e)-ni main too - ney jan - am-(e) li-ya Ye-su.
Ham - (e) sab-(e) key____ pa - pon____ ko mi-ta-ne.____
Krus____ par-(e) ap-(e)-na khoon - (e) ba-haa kar____

Ye - su hai da - ta ma - han,_____
Soo - ley pay ki-ya vish-(e) - ram,_____
Ye - su hu - a hai ba-li - dan,_____
sa - re chu-ka - ya____ daam,_____

Ye - su hai da - ta ma - han.
Soo - ley pay ki - ya vish - (e) - ram.
Ye - su hu - a hai ba - li - dan.
Sa - ra - chu - ka - ya daam.

Translation

Peace comes to you in Jesus' name,
Salvation in no other name.

Jesus is the Ocean of Grace:
You are majestic, Lord.

Jesus, You were born in a manger (made of wood:)
You were crucified on the cross (made of wood.)

For the remission of our sins,
Jesus has been sacrificed on the cross.

By shedding Your blood on the cross,
You paid the full price for our sins.

930.

My first love
(Like a child)

As a jig

2 Sam 6:14; Ps 42:7; 85:6; Song 8:6;
Mt 24:31; Jn 4:14; 1 Cor 15:52;
1 Thess 4:16;4 Rev 2:4

Stuart Townend

1. My first love is a blaz-ing fi-re, I feel His pow'r-ful love in me; for he has kin-dled a flame of pas-sion, and I will let it grow in me. And in the night I will sing Your praise, my love.— And in the morn-ing I'll seek your face, my love.——

And like a child I will dance in your pres-ence, oh, let the joy of
hea-ven pour down on me. I still re-mem-ber the first day I met You,
and I don't ev-er want to lose that fire, my first love.

2. My first love is a rushing river,
   A waterfall that will never cease;
   And in the torrent of tears and laughter,
   I feel a healing power released.
   And I will draw from Your well of life, my love,
   And in your grace I'll be satisfied, my love.

3. Restore the years of the church's slumber,
   Revive the fire that has grown so dim;
   Renew the love of those first encounters,
   That we may come alive again.
   And we will rise like the dawn throughout the earth,
   Until the trumpet announces Your return.

931. My God shall supply all my needs

Is 58:11; Phil 4:19

Ian Smale

Joyfully

My God shall sup-ply all__ my__ needs, my
God shall sup-ply all__ my__ needs, my
God shall sup-ply all my needs__ 'cause it
says so in the Bi - ble.__ 'Cause it says so (where?) in the
book that came from heav'n, 'cause it says so (where?) I-sai - ah

932.

My heart

Ps 34:4

Chris Williams

My heart,— I want to give You my heart,— in ser-vice to the Lord, the One who cares— to ask for my life.

Take me,— mould my life and make me— in-to a child who longs to stay by Your side— and learn of Your— ways. For when I sought You, Lord,— You heard—

933.
Capo 3 (D)
Steadily

My heart is not raised up too high
(Psalm 131)

Ps 131
Job 11:7-8

Maggi Dawn

1. My__ heart is not raised__ up too high, my__ eyes don't search be - yond the sky. I do not__ seek what__ can't be known, nor fret my - self ov - er mys - ter - ies.__

2. But I have calmed and soothed my soul,
   Like a child at rest in its mother's arms;
   Like this child sleeping by my side,
   My soul, in God, knows peace and calm.

3. All you who love and trust your God,
   In this God shall you put your hope,
   For there you'll find unfailing love,
   From this time forth, and forever more.

And we know that in all things God works for the good of those who love Him, who have been called according to His purpose.

ROMANS 8:28

934.

My Jesus, my lifeline

With strength

Tim Hughes

1. My Je - sus, my life - line, I need You more than__ I've ev - er__ known. There's no one quite like You, I'm__ cry - ing out for__ Your lov - ing.__ Oh, Je - sus, oh Je - sus,__ I've nev - er known a love like this be - fore. Oh Je - sus, oh Je - sus,__ ac - cept__ this__ love I give to You,__

it's all I can do._____

2. I'm searching, I'm longing,
   Please meet me just as You want to.
   I'll stand here to offer,
   Offer up this song of love to You.

935.

My Jesus, my Saviour
(Shout to the Lord)

Capo 1 (A)
Growing in strength

I Sam 2:2; 1 Chron 16:32;
Ps 46:1; 61:33; 86:8-9; 92:4;
96:10; 98:4; 100:1; Prov 10:25;
Jer 16:19; Hab 3:10; 2 Cor 1:20

Darlene Zschech

My Je - sus, my Sa - viour, Lord, there is none like__ You.__
My com-fort, my shel - ter, tow - er of re - fuge and strength,__

__ All of my days__ I want to praise__
__ let ev - 'ry breath,__ all that I am,__

1.
__ the won-ders of Your migh - ty love.

2.
__ ne - ver cease to wor - ship You.

Shout to the Lord__ all the earth__ let us sing__
I sing for joy__ at the work__ of Your hands.__ For-

936.

My life is in You, Lord

Is 40:31

Moderately

Daniel Gardner

937.
My lips shall praise You
(Restorer of my soul)

Capo 3 (D)

Ps 23:3; 63:5; 1Jn 4:18

Noel & Tricia Richards

With energy

Chorus

My lips_ shall praise You,_ my_ great Re - deem-er;_

Last time to Coda

my heart_ will wor-ship_ Al - might-y Sav - iour.

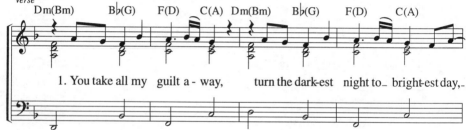

Verse

1. You take all my guilt a - way, turn the dark-est night to_ bright-est day,_

— You are the re - stor-er of_ my soul.

Coda **rall**.........

Sav - iour.

2. Love that conquers every fear,
   In the midst of trouble You draw near,
   You are the restorer of my soul.

3. You're the source of happiness
   Bringing peace when I am in distress,
   You are the restorer of my soul.

938. My trust is in the name of the Lord

Ps 20:7; Is 34:16; Acts 17:24

Laurie Jasurda

2. My hope is in the name of the Lord . . .

3. My joy is in the name of the Lord . . .

939.

Name of all majesty

1 Chron 29:11; Job 11:7;
Is 35:10; 51:11; Jn 3:16; Eph 1:21;
Phil 2:8,11; 1 Tim 2:6; 1 Jn 4:9; Jude 25

Tune: MAJESTAS

Michael Baughen
Arr. Noël Tredinnick

1. Name of all ma-jes-ty, fa-thom-less mys-te-ry, King of the a-ges by an-gels a-dored; pow'r and au-tho-ri-ty, splen-dour and dig-ni-ty, bow to His mas-te-ry - Je-sus is Lord!

2. Child of our destiny,
God from eternity,
Love of the Father on sinners outpoured;
See now what God has done,
Sending His only Son,
Christ the belovèd One -
Jesus is Lord!

3. Saviour of Calvary,
Costliest victory,
Darkness defeated and Eden restored;
Born as a man to die,
Nailed to a cross on high,
Cold in the grave to lie -
Jesus is Lord!

4. Source of all sovereignty,
Light, immortality,
Life everlasting and heaven assured;
So with the ransomed, we
Praise Him eternally,
Christ in His majesty -
Jesus is Lord!

Timothy Dudley-Smith

940. Nearer, my God, to Thee

Gen 28:12;,18-19; Is 40:31; Mt 16:24;
Mk 8:34; Lk 9:23; Heb 4:16

Tune: PROPIOR DEO

Arthur S Sullivan (1842-1900)

1. Near-er, my God, to Thee, near-er to Thee: e'en though it be a cross that rais-eth— me, still all my song would be,— near-er, my God, to Thee, near-er to Thee,— near-er to Thee.

2. Though, like the wanderer,
   The sun gone down,
   Darkness be over me,
   My rest a stone,
   Yet in my dreams I'd be
   Nearer, my God, to Thee,
   Nearer to Thee, nearer to Thee.

3. There let my way appear,
   Steps up to heaven;
   All that Thou sendest me,
   In mercy given;
   Angels to beckon me
   Nearer, my God, to Thee,
   Nearer to Thee, nearer to Thee.

4. Then, with my waking thoughts
   Bright with Thy praise,
   Out of my stony griefs
   Bethel I'll raise;
   So by my woes to be
   Nearer, my God, to Thee,
   Nearer to Thee, near

5. Or, if on joyful wing
   Cleaving the sky,
   Sun, moon, and stars forgot,
   Upwards I fly,
   Still all my song shall be,
   Nearer, my God, to Thee,
   Nearer to Thee, nearer to Thee.

Sarah Flower Adams (1805-48)

941.   Never let my heart grow cold

Song 8:6

Capo 2 (D)

Chris Roe

With feeling

Nev-er let my____ heart   grow   cold.

Lord, help my to love You____ with a love that nev-er dies.

Set my heart a - blaze with a burn-ing de - sire

to see Je - sus glo - ri - fied,____

to see Je - sus glo - ri - fied.____

He who sacrifices thank-offerings honours me, and he prepares the way so that I may show Him the salvation of God.

PSALM 50:23

942.

New covenant people

Heb 12:22-24,29; 13:15

David Fellingham

With life

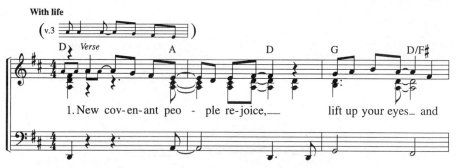

1. New cov-en-ant peo - ple re-joice,___ lift up your eyes___ and

see your King.___ Reign-ing in pow'r___ on His heav - en-ly throne,___

ang - els are joy - ful - ly sing-ing: to the Fa - ther,_____

_____ our Cre - a - tor,_____ to our

Judge and Lord._____ And to Je - sus,____

_____ Me - di - a - tor,_____ who has cleansed us

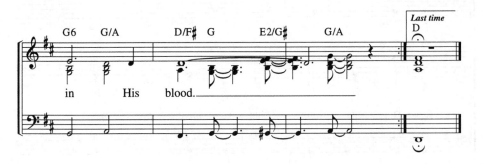

in His blood._____

2. Let us through Jesus draw near to God,
   Offering up our sacrifice,
   Confessing that Jesus is Lord over all,
   Joining with heavenly praises:

3. We give thanks to You with fear,
   Holy God, consuming fire,
   Confessing that Jesus is Lord over all,
   We bring our love and devotion:

943.

No eye has seen
(How high and how wide)

Rom 8:17; 9:22-23; 11:33;
1 Cor 2:9; Eph 2:13; 3:8,18;
1 Pet 1:8

With life

Mark Altrogge

Verse G   Am7

1. No eye— has seen, and no ear— has heard, and

G/B   C   D7sus4

no mind— has ev-er— con-ceived— the

G   Am7

glo-ri-ous things that You have— pre-pared for

G/B   Dsus4   D   F

ev-'ry-one who has— be-lieved;— You brought— us

A/C♯   Am7

near and— You called us— Your own, and made us— joint

2. Objects of mercy, who should have known wrath,
   We're filled with unspeakable joy;
   Riches of wisdom, unsearchable wealth,
   And the wonder of knowing Your voice.
   You are our treasure and our great reward,
   Our hope and our glorious King.

944.   No eye has seen, no ear has heard *1 Cor 2:9-10,12*

Paul Baloche & Ed Kerr

No eye has seen,___ no___ ear has heard,___ no

mind has con - ceived___ what the Lord___ has pre - pared;___

but by His Spi - rit, He___ has re-vealed___ His plan to those___ who___ love___

- Him.___   Him.   We've been held by___ His

ev-er-last - ing love,_____ led with lov - ing kind - ness by_ His hand;_

_____ we have hope for_ the fu - ture yet_ to come,_____ in

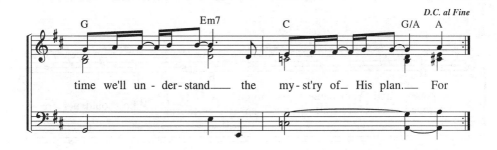

D.C. al Fine

time we'll un - der - stand_____ the my - st'ry of_ His plan._ For

945.

No one is like You, O Lord

1 Sam 2:2; Ps 8:1,9
Jer 10:6-7

Carol Owen

jes-tic is   Your name,___   as Your   peo-ple we pro - claim:

You.

But because of His great love for us, God, who is rich in mercy, made us alive with Christ even when we were dead in transgressions – it is by grace you have been saved.

EPHESIANS 2:4-5

946.

No other name

Acts 4:12; Rev 5:12

Robert Gay

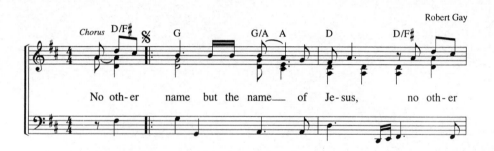

No oth-er name but the name___ of Je-sus, no oth-er

name but the name___ of the Lord; no oth-er name but the name of

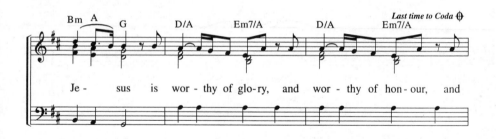

Je - sus is wor - thy of glo-ry, and wor - thy of hon - our, and

wor - thy of pow-er and all praise. No oth-er praise. His

name is ex-alt - ed far a-bove__ the earth,__ His name is high a-bove_ the hea-

vens; His name is ex-alt - ed far a-bove__ the earth,__ give

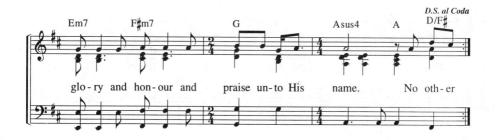

glo-ry and hon-our and praise un-to His name. No oth-er

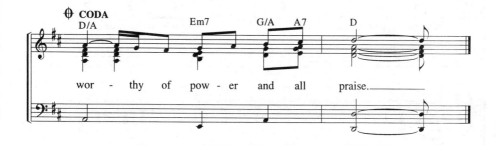

wor - thy of pow-er and all praise._____

947. Nothing shall separate us

Rom 8:2,32,34,38-39

Noel & Tricia Richards

No-thing shall se-pa-rate us from the love of God.
No-thing shall se-pa-rate us from the love of God.
1. God did_ not spare His on-ly Son, gave Him to save us____ all. Sin's price_ was met by Je-sus' death and hea-ven's mer-cy____ falls.

2. Up from the grave Jesus was raised
   To sit at God's right hand;
   Pleading our cause in heaven's courts,
   Forgiven we can stand.

3. Now by God's grace we have embraced
   A life set free from sin;
   We shall deny all that destroys
   Our union with Him.

Give thanks to the Lord, for He is good. His love endures for ever.

PSALM 136:1

948.

No weapon formed

Is 54:17; Col 2:15

Capo 5 (Am)

Tom Dowell

Fast march

No wea-pon formed,— or ar-my or king,— shall be
a-ble to stand— a-gainst the Lord and His a-noint-ed.
All prin-ci-pa-li-ties and po-wers— shall crum-ble be-fore the
Lord; and men's hearts shall be re-leased,— and—
they shall come un-to the Lord.—

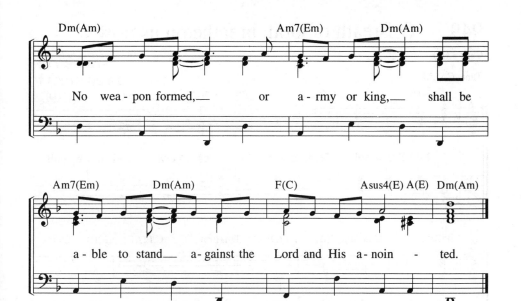

949. O Breath of God, breathe on us now

Capo 3 (D)

Rom 8:26-27,34; Jn 14:16,26;
Heb 7:25; 1 Jn 2:1

Tune: CALM

J.B.Dykes (1823-76)

2. O strangely art Thou with us, Lord,
   Neither in height nor depth to seek:
   In nearness shall Thy voice be heard;
   Spirit to spirit Thou dost speak.

3. Christ is our Advocate on high;
   Thou art our Advocate within.
   O plead the truth, and make reply
   To every argument of sin.

4. But ah, this faithless heart of mine,
   The way I know, I know my Guide:
   Forgive me, O my Friend divine,
   That I so often turn aside.

5. Be with me when no other friend
   The mystery of my heart can share;
   And be Thou known, when fears transcend,
   By Thy best name of Comforter.

Alfred Henry Vine (1845 - 1917)

Sing to the Lord a new song,
His praise from the ends of the earth.

ISAIAH 42:10

950. O Father of the fatherless
(Father me)

Ps 68:5; 119:176;
Eph 3:15; Rev 7:14

Graham Kendrick

Smoothly
Verse

1. O Father of the fatherless, in whom all families are blessed, I love the way You father me.

You gave me life, forgave the past, now in Your arms I'm safe at last, I love the way You father me.

Chorus

Father me, for ever You'll father me, and in

Your em-brace I'll be for-ev - er se-cure._____

I love the way_ You fa - ther me._____

I love the way_ You fa - ther me._____ 2. When

2. When bruised and broken I draw near
   You hold me close and dry my tears,
   I love the way You father me.
   At last my fearful heart is still,
   Surrendered to Your perfect will,
   I love the way You father me.

3. If in my foolishness I stray,
   Returning empty and ashamed,
   I love the way You father me.
   Exchanging for my wretchedness
   Your radiant robes of righteousness,
   I love the way You father me.

4. And when I look into Your eyes
   From deep within my spirit cries,
   I love the way You father me.
   Before such love I stand amazed
   And ever will through endless days,
   I love the way You father me.

951.   O for a closer walk with God

Rev 2:4

Tune: CHESHIRE

Este's *Psalter*, 1592

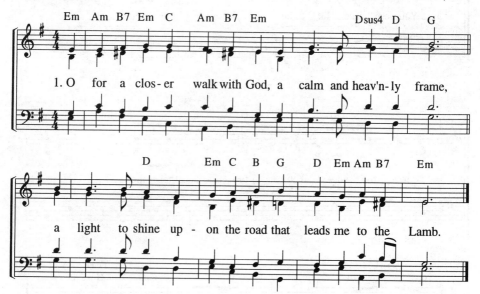

1. O for a clos-er walk with God, a calm and heav'n-ly frame,
a light to shine up - on the road that leads me to the Lamb.

2. Where is the blessèdness I knew
When I first saw the Lord?
Where is that soul-refreshing view
Of Jesus and His word?

3. What peaceful hours I once enjoyed!
How sweet their memory still!
But they have left an aching void
The world can never fill.

4. Return, O holy Dove! return,
Sweet messenger of rest!
I hate the sins that made Thee mourn,
And drove Thee from my breast.

5. The dearest idol I have known,
Whate'er that idol be,
Help me to tear it from thy throne,
And worship only Thee.

6. So shall my walk be close with God,
Calm and serene my frame;
So purer light shall mark the road
That leads me to the Lamb.

William Cowper (1731-1800)

952. O God, be my strength

Ps 28:7; 118:14

John Paculabo

Meditatively

1. O God, be my strength through my doubt and my fear. O

God, be my com-fort when dark-ness is near. O Lord of all hope, You're my

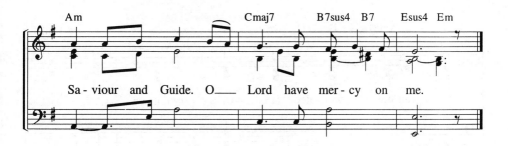

Sa - viour and Guide. O—— Lord have mer - cy on me.

2. O God of all mercy
   And God of all grace,
   Whose infinite gift
   Was to die in my place,
   Eternal Creator,
   Redeemer and Friend,
   O Lord, have mercy on me.

3. O God of all power,
   Invisible King,
   Restorer of Man,
   My life I bring.
   O Lord of my heart,
   Grant Your peace now I pray:
   O Lord, have mercy on me.

953.

O God beyond all praising

He 13:15; Jas 1:17

Tune: THAXTED
With dignity

Music: Gustav Holst (1874-1934)
Arr. David Ball

1. O— God be-yond all prais-ing, we wor-ship You to-day, and— sing the love a-maz-ing that songs can-not re-pay; for— we can on-ly won-der at— ev-'ry gift you send, at— bles-sings wit-hout num-ber and mer-cies with-out end: we—

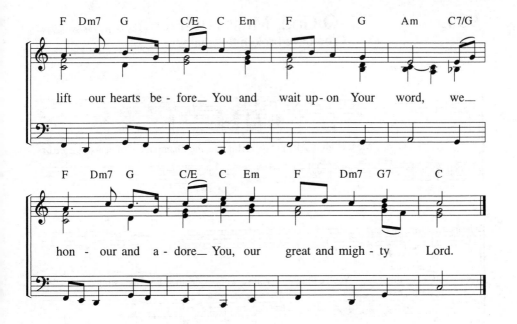

lift our hearts be - fore— You and wait up- on Your word, we—

hon - our and a - dore— You, our great and migh - ty Lord.

2. Then hear, O gracious Saviour,
   Accept the love we bring,
   That we who know Your favour
   May serve You as our King;
   And whether our tomorrows
   Be filled with good or ill,
   We'll triumph through our sorrows
   And rise to bless You still:
   To marvel at Your beauty
   And glory in Your ways,
   And make a joyful duty
   Our sacrifice of praise!

Michael Perry (1942-1996)

954.
O God, Most High
(You have broken the chains)

Ps 68:18; 1Cor 15:55; Eph 4:8

Jamie Owens-Collins

With strength

1. O God, Most High, Al-might-y King,— the Champ-i-on of hea-ven, Lord of ev'-ry-thing;— You've fought, You've won, death's lost its— sting,— and stand-ing in— Your vic-tor-y we sing.

Chorus
You have bro-ken the chains— that held our cap-tive souls.— You have bro-ken the chains— and used them on— Your foes.—

2. The power of hell has been undone,
   Captivity held captive by the risen One,
   And in the name of God's great Son,
   We claim the mighty victory You've won.

955. O God of burning, cleansing flame
(Send the fire)

1 Kings 18:38;
Acts 2:1,3; Rom 8:37; 12:1;
Rev 5:9; 7:14

William Booth
Adpt. Lex Loizides

Lex Loizides

1. O God of burn-ing, clean-sing flame: send the fi - re! Your

blood - bought gift to - day we—claim: send the fire to - day! Look

down and see this wait-ing host, and send the prom-ised Ho-ly Ghost; we

need a - no-ther Pen-te - cost! Send the fire to - day! Send the fire to-

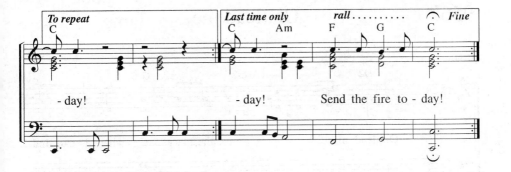

2. God of Elijah, hear our cry: send the fire!
   And make us fit to live or die: send the fire today!
   To burn up every trace of sin,
   To bring the light and glory in,
   The revolution now begin!
   Send the fire today!
   Send the fire today!

3. It's fire we want, for fire we plead: send the fire!
   The fire will meet our every need: send the fire today!
   For strength to always do what's right,
   For grace to conquer in the fight,
   For power to walk the world in white:
   Send the fire today!
   Send the fire today!

4. To make our weak hearts strong and brave: send the fire!
   To live, a dying world to save: send the fire today!
   Oh, see us on Your altar lay,
   We give our lives to You today,
   So crown the offering now we pray:
   Send the fire today!
   Send the fire today!
   Send the fire today!

William Booth (1829-1912)

956.

Oh, lead me

Jn 20:22

Gently

Martin Smith

Oh, lead me___ to the place___ where I can find___

_ You.___ Oh, lead___ me___ to the place___

_ where You'll be. Lead me to the cross where we first met;___

_ draw me to my knees, so we can talk.___ Let me feel your

breath, let me know You're here with me. Oh,

"I will refine them like silver and test them like gold. They will call on My name and I will answer them; I will say, 'They are My people,' and they will say, 'The Lord is our God.'"

ZECHARIAH 13:9

957.

Oh our Lord and King
(King forever)

Ps 18:31; Lam 3:22;
Rev 1:17; 2:8; 22:13

Alan Rose

With strength

Oh our Lord and King,— our praise to You— we bring,—
Seat - ed high a - bove,— You are the One— we love,—

there is no o - ther Rock— but You.
this is our song of praise— to You.

1. King for- ev- er! You are the first and You're the last,

You are sove-reign;

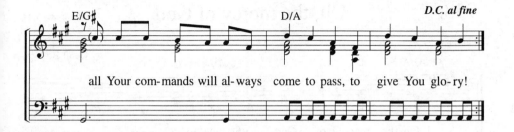

all Your com-mands will al-ways come to pass, to give You glo-ry!

2. Who is like You?
   Who else is worthy of our praise?
   We exalt You;
   You reign in majesty and
   Awesome splendour,
   King forever!

3. Abba Father,
   Your steadfast love will never fail.
   You are faithful,
   You are God and I will
   Worship in Your
   Courts forever.

958.
Oh, the mercy of God

Eph 1:4; Col 1:15

Flowing

Geoff Bullock

1. Oh, the mer-cy of God,___ the glo-ry of grace, that You chose to re-deem us, to for-give and re-store, and You call us Your chil-dren, cho-sen in Him to be ho-ly and blame-less to the glo-ry of God.

Chorus To the praise of His glo-ri-ous grace, to the praise of His glo-ry and pow'r;

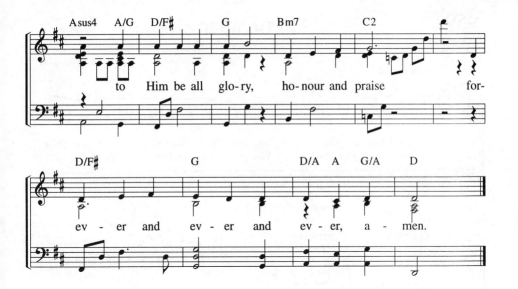

to Him be all glo-ry, ho-nour and praise for-
ev – er and ev – er and ev – er, a – men.

2. Oh, the richness of grace, the depths of His love,
In Him is redemption, the forgiveness of sin.
You called us as righteous, predestined in Him
For the praise of His glory, included in Christ.

3. Oh, the glory of God expressed in His Son,
His image and likeness revealed to us all;
The plea of the ages completed in Christ,
That we be presented perfected in Him.

959.

O Lord, arise
(Lord of every man)

Capo 2 (D)

Ps 68:1,33

Craig Musseau

With strength

Verse   E(D)   B(A)

O Lord, a - rise,   re - lease Your pow'r,   scat - ter Your
You hold our lives,   You give us breath,   You freed us

F♯m7(Em)   C♯m7(Bm)   *1.* A(G)

foes   this ver - y hour.__ May we hold on to Your ho - ly com - mands.
from   the pow - er of death.__ You're our sal -

E(D)   B(A)   A A2 (G) (G)

___ You are the Lord_ of ev - 'ry man.___

2. A(G)   E(D)   B(A)

va - tion, our on - ly hope,___ You are the Lord_ of ev - 'ry man.__

A(G)   *Chorus*   E(D)

___ Your voice,_____ it is like

960. O Lord, how I love to sing Your praises

Ps 47:6

(Face to face)

Brightly

Chris DuPré

O Lord, how I love— to sing Your prais- es. O Lord,
La, la, la..... Oh,—

how I love— to dance for You. O Lord, You have cap- tured my af-fec-tion,
la, la, la..... Oh,— la, la, la.....

2nd time to Coda ⊕

for - ev - er I will sing of— Your love, for - ev - er
for - ev - er

I— will bring— to You— my life. For - ev - er I will wor - ship

You. And when I think— of what You've

961. O Lord, I want to sing Your praises

(La Alleluia)

Ps 63:1, 3-5

In a 'Latin' style

Traditional Arr. Bryn Haworth
Words: Andy Park

O Lord, I want to sing Your praises, I want to praise Your name e-ve-ry day.

O Lord, I want to sing Your Al - le - lu - ia, al - le - lu. Al - le - lu - ia, al - le - lu.

Let everything that has breath praise the Lord.

PSALM 150:6

962.

O Lord, our Lord
(How majestic is Your name)

Ps 8:1; Is 9:6

Michael W. Smith

Steadily

Lyrics:

O Lord our Lord, how ma-jes-tic is Your name in all the earth. O Lord our Lord, how ma-jes-tic is Your name in all the earth. O Lord, we praise Your name, O Lord we

963. O Lord, You are my Rock and my Redeemer

Capo 3 (D)

Is 53:4; Ps 19:14; 107:14; Mt 2:6;
Acts 2:4; Eph 5:18; 1 Pet 2:9; 1 Jn 1:7

Brightly

Jon Soper, Mark Robinson
& John Peters

O Lord, You are my Rock and my Re-deemer; my song, You are the Strength of my life. O Lord, You are the Shep-herd of Your peo-ple; You keep us

964.

O Lord, You're great

As a 'twist'

Ian Smale

1. O Lord, You're great, You are fab-u-lous,— we love You more than an-y words can sing,—— sing, sing. O Lord, You're great, You are so gen-er-ous,— You lav-ish us with gifts when we

2. O Lord, You're great, You are so powerful,
   You hold the mighty universe in Your hand, hand, hand.
   O Lord, You're great, You are so beautiful,
   You've poured out You love on this undeserving land.

965.

Only one thing

Ps 27:4-5

Flowing

Maggi Dawn

On - ly one thing I ask of the Lord:_ on - ly one thing_
Ev - en when days of trou - ble may come, I will be safe if

do I de - sire:_ that I may dwell, may_ dwell in God's house
God is my home, for I will hide in the shel - ter of love

Last time to Coda

all of the days_ of my life, all of the days_ of my

1st time
life._

2nd time
life._ I'll gaze_ on His

beau - ty,_ and sing_ of His glo - ry;_ while

966.
Open the doors of praise

Ps 22:3; Mk 16:17; Eph 6:12

Ian White

With energy

Chorus

Op-en the doors__ of praise. Op-en the doors__ of

praise. Op-en the doors__ of praise and

let the Lord come in.__ __ 1. In the spi - rit world__

__ there's a bat-tle go-ing on, and it rag-es end-less -

ly.__ But in the name of the Lord,__ we can

2. And the demons will flee,
   As He said it would be,
   And the skies will ring with shouts of praise.
   And the Lord Jesus Christ
   Will be lifted high,
   The Holy One who truly saves!
   For He lives . . .

967.

O righteous God

Ps 7:1,9-10,17

With awe

Mal Pope

Verse

1. O righ-teous God who search-es minds and hearts, bring to an end the vio-lence of my foes, and make the righ-teous__ more se-cure, O__ righ - teous God.

Chorus

Sing praise to the name of the Lord most__ high. Sing praise to the name of the Lord most__ high. Give__ thanks to the

Lord who re - scues me, O__ righ - - teous God.__

2. O Lord my God, I take refuge in You;
   Save and deliver me from all my foes.
   My shield is God the Lord most high,
   O Lord my God.

968. O the deep, deep love of Jesus

Ps 42:7; Rom 8:34; Eph 3:18; Heb 13:8

Tune: EBENEZER

Thomas John Williams (1869-1944)

Capo 1 (Em)

Lyrics:

O the deep, deep love of Je-sus! Vast, un-mea-sured, bound-less, free; roll-ing as a migh-ty o-cean in its ful-ness o-ver me. Un-der-neath me, all a-round me, is the cur-rent of Thy love; lead-ing on-ward,

Music Copyright © E Crump & D Evans

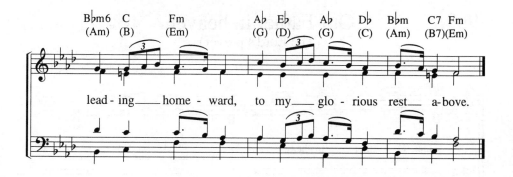

lead - ing___ home - ward, to my___ glo - rious rest___ a-bove.

2. O the deep, deep love of Jesus!
   Spread His praise from shore to shore,
   How He loveth, ever loveth,
   Changeth never, nevermore;
   How He watches o'er His loved ones,
   Died to call them all His own;
   How for them He intercedeth,
   Watches over them from the throne.

3. O the deep, deep love of Jesus!
   Love of every love the best:
   'Tis an ocean vast of blessing,
   'Tis a haven sweet of rest.
   O the deep, deep love of Jesus!
   'Tis a heaven of heavens to me;
   And it lifts me up to glory,
   For it lifts me up to Thee.

Samuel Trevor Francis (1834-1925)

969.

Our Father in heaven
(The Lord's prayer)

Mt 6:9-13; Lk 11:2-4

Brian Doerksen
& Michael Hansen

Quite slow

Our Fa- ther in heav- en { ho- ly is Your— name.
give us our bread.

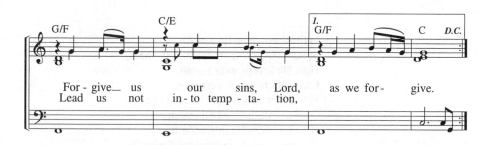

For- give— us our sins, Lord, as we for- give.
Lead us not in- to temp- ta- tion,

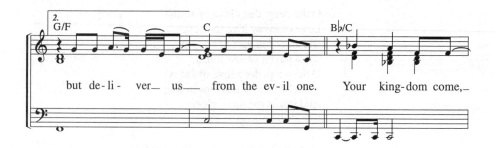

but de- li- ver— us— from the ev- il one. Your king- dom come,—

— Your will be— done. Your king- dom come,— Your will be—

done.　　　　　　　done　　on　the　earth

as it is‿ in heav - en.＿＿＿ Let it be‿ done on the　earth.　　A-

men.＿＿＿＿＿＿　　　A　-　men.＿＿＿＿＿

970. Our Father in heaven
(The Lord's prayer)

Mt 6:9-13; Lk 11:2-4

Smoothly

Keith Routledge

971.

Our God is awesome in power
(Warrior)

Ex 15:3; Deut 20:4;
Ps 18:34; 68:1; 144:1; Prov 21:31;
Jer 20:11; 1 Cor 15:57; Eph 6:13

Noel & Tricia Richards

1. Our God is awe-some in pow-er, scat-ters His en-em-ies; our God is migh-ty in bring-ing the pow-er-ful to their knees. He has put on His ar-mour, He is pre-pared for war; mer-cy and jus-tice tri-umph when the Li-on of Ju-dah roars.

Lyrics within the music:

The Lord is a war-ri-or,___ we will_ march with Him.___ The Lord is a war-ri-or,___ lead-ing us_ to win.___ The _

(fine)

1st & 2nd times - Tacet

War - ri-or,___

lead-ing us_ to win.___ (The)

2. Waken the warrior spirit,
Army of God, arise;
Challenge the powers of darkness,
There must be no compromise.
We shall attack their strongholds,
Our hands are trained for war;
We shall advance the kingdom,
For the victory belongs to God.

972.

Our God is great

Bright and rhythmic

Dave Bilbrough

Our God is great. Our God is great.

Our God is great. Our God is great.

Our God is 1. He gave us the wind, the sun and the snow, the

sand on the sea shore, the flowers that grow. Morning and evening,

winter and spring; come join all creation and sing.

6.

G♯m For mu - sic_ and dan - cing,_ the

Our God is

F♯m7 sounds that_ we hear; **A** for co - lours_ and words,

the

B life that_ we share,___ we say: *D.C. al fine* Our God is

2. The gifts that He brings
   Are new every day,
   From glorious sunset
   To soft falling rain.
   The mist on the hills,
   The light and the shade;
   Come join all creation in praise.

973. Our passion is for You

John Gibson

With strength

Our pas-sion is__ for You,__ Lord Je - sus; Your grace has fuelled__ a fi - re that burns with-in our hearts.__ There's no-where that__ com-pares_____ with Your pre - sence; we've tas - ted of__ Your Spi - rit, so there's just one thing__ we ask:__ More, more, more, more,

974.

Over the heavens above
(Great are You, Lord, and mighty)

Capo 2 (D)

Nigel Leppitt

Moderately, with strength

Verse

Ov-er the heav'ns a - bove, un-der the earth be - low, deep-er than an-y sea shines the pre-sence of Your glo-ry. A ri-ver with ma-ny streams flows to the heart of the ho-ly King; full of such won-der and

975.
Over the mountains and the sea
(I could sing of Your love forever)

Capo 3 (D)

Martin Smith

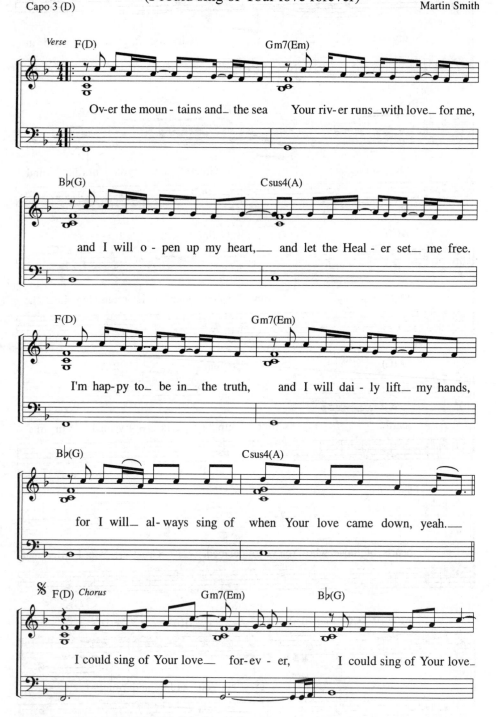

Verse F(D) Gm7(Em)

Ov-er the moun - tains and_ the sea   Your riv-er runs_with love_ for me,

Bb(G) Csus4(A)

and I will o - pen up my heart,___ and let the Heal - er set_ me free.

F(D) Gm7(Em)

I'm hap-py to_ be in_ the truth,   and I will dai - ly lift_ my hands,

Bb(G) Csus4(A)

for I will_ al - ways sing of   when Your love came down, yeah.___

F(D) Chorus   Gm7(Em)   Bb(G)

I could sing of Your love___ for-ev - er,   I could sing of Your love_

976.

Overwhelmed by love

Ps 42:7; Is 53:6; 1 Pet 2:24

Noel Richards

With feeling

1. O-ver-whelmed by love, deep-er than o-ceans, high as the heav-ens. Ev - er liv-ing God. Your love has res-cued me. No one could ev - er earn Your love, Your grace and mer-cy is free.____ Lord, these words are true, so is my love for You.

2. All my sin was laid
On Your dear Son,
Your precious One.
All my debt He paid,
Great is Your love for me.

977.

Peace, perfect peace

Mt 11:28; Jn 14:27; 1 Cor 15:54

Tune: SONG 46

Orlando Gibbons (1583-1625)

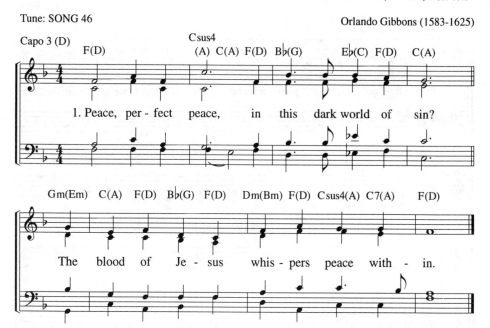

1. Peace, per - fect peace, in this dark world of sin?
The blood of Je - sus whis - pers peace with - in.

2. Peace, perfect peace, by thronging duties pressed?
   To do the will of Jesus, this is rest.

3. Peace, perfect peace, with sorrows surging round?
   In Jesus' presence nought but calm is found.

4. Peace, perfect peace, with loved ones far away?
   In Jesus' keeping we are safe, and they.

5. Peace, perfect peace, our future all unknown?
   Jesus we know, and He is on the throne.

6. Peace, perfect peace, death shadowing us and ours?
   Jesus has vanquished death and all its powers.

7. It is enough: earth's struggles soon shall cease,
   And Jesus call us to heaven's perfect peace.

E H Bickersteth (1825-1906)

978.

Power from on high

Lk 24:49; Jn 3:3

Ian White

With feeling

Pow'r from on high, pow'r from on high, Lord, we are waiting— for

pow'r from on high. Pow'r from on high, pow'r from on high,

Lord, we are wait-ing— for pow'r from on high. 1. May we taste Your

heav-en here on the earth,— may Your Spi-rit bring us new birth.—

2. May we take Your heaven
To those on the earth,
May Your Spirit bring them new birth.

3. May the truth and power
Of life that You give
Very soon be ours to live.

979.
Praise and glory
(Revelation 7:12)

Rev 7:12

Capo 3 (D)

Eddie Espinosa

Praise and glo-ry, wis-dom and hon-our, pow-er and strength and thanks-giv-ing be to our God for ev-er and ev-er, a-men. a-men. a-men, a-men.

980. Praise God from whom all blessings flow
(Doxology)

Rev 5:12

Andy Piercy & Dave Clifton

Steady rock feel

Praise God from whom all bles - sings flow, praise Him all crea - tures here be-low. Praise Him a-bove, you heav- 'nly host, praise Fa-ther, Son and Ho - ly Ghost. Give glo-ry to the Fa - ther, give glo-ry to the Son, give glo-ry to the Spi-

To finish repeat twice   *3rd time to CODA*   *Fine*   *Verse*

981. Praise the Lord, all you servants of the Lord

Ps 134: 1-3

Moderately

Ian White

Praise the Lord, all you ser - vants of the Lord,
who mi - ni - ster by night with - in His house.
Lift up your hands with - in the sanc - tua - ry, and
praise the Lord. May the Lord, the
mak - er of hea - ven and earth, may this Lord

982. Promise of the Father
(Catch the fire)

Joel 2:8; Acts 2:28,33; Heb 7:25

David Fellingham

1. Pro-mise of the Fa-ther,— giv-en— through— the Son, of pow-er— for— His chil-dren,— the Ho-ly Spi-rit's come. Young men will see vi - sions,—

pow'r will set me free.   Let Your pow-er fall on me.____

2. Jesus in His glory sends His Spirit now,
   That we might be proclaimers of the gospel's power.
   In worship and in witness we declare God's love,
   Speaking to a dying world,
   Jesus has the power to save, I'll...

"Behold, I am coming soon! My reward is with me, and I will give to everyone according to what he has done."

REVELATION 22:12

983.

Quiet my mind

EX 17:12; Ps 37:7; 46:10;
Zeph 3:16-17; Heb 12:12

Tracy Orrison

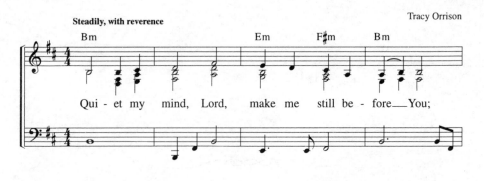

Qui - et my mind, Lord, make me still be - fore___You;

calm my rest - less heart, Lord, make me more like You.

Raise up my hands that are hang - ing down;

strength - en my fee - ble___knees.___

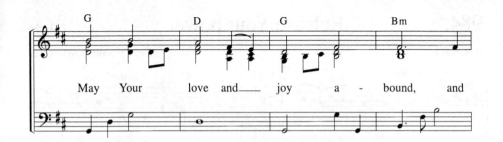

May Your love and___ joy a - bound, and

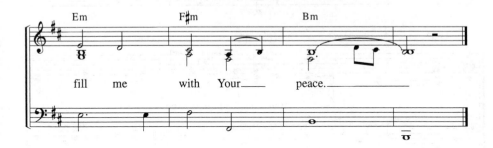

fill me with Your___ peace._____

984. Release Your power

Ps 37:5-6

With energy

Luke & Nathan Fellingham

Re-lease Your pow'r a-mong us, Lord, that all may see Your glo - ry. Re-lease Your pow'r

1. Lord, I give my life to You, and trust Your ho - ly name; help me grow in ho - li-ness, and fol-low You in all

2. Teach me, Lord, to listen to the calling of Your Spirit,
   Helping me and guiding me to live my life as Jesus did.
   I long to know Your power and see the sick get healed;
   Come and move among us, Lord, that truth will be revealed.

985.
Release Your power, O God

Capo 1 (D)

Stuart Garrard

With awe

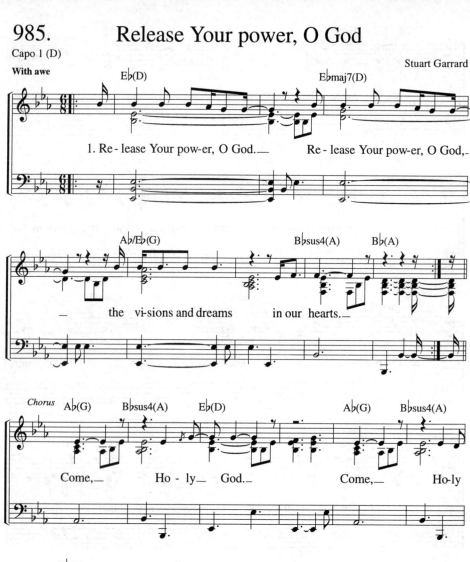

1. Re - lease Your pow-er, O God.— Re - lease Your pow-er, O God,— the vi-sions and dreams in our hearts.—

Chorus

Come,— Ho - ly— God.— Come,— Ho-ly

God.—

2. Release Your fire, O God.
Release Your fire, O God,
A passion that burns in our hearts.
(Repeat)

"No eye has seen, no ear has heard, no mind has conceived what God has prepared for those who love Him"

1 CORINTHIANS 2:9

986.
Remember your Creator

Capo 3 (D)

Ecc 12:1

Jim Bailey

Calypso

Re - mem-ber your Cre-a-tor in the days of your youth. Re-mem-ber your Cre-a-tor in the days— of your youth. Re-mem-ber your Cre-a-tor in the days of your youth. Re-mem-ber your Cre-a-tor in the days— of your youth.

Verse

1. See peo-ple old and grey, hear them
2. While you are young and strong you can sing this

987. Righteousness, peace, joy in the Holy Ghost

With an 'island' feel

Rom 14:7

Helena Barrington

Verse

Right-eous-ness, peace,___ joy___ in the Ho-ly Ghost;___ right-eous-ness, peace___ and joy___ in the Ho-ly Ghost,

1. that's the king - dom of God.___

2. that's the king - dom of God.

Chorus Don't you want to be a part of the king-dom, don't you want to be a part of the king-dom, don't you want to be a part of the king-dom?

2. There's peace in the kingdom, so much peace in the kingdom . . .

3. There's joy in the kingdom, so much joy in the kingdom . . .

4. I'm an heir of the kingdom, I'm an heir of the kingdom . . .

988. Rise up

Is 60:1-3; Rom 8:19; Col 1:27;
Rev 5:8; 8:3-5; 12:11

Peter Arajs

With energy

Rise up, let Your king-dom a-rise_ in us; we lift our
eyes to the skies,_ and rise up to the bright-ness of_ His ris-
- ing.
1. All cre-a-tion a-waits_ the re-
veal-ing of the sons of God,_ and all the an-gels of heav-en are

Last time to coda

list-ening for the prayers of us:—   Hear-ing the sound of a

pow-er-ful flood,   saints of our God who've been   bought by His blood.

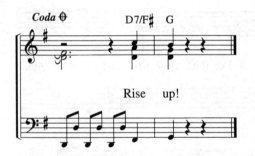

Rise   up!

2. The redemption of God has given us a kingdom view,
   And His promise to us, the hope of glory, Christ in you.
   Darkness shall run from the strength of His hand,
   Our testimony, the blood of the Lamb.

989.

River of God

Ps 34:8; 42:7; Is 43:19
Mt 9:38; Lk 10:2; Acts 2:2

Paul Oakley

Quite slow

Ri-ver_ of God,_ flood o - ver me, and lift my feet up off the ground._

Car-ry_ me out_ in-to_ Your sea, and in Your pres-ence I'll be found._

Last time to Coda

1. I've felt_ Your fire and I've felt_ Your

rain;_____ and I've heard_ Your voice whis-per_ my

name._____ I've been wa-ding in Your ri-ver, I've

rid-den on Your waves;_____ I've tas-ted of Your good-ness,

still I'm long-ing to be changed._____ I've

had e-nough of hold-ing back,_ I see Your good-ness all a-round,_ this

time I'm op-ening up my heart,_ so come and fill me now._____

Coda

2. There's something inside me that just
                              won't let go;
   Why am I afraid of losing control?
   Oh, I know Your love is for me,
   And You'll never do me harm;
   So melt away my fears,
   And Holy Spirit come!

3. Please help me, Lord, to be more like You,
   To do all the things You've called me to do.
   Let me help bring in Your harvest,
   Oh, I want it for Your Son;
   So fill me with Your power,
   Holy Spirit come!

4. Come like a mighty rushing wind,
   A tidal wave or a monsoon rain,
   Like a stream in the desert,
   Or a warm summer breeze;
   Gentle Dove of heaven,
   Bring me to my knees!

990.

Ruach

Mt 3:11; Lk 3:16; Jn 3:8
Acts 2:2; 2 Tim 1:6

With a sense of awe

David Fellingham

Ru - ach, Ru - ach,

ho-ly wind of God, blow on me.

Touch the fa-ding em-bers, breathe on me.

Fan in-to a flame all that You've placed in me.

Let the fire— burn   more   pow'r-ful-ly.

Ru   -   ach,

Ru   -   ach,

ho - ly wind of God,   ho - ly wind of

God,   breathe on me.—

991. Safe in the shadow of the Lord

Ps 57:1; 63:6-7; 91:11-12

Tune: CREATOR GOD

Norman Warren

1. Safe in the sha-dow of the Lord, be-neath His hand__ and pow'r,_____ I trust in Him,__ I trust in Him,__ my fort-ress and__ my tower.__

2. My hope is set on God alone,
   Though Satan spreads his snare,
   I trust in Him,
   I trust in Him
   To keep me in His care.

3. From fears and phantoms of the night,
   From foes about my way,
   I trust in Him,
   I trust in Him
   By darkness as by day.

4. His holy angels keep my feet
   Secure from every stone;
   I trust in Him,
   I trust in Him,
   And unafraid go on.

5. Strong in the everlasting Name,
   And in my Father's care,
   I trust in Him,
   I trust in Him
   Who hears and answers prayer.

6. Safe in the shadow of the Lord,
   Possessed by love divine,
   I trust in Him,
   I trust in Him,
   And meet His love with mine.

Timothy Dudley-Smith

*O Lord, You are my God; I
will exalt You and praise Your name.*

ISAIAH 25:1

992. Salvation belongs to our God

Rev 7:10,12

Adrian Howard and Pat Turner

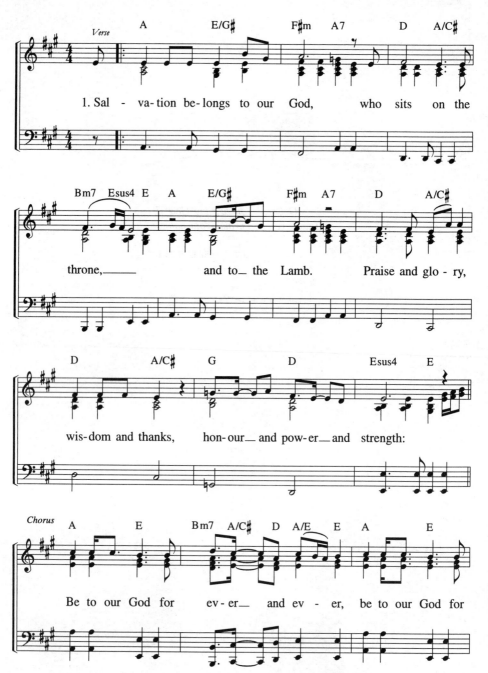

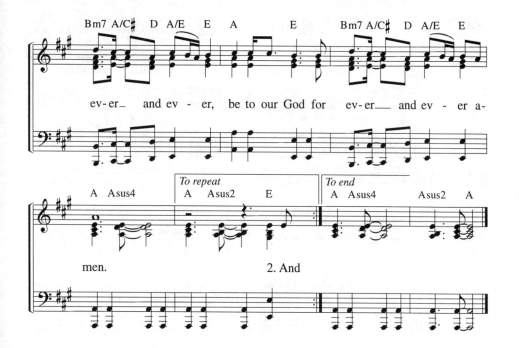

ev-er— and ev - er, be to our God for ev-er— and ev - er a-

men.   2. And

2. And we, the redeemed shall be strong
   In purpose and unity,
   Declaring aloud,
   Praise and glory, wisdom and thanks,
   Honour and power and strength:

993.

Say the word

Is 53:11; Hos 6:3; Joel 2:23; Mt 5:5-6; 8:8; Lk 7:7; Jn 4:14; 2Cor 8:9; 12:9; Phil 1:6

Capo 1 (D)

Stuart Townend

1. Say the word, I will be healed; You are the great Phy-si-cian, You meet ev-'ry need.— Say the word, I will be free; where chains have held me cap-tive, come sing Your songs to me, say the word.

2. Say the word, I will be filled; my hands reach out to hea-ven, where stri-ving is stilled.— Say the word, I will be changed; where I am dry and thir-sty, send cool, re-fresh-ing rain, say the word.

Chorus His tears have fal-len like rain_

3. Say the word, I will be poor,
   That I might know the riches
   That You have in store.
   Say the word, I will be weak;
   Your strength will be the power
   That satisfies the meek.
   Say the word.

   The Lord will see the travail of His soul,
   And He and I will be satisfied.
   Complete the work You have started in me:
   O, come Lord Jesus, shake my life again.

994.
Search me, O God
(All consuming fire)

Deut 4:24; Ps 25:4-5 51:7,10,13
139:23; Mt 5:8; Heb 12:29; Acts 1:8

Slowly, with feeling

Paul Oakley

1. Search me, O God,— and know my heart; know all my thoughts and my— ways. Cleanse me, O God,— give me a pure heart, that I may see Your— face. For You are an all-con- su - ming fire! For You are an all-con-

su - ming fire!

2. Teach me, O God,
   Show me Your ways,
   And I will walk in Your truth.
   Keep me, O God,
   Keep me from falling,
   That I may stand before You.

3. Fill me, O God,
   And send me out,
   And I will make You known.
   Give me Your heart
   And Your compassion,
   And let Your mercy flow.

995.

Send forth Your light

Ps 16:11; 43:3-4;
Jn 14:6; Rom 12:1

Capo 2 (D)

Geoff Twigg

Brightly with a swing

Chorus E(D)   E/G♯(D)   A(G)   B(A)

Send forth Your light and Your truth,— let them guide—

E(D)   E/G♯(D)   A(G)   B(A)

— me, let them bring— me to Your ho-ly moun-

Last time to Coda ⊕

C♯m(Bm)   F♯m7(Em)   A/B(G)

tain, to the place— where You dwell.—

Verse A(G)   B(A)   E(D)   E/G♯(D)   F♯m7(Em)

1. Then I will come— to the al - tar of God,— my joy and my de-

light; then I will of - fer the whole___ of my life,___ a

liv - ing sac - ri - fice.

✠ *Coda*

___ where You dwell,___ O___ Lord.___

2. Jesus, the Way and the Truth and the Life,
   My Saviour and my Lord;
   Knowing Your presence will be my delight,
   Your glory my reward.

996.
Send me out from here

Ps 23:5; 6:8; Mt 10:10; 28:19; Mk 6:8; Lk 9:3

With conviction

John Pantry

Send me out from here, Lord, to serve a world in need. May I know no man by the coat he wears, but the heart that Je-sus sees. And may the light of Your face shine up-on me, Lord. You have filled my heart with the great-est joy, and my cup is ov-er-

flow - ing. 1. "Go now, and car-ry the news to all cre - a - tion ev - 'ry race___ and tongue. Take no purse___ with you, take no-thing to eat for He will sup - ply___ your needs."

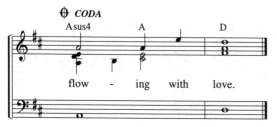

flow - ing with love.

2. "Go now, bearing the light, living for others,
   Fearlessly walking into the night;
   Take no thought for your lives, like lambs among wolves,
   Full of the Spirit, ready to die."

997.
Send us the rain, Lord

Capo 1 (A)

Deut 4:24; 28:12;
1 Kings 18:38; Ps 85:6;
Ezek 37:5; Jn 2:10; 20:22; Heb 12:29

Gently, with increasing intensity

Dave Wellington

1. Send us the rain, Lord, rain of Your Spi - rit, rain on this dry bar-ren land. Send us the rain, Lord, rain to re- -vive us; cleanse us and fill us a - gain. Here we are, of one ac-cord, cal-ling to You, sing-ing: send_ Your Spi - rit, send_ Your

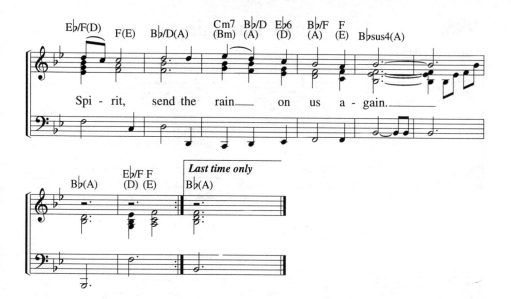

Spi - rit, send the rain___ on us a - gain.___

Last time only

2. Pour out Your wine, Lord,
   Wine of Your Spirit,
   Wine that would teach us to love.
   Pour out Your wine, Lord,
   Oh, how we need You
   To quench the thirst of our hearts.
   Here we are of one accord,
   Calling to You, singing:
   Send Your Spirit,
   Send Your Spirit,
   Pour Your wine on us again.

3. Breathe now upon us,
   Breath of Your Spirit,
   Breath to bring life to these bones.
   Breathe now upon us
   Life of abundance,
   Holiness, wisdom, love, truth.
   Here we are of one accord,
   Calling to You, singing:
   Send Your Spirit,
   Send Your Spirit,
   Breathe Your life on us again.

4. Send down the fire,
   Fire of Your Spirit,
   Refiner's fire to fulfil.
   Send down the fire,
   Fire to consume us,
   Reveal Your power once more.
   Here we are of one accord,
   Calling to You, singing:
   Send Your Spirit,
   Send Your Spirit,
   Send the fire on us again.

998.

Send Your rain

Deut 28:12; Ps 85:6

Steadily, with rhythm

Dave Bilbrough

1. Send Your rain down from the hea-vens;
2. Send Your fire down from the hea-vens.

send Your rain to this earth.____
The fire of re - vi - val to Your church.____

Let there be a great____ out-pour-
We can see the world____ is wait-

ing; Ho-ly Spi - rit, come to____
ing; Ho-ly Spi - rit, come to____

999.
Show me, dear Lord
(Precious child)

Capo 2 (G)

Ps 103:10-11,13; Is 43:1;
Lam 3:22; Eph 1:4; 1Pet 2:4

Andy Park

Steadily
Verse

1. Show me, dear Lord, how You see me in Your eyes, so that I can re-al-ise Your great love for me. Teach me, O Lord, that I am pre-cious in Your sight, that as a fa-ther loves his child, so You love me.

I am Yours___ be-cause You have cho-sen me.

I'm Your child___ be-cause You've called my___ name,

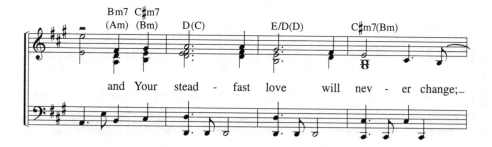

and Your stead - fast love will nev - er change;___

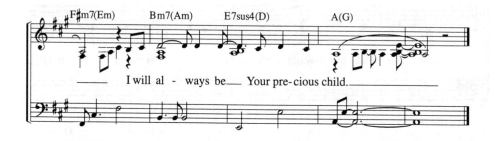

___ I will al - ways be___ Your pre-cious child.___

2. Show me, dear Lord, that I can never earn Your love,
   That a gift cannot be earned, only given.
   Teach me, O Lord, that Your love will never fade,
   That I can never drive away Your great mercy.

1000. Show me the way of the cross
(The way of the cross)

Mt 16:24; Mk 8:34;
Lk 9:23; 12:48

With feeling

Matt Redman

1. Show me the way of the cross once a-gain, de-ny-ing my-self for the love that I've gained. Ev-'ry-thing's You now, ev-'ry-thing's changed; it's time You had my whole life, You can have it all.

Chorus

Yes, I re-solve to give it all;

2. I've given like a beggar, but lived like the rich,
   And crafted myself a more comfortable cross.
   Yet what I am called to is deeper than this;
   It's time You had my whole life,
   You can have it all.

1001

Sing a song of celebration
(We will dance)

2 Sam 6:14; 1 Cor 13:12;
Rev 5:9; 7:9; 19:7; 21:2,18,21

With strength

David Ruis

Sing a— song of cel-e-bra-tion, lift up a shout of—
Dance with— all your might, lift up your hands and clap for—

praise, for the Bride-groom will come,_____ the
joy: the time's draw-ing near_____ when

glo-ri-ous One._____ And oh,_____
He will ap-pear._____ And oh,

— we will look on His face;_____ we'll
— we will stand by His side;_____ a

go_____ to a much bet-ter place._____
strong_____

1002.

Sing to God new songs

Ps 98: 1-9

Tune: ODE TO JOY

Ludwig van Beethoven (1770-1827)

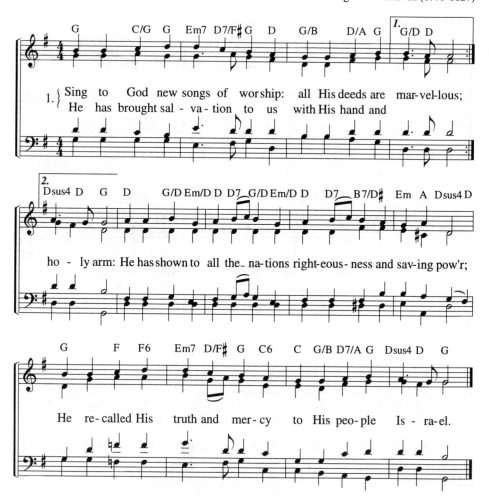

1. Sing to God new songs of worship: all His deeds are mar-vel-lous;
   He has brought sal-va-tion to us with His hand and ho-ly arm: He has shown to all the na-tions right-eous-ness and sav-ing pow'r; He re-called His truth and mer-cy to His peo-ple Is-ra-el.

2. Sing to God new songs of worship:
   Earth has seen His victory;
   Let the lands of earth be joyful
   Praising Him with thankfulness:
   Sound upon the harp His praises,
   Play to Him with melody;
   Let the trumpets sound His triumph,
   Show your joy to God the King!

3. Sing to God new songs of worship:
   Let the sea now make a noise;
   All on earth and in the waters
   Sound your praises to the Lord:
   Let the hills be joyful together,
   Let the rivers clap their hands,
   For with righteousness and justice
   He will come to judge the earth.

Michael Baughen

1003. Sing to the Lord
(Awaken the dawn)

Deut 6:5; Ps 57:8; 108:1-2
Mt 22:37; Mk 12:30; Lk 10;27

Capo 3 (D)

Stuart Garrard

With a lilt

1. Sing to the Lord___ with all of your heart; sing of the glo - ry that's

due to His name. Sing to the Lord___ with all of your soul,

Chorus

join all of heav-en and earth to pro-claim: You are the Lord,___ the

Sa - viour of all,___ God of cre - a - tion, we praise You.

We sing the songs— that a - wa-ken the dawn,— God of cre-a - tion, we

praise You.

2. Sing to the Lord with all of your mind,
   With understanding give thanks to the King.
   Sing to the Lord with all of your strength,
   Living our lives as a praise offering.

1004.

Soften my heart

Capo 1 (D)

Michael Sandeman

Soft - en my heart, that I may know the
Soft - en my heart for love to grow, the

love You have for me, more than words or well-worn
love I have for You, that keeps my mo - tives pure and

phra - ses. En - ter in, come and
blame - less. Ris - en Lamb,

have free reign as I walk with You to -
Ho - ly One, ov - er - sha - dow

day. me to - day.

1005. Sometimes when I feel Your love
(I love Your love)

Capo 4 (G)

Paul Oakley

Some-times when I feel___ Your love___ as I walk__ a-long__ the bu-sy street,___ I whis - per Your name__ un-der__ my breath.___ And some-times when I feel__ Your touch___ in the qui - et place___ of my room,___ I__ sing Your name in a-dor-a - tion. And there are times__

1006.

Son of man
(You're making me like Jesus)

Ps 40:2-3; Mt 11:19; Lk 7:34;
Jn 1:14; 3:13; Rom 8:29;
Phil 1:6; Heb 4:15

Paul Oakley

With a rocky feel

1. Son of Man and Man of heav'n, full of grace and truth; sin-ner's friend yet with-out sin, I want to be like You: per-fect in ho-li-ness, full of faith-ful-ness and love.

2. from sin and from shame You set me free, and I know Your ten-der-

2. You began a work in me,
   I know You'll see it through.
   There's a new song in my heart,
   And I want to sing to You.
   You lifted me from the mire,
   From sin and from shame You set me free,
   And I know Your tenderness,
   I know Your power at work in me.

   You're making me like Jesus . . .

You also, like living stones, are being built into a spiritual house to be a holy priesthood, offering spiritual sacrifices acceptable to God through Jesus Christ.

1 PETER 2:5

1007.

Soon, and very soon

Is 25:5; Rev 21:4

Capo 1 (E)

With a 'gospel' feel

Andrae Crouch

Soon, and ve-ry soon,___ we are go-ing___ to see the King;___

soon, and ve-ry soon,___ we are go-ing___ to see the King;___

soon, and ve-ry soon,___ we are go-ing___ to see the King;___

al-le-lu-ia,___ al-le-lu-ia,___ we're going to see the King!___

Al - le - lu - ia, al - le - lu - ia, al - le - lu - ia, al - le - lu - ia.

2. No more crying there,
   We are going to see the King;
   No more crying there,
   We are going to see the King;
   No more crying there,
   We are going to see the King;
   Alleluia, alleluia,
   We're going to see the King!

3. No more dying there,
   We are going to see the King;
   No more dying there,
   We are going to see the King;
   No more dying there,
   We are going to see the King;
   Alleluia, alleluia,
   We're going to see the King!
   Alleluia, alleluia, alleluia, alleluia.

4. Soon, and very soon,
   We are going to see the King;
   Soon, and very soon,
   We are going to see the King;
   Soon, and very soon,
   We are going to see the King;
   Alleluia, alleluia,
   We're going to see the King!
   Alleluia, alleluia, alleluia, alleluia.

1008.

Sound the trumpet

Ps 24:7; 150:3; Rev 1:18

Dave Bilbrough

Strong and rhythmic

Sound the trum-pet, strike the drum, see the King of glo-ry come,

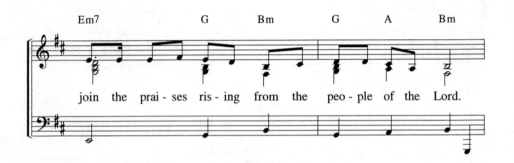

join the prai-ses ris-ing from the peo-ple of the Lord.

Let your voic-es now be heard, un-re-strained and un-re-served, pre-

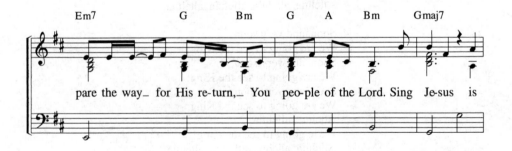

pare the way_ for His re-turn,_ You peo-ple of the Lord. Sing Je-sus is

Lord; Je-sus is— Lord.————— Bow down to His au-

tho-ri-ty, for He has slain the en-e-my. Of heav'n and hell He

holds the key. Je-sus is Lord; Je-sus is— Lord.—————

1009. Spirit of God, show me Jesus

Capo 1 (D)

A cappella

Chris Bowater

Spi - rit of God show me Je - sus,

Re - move the dark - ness, let truth shine through!

Spi - rit of God, show me Je - sus,

Re - veal the ful - ness of His love to me.

On coming to the house, they saw the child with His mother Mary, and they bowed down and worshipped Him.

MATTHEW 2:11

1010.

Spirit of holiness

Jn 3:8; 14:16,26; 15:26; 16:15;
Acts 1:4; Rom 1:4; 5:5;
1 Cor 12:4; Gal 5:22

Tune: Blow the wind southerly

Traditional melody
Arr. John Barnard

Chorus

Spi-rit of hol-i-ness, wis-dom and faith-ful-ness, Wind of the
Lord, blow-ing strong-ly and free: strength of our serv-ing and
joy of our wor-ship-ping; Spi-rit of God, bring Your ful-ness to me!

Verse

1. You came to in-ter-pret and teach us ef-fec-tive-ly all that the

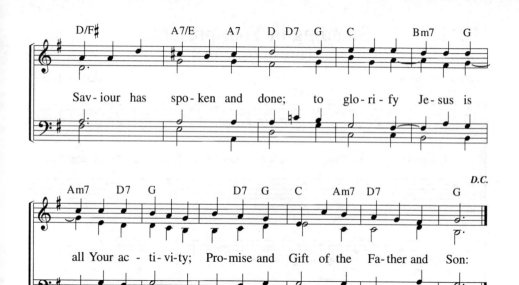

Sav-iour has spo-ken and done; to glo-ri-fy Je-sus is all Your ac-ti-vi-ty; Pro-mise and Gift of the Fa-ther and Son:

2. You came with Your gifts
To supply all our poverty,
Pouring Your love
On the church in her need;
You came with Your fruit
For our growth to maturity,
Richly refreshing
The souls that you feed:

Christopher Idle

1011. Standing in Your presence
(I live to know You)

Rev 11:15

Building, with strength

Darlene Zschech

1. Stand-ing in Your pre-sence, Lord, my heart and life are changed;

just to love You and to live to see Your

beau-ty and Your grace. Hea-ven and earth cry out Your name,

na-tions rise up and see Your face;

and Your king - dom is es-tab - lished as I

2. You've called me, I will follow,
   Your will for me I'm sure.
   Let Your heart beat be my heart's cry,
   Let me live to serve Your call.

1012. Take me past the outer courts
(Take me in)

Ex 38:30; Is 6:6-7
Mt 5:6; Heb 10:19-20

Dave Browning

Reverently

Take me past the out-er courts,— and through the ho-ly place,— past the bra-zen al-tar, Lord, I want to see— Your face.— Pass me by the crowds— of peo-ple, and the priests who sing— their praise;— I hun-ger and thirst for Your righ-teous-ness, but it's on-ly found one place,. so take me in—

1013.
Teach me to dance

Lively

Graham Kendrick
& Steve Thompson

Teach me to dance to the beat of Your heart,____ teach me to move
Teach me to love with your heart of com - pas - sion, teach me to trust

in the pow'r of Your Spi - rit, teach me to walk
in the word of Your pro - mise, teach me to hope

in the light of Your pre - sence, } teach me to dance
in the day of Your com - ing, }

to the beat of Your heart.____

Verse

1. You wrote the rhy - thm of life, cre - a - ted hea - ven and earth,

in You is joy with-out mea - sure. So, like a child in Your sight,

I dance to see Your de-light, for I was made for Your plea -

sure, plea - - sure.

2. Let all my movements express
A heart that loves to say 'yes',
A will that leaps to obey You.
Let all my energy blaze
To see the joy in Your face;
Let my whole being praise You,
Praise You.

1014.

Teach us, O Lord
(Break our hearts)

Job 28:28; Joel 2:13; Ps 126:5;
Prov 1:7; 9:10; Mal 3:2; Phil 2:10

Capo 2 (D)

Kevin Prosch

1. Teach us, O Lord,___ what it real - ly means___ ___ to rend our___ hearts in - stead of out - er___ things.___ ___ And teach us, O God,___ what we do not___ see___ ___ a - bout our___ hearts___ and of Your___ ways.. ___ And Fa - ther deal___ with our car - nal de - sires,___

2. Raise up an army like Joel saw,
   Your church that is stronger than ever before.
   They do not break ranks when they plunge through defences,
   But the fear of the Lord will be their wisdom.
   That they might weep as Jesus wept,
   A fountain of tears for the wounded and lost;
   Whoever heard of an army, O God,
   That conquered the earth by weeping,
   And mourning, and brokenness?

   But there will be a day when the nations will bow
   And our Lord will be King over all the earth;
   And He will be the only One,
   And also His name will be the only One.

Through Jesus, therefore, let us continually offer to God a sacrifice of praise – the fruit of lips that confess His name.

HEBREWS 13:15

1015. Thank You for saving me

Ps48:1; 96:4; 99:2; 145:33;
Mt 6:10; Lk 11:2; Jn 8:32; Rom 5:5;
Eph 1:6; Col 1:27; 1 Tim 4:10;
Heb 4:16; 1 Pet 2:6; 1 Jn 4:14

Capo 2 (D)

With a steady rhythm

Martin Smith

1. Thank You for sa-ving me; what can I say?

You are my ev-'ry-thing, I will sing Your praise.

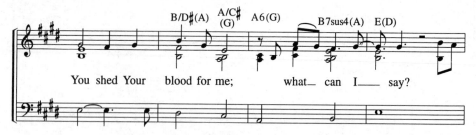

You shed Your blood for me; what can I say?

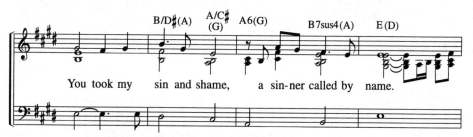

You took my sin and shame, a sin-ner called by name.

Great is the Lord.

Great is the— Lord.

For we know Your truth has set us free;

You've set Your hope in me.

Last time only

Thank You for sa-ving me; what— can I say?

2. Mercy and grace are mine, forgiven is my sin;
   Jesus, my only hope, the Saviour of the world.
   "Great is the Lord," we cry; God, let Your kingdom come.
   Your word has let me see, thank You for saving me.

1016.   The angels around Your throne

Rev 5:12

Worshipfully

Richard Lewis

2. The angels around Your throne,
They cry "worthy is the Lamb" . . .

1017. The angels, Lord, they sing

Rev 4:8

With awe

Matt Redman

1. The an-gels, Lord, they sing a - round Your throne; and we will join their song: praise You a - lone. The lone. Ho-ly, ho-ly, ho-ly, Lord our God, who was and is and is to come. come, 2. The come. A - men. A - men.

2. The living creatures, Lord, speak endless praise;
   And joining at Your throne, we'll sing their sweet refrain. } (x2)

3. The elders, Lord, they fall before Your throne; } (x2)
   Our hearts we humbly bow to You alone.

1018.

Capo 3 (Em)

The battle is the Lord's

1 Sam 17:47; 2 Cor 10:4

With drive

Doug Horley

The bat-tle is the Lord's,_____ the bat-tle is the Lord's,_____

_ the bat-tle is the Lord's,_____ that is our vic-

to- ry cry. The 1. We re-

fuse to bow_ to Sa - tan's schemes, set our wills_ for right-

eous-ness; we de-clare we'll choose— for truth— in ev-'ry sit-u-

a-tion.— We could bat-tle in— the hea-ven-lies, yet

in our lives— ne-glect— to fight: say-ing no to self— and no— to sin— is

where our war - fare must— be-gin.— The

2. As we're taking ground in daily war,
   Living lives of righteousness,
   We will grow in strength to face the bigger situations.
   And the more of us that battle through,
   Purer then this church will be;
   Who will stop us then as we proclaim:
   "Strongholds, you have had your day!"

1019.
The cross has said it all

Ps 103:11-13; 1 Cor 1:18
Eph 3:18; 1 Pet 1:19

With energy

Matt Redman & Martin Smith

1. The cross has said it all, the cross has said it all. I can't de-ny what You have shown, the cross speaks of a God of love; there dis-played for all to see, Je-sus Christ, our on-ly hope, a mess-age of the Fa-ther's heart:

from_ us._ How high, how wide, how deep,

how high,_ how_ wide, how_ deep,_ how high!_____ As

from_ us._

2. The cross has said it all,
   The cross has said it all.
   I never recognised Your touch
   Until I met You at the cross;
   We are fallen, dust to dust,
   How could You do this for us?
   Son of God shed precious blood,
   Who can comprehend this love?

For God so loved the world that He gave His only Son, that whoever believes in Him shall not perish but have eternal life.

JOHN 3:16

1020. The crucible for silver

1 Chron 16:29; Ps 29:2; 96:9;
Prov 17:3; Is 6:6-7; Rev 17:14; 19:16

Martin Smith

With anticipation

Verse

1. The cru-ci-ble for sil-ver and the fur-nace for gold, but the

Lord tests the heart of this child.

Stand-ing in all pu-ri-ty, God, our pas-sion is for ho - li-ness,

lead us to the se - cret place of praise.

Je-sus, Ho-ly One, You are my heart's—de-sire.—

King of kings, my ev-'ry-thing,— You've

set this heart— on fire. ——

2. Father, take our offering, with our song we humbly praise You.
   You have brought Your holy fire to our lips.
   Standing in Your beauty, Lord, Your gift to us is holiness;
   Lead us to the place where we can sing:

1021. The day of the streams

Rev 22:1-2

Capo 3 (D)

Dave Bilbrough & Andy Piercy

The day of the streams is ov-er,— the time of the ri-ver is here. *(4x)*

1. I hear the sound of a migh - ty ri - ver, of rush-ing wa-ter run-ning free— to ev-'ry land, through— ev-'ry bor - der, flow-ing now a - cross this earth.

F(D) *Vamp*

15

And the ri-ver is flow-ing, get-ting wi-der and wi-der,

deep-er and deep-er as it flows from the throne;— and the

leaves on the trees— are for the heal-ing of the na-tions, it's as

D.C. al Fine

clear as crys-tal, it's the wa-ter of life.

2. There is a time I know is coming,
   When all God's people join as one;
   They will become a great awakening,
   Bringing life to all the world.

1022. The earth resounds in songs of praise
(We proclaim Your kingdom)

Ps 19:1; Is 40:22;
Rev 7:9; 11:15; 17:14; 19:16

With energy

Geoff Bullock

The earth re-sounds in songs of praise;___ cre-
king-dom rules from age to age;___ ev-'ry

-a-tion shouts Your glo-rious name,___ and the
tribe and tongue shall bring You praise,___ and we

skies speak forth Your ma-jes-ty,___ and the
come to bow be-fore the throne

hea-vens de-clare Your___ glo-ry. Your _ of the

Lord of___ the hea-vens and earth.___

1023.
The grace of God

Eph 2:8; Titus 3:4-5,7

Judy Pruett

1024.

The heavens they preach

Ps 19:1-4; Is 55:6
Lk 19:47; 21:37; Rom 1:19-20; 8:34
2 Cor 5:15; Eph 3:8

Lex Loizides

With an 'African' feel

1. The hea- vens— they preach, they preach, they— preach the glo- ri - ous splen- dour— of God.___ The stars in— the sky seem so out— of reach, yet— they whis - per— His won - der - ful love.___ Day af - ter day in— a ser- mon— of na- ture— the works of— His hands lift— their voice:___

2. The prophets, they preached, they preached,
   They preached that one day a Saviour would come;
   And suddenly men heard a heavenly speech,
   The voice of God's only Son.
   Day after day in the streets and the temple
   He taught them and met their needs,
   And now through His death and His great resurrection
   His glorious purpose succeeds.

3. Your people will preach, we'll preach,
   We'll preach the unfailing riches of Christ;
   There's no one who's fallen too far from His reach,
   Who can't come from death into life.
   Day after day at the dawn of revival
   The multitudes seek His face,
   As we work to speed on His final arrival
   And crown Him with glory and praise!

The Lord will be king over the whole earth. On that day there will be one Lord, and His name the only name.

ZECHARIAH 14:9

1025.

Capo 3 (D)

With life

The King of love
(The King has come)

Song 6:3; 7:9; Is 61:1; Lk 4:18
Jn 20:25-27; Rev 1:14-18; 5:9

Stuart Townend & Kevin Jamieson

1. The King of love is my de-light,— His eyes are
   mouth there comes a sound— that shakes the

fire, His face is light,— the First and Last, the Liv-ing One,—
earth and splits the ground,— and yet this voice is life to me,—

— His name is Je - sus.— And from His — And I—
— the voice of Je - sus.—

Chorus

— will sing— my songs— of love,— cal - ling out— a-cross—
- led minds— can know— His peace,— cap - tive hearts— can be—

— the earth; {
— re-leased; {
the King— has come,— the King— of love— has come.—

Last time to Coda ⊕

F(D)

1.3.

And troub-

2.5.

2. My Lov - er's

D.C.

4.

C(A)

And— my— de - sire— is to have— You near,— Lord You

Gm7(Em)

C(A)

know that You— are wel - come here.— Be- fore— such love,— be-fore—

Gm7(Em)

F/A(D) B♭(G)

D.%. al Coda

— such grace— I will let the walls— come down.—— And I—

Coda ⊕

2. My Lover's breath is sweetest wine,
I am His prize, and He is mine;
How can a sinner know such joy?
Because of Jesus.
The wounds of love are in His hands,
The price is paid for sinful man;
Accepted child, forgiven son,
Because of Jesus.

1026.

The light of Christ

Jn 1:9; 3:5-7,16,19; 2 Cor 4:6

Donald Fishel
Arr. Betty Pulkingham

Flowing

Part 2

The light_ of_Christ_____ has come in-

Part 1

The light_ of_ Christ has come in-to the

G   C   F   G7   C

Last time to Coda

to the world;_____ the light_ of_Christ____ has come.____

world; the light_of_ Christ has come in-to the_world.

F   C   F   G   C

(v.3)   (v.2&3)   (v.2&3)

1. All men must be_born a-gain to see the king-dom of God; the

wa - ter and the Spi - rit bring new___ life___ in God's love.___

world.

2. God gave up His only Son
   Out of love for the world,
   So that all men who believe in Him
   Will live for ever.

3. The light of God has come to us
   So that we might have salvation;
   From the darkness of our sins we walk
   Into glory with Christ Jesus.

1027. The Lord fills me with His strength

Ps 18:32;
Prov 2:8

Merrilyn Billing

Brightly

The Lord fills me with His strength, and pro-tects me wher-ev-er I go. The Lord fills me with His strength, and pro-tects me wher-ev-er I go. Wher-ev-er I go, wher-ev-er I go, the Lord pro-tects me wher-ev-er I go. Wher-ev-er I go, wher-ev-er I go, the Lord pro-tects me wher-ev-er I go.

1028.

The Lord has spoken
(Raise up a church)

Gen 17:8; Num 14:24

Paul Oakley

The lyrics:

The Lord has spo-ken (the Lord has spo-ken) His pur-pose stands.__ (His pur-pose__ stands) __

1. Does God__ speak__ and then not__ act? Make a__ vow__ and not ful-fil? I will__ choose__ to serve the__Lord__ whole heart-ed-ly,__ whole-heart-ed-ly.__

2. You be-gan__ with just one__man, a cov-en-ant__ with A-bra-ham, pro-mis-ing__ that through his__seed__ all na-tions would__be blessed, and now Your plan is man-i-fest__

(Ch 1.) Oh, raise up a church__with a

(Chorus 2)
Oh, raise up a church who walk by faith,
In the fear of God they overcome.
Oh, raise up a church whose God is with them,
They walk in wisdom, they fear no harm.

(Chorus 3)
Oh, raise up a church who revere Your judgements,
They lift up a banner of mercy and love.
Oh, raise up a church who'll not keep silent,
They speak of the glory of Your dear Son.

1029. The Lord reigns

Ps 97:1,3,5-6,9

Daniel C. Stradwick

Joyfully

The Lord reigns, the Lord reigns, the Lord reigns, let the earth re-joice,___ let the earth re-joice,___ let the earth re-joice.___ Let the peo-ple be glad___ that our God reigns.___ The reigns.___ 1. A fi-re goes be-fore___ Him___ and

burns up all His en - e mies; the hills melt like wax at the pres-ence of the

Lord, at the pres-ence of the Lord._____ The

reigns._____ Our God reigns,_____ our God reigns!_____

2. The heavens declare His righteousness,
   The peoples see His glory;
   For You, O Lord, are exalted over all the earth,
   Over all the earth.

1030.
The Lord's my Shepherd
(Psalm 23)

Capo 1 (D)

Ps 23:1-6; 36:8; 56:3

Stuart Townend

Thoughtfully

(Descant) I will trust, I will trust in You.

1. The Lord's my Shep - herd, I'll not want. He makes me
And I will trust in You a - lone. And I will

I will trust, I will trust in You.

lie in pas - tures green. He leads me
trust in You a - lone, for Your

End - less mer - cy fol - lows me,
by the still, still wa - - - ters, His
end - less mer - cy fol - lows me, Your

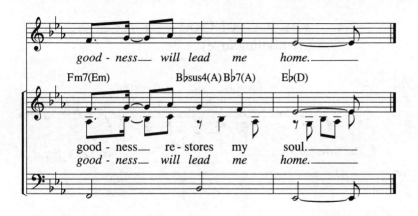

good - ness___ will lead me home._____

Fm7(Em)   B♭sus4(A) B♭7(A)   E♭(D)

good - ness___ re - stores my soul._____
good - ness___ will lead me home._____

2. He guides my ways in righteousness,
   And He anoints my head with oil,
   And my cup, it overflows with joy,
   I feast on His pure delights.

   And though I walk the darkest path,
   I will not fear the evil one,
   For You are with me, and Your rod and staff
   Are the comfort I need to know.

1031.

The love of God
(Unfailing love)

Mt 11:28; 26:2; Mk 16:4; Lk 24:2;
Jn 14:27; 20; Col 1:20; 1 Pet 2:24

Capo 1 (D)

Flowing

Geoff Bullock

1. The love of God,___ hea-ven's hope;___ this per-fect peace,___ this rest for my soul.___ This love___ di-vine,___ por-trayed___ in pain,___ the cross stands a-lone,___ un-fail-ing love._____ The love of God___

un - fail - ing love._____

2. The love of God, creation's cry,
Perfection portrayed, broken for me.
The Author of life has suffered our pain.
The cross stands alone, unfailing love.

3. The love of God, written in blood;
This empty grave, the stone rolled away!
The mercy of God has triumphed in Christ.
The cross stands alone, unfailing love.

1032.

The name of the Lord
(You alone are God)

Ps 34:8; 46:1; 120:1; 124:8
Prov 18:10; Lam 3:22-23
Mal 3:6; Heb 13:8

Brightly

Louise Hunt & Nathan Fellingham

1. The name of the Lord is a strong tow-er; the name of the Lord brings re-fuge and strength. The name of the Lord gives hope to the hope-less; the name of the Lord breathes life to the dead.

2. The heal the op-pressed.

2. The name of the Lord give strength to the weary,
   The name of the Lord brings freedom from fear;
   The name of the Lord gives peace to the restless,
   The name of the Lord will heal the oppressed.

3. The name of the Lord covers me with mercy,
   The name of the Lord brings everlasting joy;
   The name of the Lord will lift all my burdens,
   The name of the Lord, it makes me complete.

1033.

There is a home
(Tender mercy)

Is 9:7; 40:29;
Lk 1:78-79; Jn 20:27

Flowing

Stuart Townend

1. There is a home— that wand-'rers seek, there is a strength— that
   There is a cup— that sa - tis - fies, there is a Friend— who

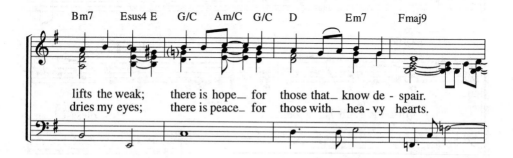

lifts the weak; there is hope— for those that— know de - spair.
dries my eyes; there is peace— for those with— hea - vy hearts.

Chorus

Ten-der mer - cy, the ten-der mer-

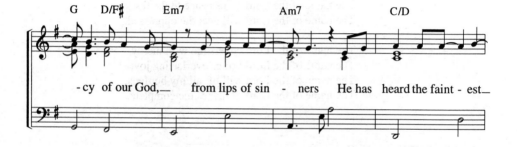

-cy of our God,— from lips of sin - ners He has heard the faint - est—

2. I have resolved to know Him more,
He whom the hosts of heaven adore,
Mighty King, whose reign will never end.
Yet as I gaze at the Holy One,
He beckons me to closer come,
Bares the scars that show to me my worth.

1034.   There is a louder shout to come _1 Cor 13:12; Rev 7:9_

With conviction

Matt Redman

1. There is a loud - er shout to come,____
   Bow - ing down__ be - fore Your throne,____

there is a sweet - er song to hear;____
ev - 'ry tribe__ and tongue will be;____

all   the na - tions with one voice,____
all   the na - tions with one voice,____

all   the peo - ple with one fear.____ __ And
all   the peo - ple with one King.____

what a song we'll sing up - on that day.

2. Now we see a part of this,
One day we shall see in full;
All the nations with one voice,
All the people with one love.
No one else will share Your praise,
Nothing else can take Your place;
All the nations with one voice,
All the people with one Lord.
And what a song we'll sing upon that day.

3. Even now upon the earth
There's a glimpse of all to come;
Many people with one voice,
Harmony of many tongues.
We will all confess Your name,
You will be our only praise;
All the nations with one voice,
All the people with one God.
And what a song we'll sing upon that day.

1035.
There is none like You
Ps 86:8; Is 46:9; Jer 10:6-7

Capo 1 (G)

Lenny LeBlanc

There is none like You, no one else can touch my heart like You do. I could search for all e- ter-ni-ty long and find there is none like You. Your mer-cy flows like a riv-

1036. There is no one like our God

Gen 2:4; 1 Sam 2:2; Neh 9:6
Ps 86:8; 147:4,8; Is 40:8; 45:12
46:9; Jer 10:6-7; 1Pet 1:25; Rev 14:7

With life

Noel & Tricia Richards

Chorus

There is   no one like— our God— (in all— the earth.—

—)   There is   no— one like— our God— (in all— the earth.—

—)   No one like— our God,— no one like— our God.—

Last time to Coda — *Verse*

—   1. Our God has made the

heav'ns,   our God has made the   earth;

2. He numbers every star
   And calls each one by name;
   He fills the skies with clouds,
   Supplies the earth with rain.

3. Sing praises to our God,
   Sing praises to His name;
   His love will never end,
   His word will never fail.

1037.
There is no other friend
(There is no other love)

PS 87:6-7; Mt 9:20; 14:36;
Mk 5:28; 6:56; Lk 8:44

David Ruis

Steadily, building in strength

There is no oth-er friend,___ there is no oth-er friend___ like
There is no oth-er love,___ there is no oth-er love___ like

You, O_ Lord;___ no oth-er bro-ther,
You, O_ Lord;___ no oth-er sweet-er,

no oth-er sis-ter_ like You.___
no oth-er foun-tain_ but You.

How long un-til I'm sa-tis-fied?_ I must have more of_

_ You.___ For I was born in Zi-on, a-wak-ened love is cry-ing

in - to the val - ley, I will run with__ You._____

Ah,_____ all my foun - tains are in You.

*Love the Lord your God with
all your heart and with all your soul
and with all your strength.*

DEUTERONOMY 6:5

1038.

There is one name

Acts 4:12; Heb 9:12; 10:12

Capo 3 (G)

Worshipfully, with strength

Robert Critchley

There is one name____ un-der hea-ven____ by which men can be saved,____ Je-sus a-lone.____ On-ly one name____ un-der hea-ven:____ Je-sus,____ and Je-sus__ a-lone.____ One sa-cri-fice,____ one ho-ly Lamb__ shed His__ own blood,

1039.

There's a light that shines
(You call us near)

Ps 22:27-28; Is 61:11;
Rev 15:4

Geoff Bullock

With strength

E Em7 D/E E Bm A

1. There's a light that shines, a lamp that burns, the hope, the peace of

Bm7 A/C# D E Em7 D/E E

right - eous - ness. And You who hear the prayers of all, You

Bm A/C# D E | **1.3.** D/E A/E | **2.4.** *Chorus* D/F#

call us near to You.   2. There's a   And the

C D E Esus4 E Esus4 C

light shines so we can see,   and the truth came so

D E Esus4 E Esus4 G Asus4 A Bm7

we could know.   And the light of God is the

2. There's a path that leads, a way that's true,
   The life, the light, the perfect truth.
   We come to You, forgiven, free,
   You call us near to You.

3. No other way, no other life,
   No other truth, no other light.
   The way ahead is found in Christ,
   You call us near to You.

4. We will dance and sing, for freedom comes
   To heal our hearts and dry our tears.
   Forever more in glorious light
   You call us near to You.

1040.

There's an awesome sound
(Send revival)

Ps 85;6; Rev 7:9-10;14:2

Building in strength

Richard Lewis

1. There's an awe - some sound_____ on the
   mor - tal King._____ who will

winds of hea - ven,_____ migh - ty thun - der clouds_____
reign for - ev - er,_____ is_____ reach - ing out_____

in the skies a - bove. The im -
with His arms of

love, His arms of_ love,

His arms of_ love. 2. All cre -

Send re - vi - val to this land, fill this na - tion with Your love. love.

2. All creation sings
   Of the Lamb of glory,
   Who laid down His life
   For all the world.
   What amazing love,
   That the King of heaven
   Should be crucified,
   Stretching out His arms,
   His arms of love,
   His arms of love.

After this I heard what sounded like the roar of a great multitude in heaven shouting: "Hallelujah! Salvation and glory and power belong to our God, for true and just are His judgements.

REVELATION 19:1-2

1041. There's a place where the streets shine
(Because of You)

Strongly rhythmic

Acts 22:16;
1 Cor 13:12; Rev 7:14;
19:9; 21:4,11,21,23

Paul Oakley

1. There's a place where the streets shine with the glo-ry of the Lamb. There's a way, we can go there, we can live there be-yond time.

Be-cause of You, jus-tice no more death. Be-cause of You,

To next section

Oh,_____ we'll see You face to face,_____ and we will dance_ to-geth - er in the ci-ty of_ our God,_ _ be-cause of_ You._____

2. No more pain, no more sadness,
No more suffering, no more tears.
No more sin, no more sickness,
No injustice, no more death.
Because of You . . .

3. There is joy everlasting,
There is gladness, there is peace.
There is wine ever flowing,
There's a wedding, there's a feast.
Because of You . . .

1042.

There's a river

Ps 36:8; Rev 19:9; 22:1-2

Malcolm du Plessis

Lively, with a swing feel

1. There's a riv-er flow-ing from the throne,
2. You in-vi-ted me to come for free,

not a gen-tle stream but pow'r-ful flow.
en-joy the feast You had pre-pared for me;

It brings the ci-ty of our God such joy, and springs up
draw with laugh-ter from Your spark-ling wells, bathe in Your

2nd time to Coda

foun-tains in her midst.
riv-er of de-lights.

On the banks the trees are

1043.

There's a river of joy

Is 40:31; Rev 22:1

Taran Ash, James Mott
& Matthew Pryce

With energy

Chorus: There's a ri-ver of joy_ that_ flows_ from Your throne,_ O ri-ver of joy_ flow_ through_ me._ There's a ri-ver of joy_ that_ flows_ _ from Your throne:_ come, Ho-ly Spi - rit, with joy,_ come, Ho - ly Spi - rit, with joy._ There's a _

Last time to Coda

1.

2.

Verse: I will_ rise_ up_ on the wings of_ an_ ea - gle;_ with

1044.

There's a wind a-blowing
(Sweet wind)

1 Kings 18:38; Ezek 3:4;
Joel 2:23; Jn 3:8; Acts 2:2-3

David Ruis

Rhythmically

1. There's a wind a-blow-ing all a-cross the land; fra - grant breeze of hea-ven blow - ing once a-gain. Don't know where it comes from, don't know where it goes, but let it blow ov-er me. Oh, sweet

2. There's a rain a-pouring,
   Showers from above;
   Mercy drops are coming,
   Mercy drops of love.
   Turn Your face to heaven,
   Let the water pour,
   Well, let it pour over me.
   Oh, sweet rain,
   Come and pour over me.

3. There's a fire burning,
   Falling from the sky;
   Awesome tongues of fire,
   Consuming you and I.
   Can you feel it burning,
   Burn the sacrifice?
   Well, let it burn over me.
   Oh, sweet fire,
   Come and burn over me.

1045. There's no one like You

Ps 86:8; Is 46:9; Jer 10:6-7

Capo 2 (D)

Eddie Espinosa

2. There's no one like You, my Lord,
   No one could take Your place;
   I long for Your presence, Lord,
   To serve You is my reward.
   There's no one like You, my Lord,
   No one could take Your place;
   There's no one like You, my Lord,
   No one like You.

1046. There's nothing I like better than to praise

Brightly

Ian Smale

There's no-thing I like bet-ter than to praise.

There's no-thing I like bet-ter than to praise.

'Cause Lord, I love You, and there's no-thing I would

ra-ther do than whis-per a-bout it, talk all a-bout it.

shout all a-bout it all my days.

shout all a-bout___ it all my days.

1047.

These are the days of Elijah
(Days of Elijah)

Capo 3 (Em)

With confidence

Lev 25:54; 1Kings 5:5
Ps 14:7; 53:6; Is 40:3; Ezek 37:6; Dan 7:3
Mal 3:1; 45; Mt 3:3; 24:30; 26:64; Mk 1:3
13:26; 14:62; Jn 1:23; 4:35; Acts 3:22; Rev 6:8

Robin Mark

1. These are the days of Elijah, declaring the word of the Lord: and these are the days of Your servant Moses, righteousness being restored. And though these are days of great trial, of famine and darkness and sword, still

2. These are the days of Ezekiel,
The dry bones becoming as flesh;
And these are the days of Your servant David,
Rebuilding the temple of praise.
These are the days of the harvest,
The fields are as white in the world,
And we are the labourers in the vineyard,
Declaring the word of the Lord.

1048.

The sky is filled

Mt 1:23; Lk 2:10,13;
Rev 17:14; 19:16

Mick Gisbey

Capo 2 (G)

Rocky

1. The sky is filled with the glo - ry of God. Tri - um - phant - ly the an - gels sing: "Re - joice, good news, a Sa - viour is born, and life will ne - ver be the same."

2. Praise and adoration spring from our hearts,
   We lift our voices unto You;
   You are the One, God's only Son,
   King of kings forever more!

The Spirit of the Sovereign Lord is on me, because the Lord has anointed me to preach good news to the poor.

ISAIAH 61:1

1049. The Spirit of the Sovereign Lord

Capo 3 (Em)

Is 61: 1-3; Lk 4:18-19

Andy Park

Resolutely

1.The Spi- rit of— the Sov-'reign Lord is up - on—— you, be-

cause He has— a-noint-ed you to preach good— news.—— The

2. news.—— He has sent you to— the poor,—

— (this is the year,—) to bind up the bro - ken- heart-

of the ven-geance of our God._____ 2. The

2. The Spirit of the Sovereign Lord is upon us,
   Because He has anointed us to preach good news.
   (Repeat)

   He will comfort all who mourn,   *(this is the year)*
   He will provide for those who grieve; *(this is the day)*
   He will pour out the oil of gladness, *(this is the year)*
   Instead of mourning you will praise.

1050. The Virgin Mary had a baby boy

Mt 1:23,25; 2:20;
Lk 1:31,31; 2:7,13

Melody: Edric Connor Collection
Arr. Stuart Townend

Brightly, with a 'calypso' feel

1. The Vir- gin Ma - ry had a ba - by boy,___ the Vir- gin Ma - ry had a ba - by boy,___ the Vir- gin Ma - ry had a ba - by boy,___ and they said that His name was Je - sus.

Chorus

He come___ from the glo - ry, He come___ from the glo - ri - ous king - dom. Oh, yes! be- liev - er.

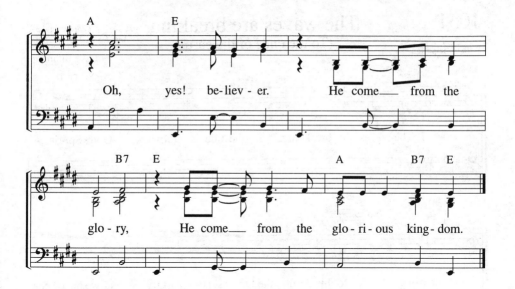

2. The angels sang when the baby was born,
   The angels sang when the baby was born,
   The angels sang when the baby was born,
   And proclaimed Him the Saviour Jesus.

3. The wise men saw where the baby was born,
   The wise men saw where the baby was born,
   The wise men saw where the baby was born,
   And they saw that His name was Jesus.

1051.

The waves are breaking
(To the ends of the earth)

Mt 28:19; Jn 4:35;
Acts 1:8; 2:2-3; Rev 14:15

Dave Bilbrough

With anticipation

1. The waves are break-ing, the tide is turn-ing, God's Spi-rit is com-ing to this earth; the har-vest is wait-ing, and we have been called to go— to the na-tions of this— world. To the ends of— the earth, to the ends of— the earth, to the ends of— the earth we will—

go; bear-ing the mes - sage__ that our God can be known, to the ends of__ the earth we will__ go.

2. The fire is falling, the wind is blowing,
   The flame is spreading across our land;
   Revival is coming, let the world hear,
   Tell every woman, child and man.

3. The drums are beating, the trumpet is sounding,
   A warrior spirit He's put in our hearts;
   In the name of the Father, Spirit and Son,
   We'll take this word to everyone.

1052. The world is looking for a hero
(Champion)

Phil 2:7-8; Rev 17:14; 19:11,15-16

With strength

Noel & Tricia Richards

1. The world is look-ing for a he-ro;— we know the
great-est one of all: the migh-ty Ru-ler of the na-tions,—
King of kings and Lord of lords, who took the

na-ture of a ser-vant,— and gave His life to save us all.

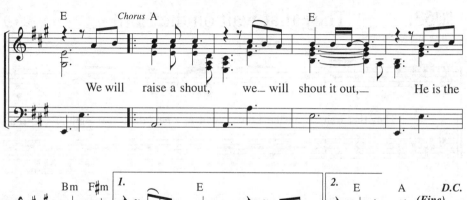

We will raise a shout, we will shout it out, He is the

Cham-pion of the world. We will of the world.

2. The Lord Almighty is our hero,
   He breaks the stranglehold of sin.
   Through Jesus' love we fear no evil;
   Powers of darkness flee from Him.
   His light will shine in every nation,
   A sword of justice He will bring.

1053. They that wait on the Lord

With a driving rhythm

Is 40:28-31

Kevin Prosch

They that wait— on the Lord— will re - new their— strength,— run— — and not get wea-ry,— walk— and not faint.—

They that wait

Do you not know?— Have you not heard?—

My— Fa - ther does not get— wea - ry.—

who— wait.— I will wait—— I will wait,—
I will wait—— on— You;— I will run,—
I will run—— with— You;— my— love,
my— love—— for— You.—

I will wait,—
I will run,—
my— love,—

Keep yourselves in God's love as you wait for the mercy of our Lord Jesus Christ to bring you eternal life.

JUDE: 21

1054. This earth belongs to God

Tune: TRUMPET VOLUNTARY

Music: Jeremiah Clarke (1670-1707)
Arr. David Ball

March style ♩ = 128

This earth be - longs to God, the world, its wealth, and all its peo - ple; He formed the wa - ters wide and fa - shioned ev - 'ry sea and shore. *(Fine)* Who may go up the hill of the Lord and stand in the place of ho - li - ness?

Only the one whose heart is— pure, whose hands and— lips are

clean.

2. Lift high your heads, you gates,
   Rise up, you everlasting doors,
   As here now the King of glory
   Enters into full command.
   Who is the King, this King of glory,
   Where is the throne He comes to claim?
   Christ is the King, the Lord of glory,
   Fresh from His victory.

3. Lift high your heads, you gates,
   And fling wide open the ancient doors,
   For here comes the King of glory
   Taking universal power.
   Who is the King, this King of glory,
   What is the power by which He reigns?
   Christ is the King, His cross of glory,
   And by love He rules.

4. All glory be to God
   The Father, Son and Holy Spirit;
   From ages past it was,
   Is now, and evermore shall be.

   Christopher Idle

1055.

This God is our God

Ps 48:8-11,13-14

With energy

Kent Henry & David Ortinau

2. As we have heard, so we have seen
   The safety of our God,
   That we might tell all generations
   You will be, forever be
   Our guide unto the end.

1056.

This I know

Brightly, with a 'pop' feel

Mt 7:11; Lk 11:13;
Rom 8:31-32,34; Heb 4:16; 7:25

Mark Altrogge

Chorus

This I know, my God is for me, this I know.

This I know, my God is on my side; my God is

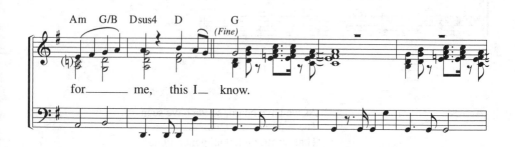

for me, this I know.

Verse

1. If God did not spare His on-ly Son, but de-

liv-ered__ Him up for__ us all,   will He__ not give us

ev-'ry__ good thing when__we come in__ His name and__ call?   Oh,__

2. Let us draw near the throne of grace
   For mercy and help in our need;
   For Jesus is ever praying for us,
   He is living to intercede.

1057.

This is holy ground
(Holy ground)

Ex 3:5; 1 Tim 2:8

Capo 1 (D)

Worshipfully

Christopher Beatty

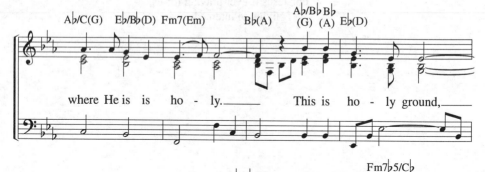

This is ho - ly ground,_____ we're stand - ing on
ho - ly ground,_____ for the Lord is here___ and
where He is is ho - ly._____ This is ho - ly ground,_____

_ we're stand - ing on ho - ly ground,_____ for the

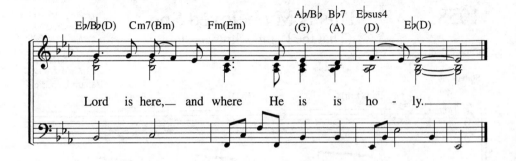

Lord is here, and where He is is ho - ly.

2. These are holy hands,
   He's given us holy hands,
   He works through these hands
   And so these hands are holy.
   These are holy hands,
   He's given us holy hands,
   He works through these hands
   And so these hands are holy.

1058.
This is My belovèd Son
(That the Lamb who was slain)

Capo 2 (Em)

Is 53:11; Mt 3:17;
9:37-38; 28:19;
Mk 1:11; 4:29;
Lk 3:22; 1 :2;
Jn 3:16; 4:35;
Rev 5:12; 19:7

Graham Kendrick

Stately

This is my be - lo-vèd Son who tast-ed death that you, my child, might live. See the blood He shed for you, what suf-fer-ing, say what more could He give? Clothed in His per-fec-tion bring praise, a fra-grance sweet,

Boldly

Chorus

gar-land-ed with joy, come wor-ship at His feet: that the Lamb who was slain might re - ceive the re - ward, might re - ceive the re - ward of His suf-fer-ing.

To end

2. Look, the world's great harvest fields
   Are ready now,
   And Christ commands us: "Go!"
   Countless souls are dying
   So hopelessly,
   His wondrous love unknown.
   Lord, give us the nations
   For the glory of the King.
   Father, send more labourers,
   The lost to gather in.

3. Come the day when we will stand
   There face to face,
   What joy will fill His eyes.
   For at last His Bride appears,
   So beautiful,
   Her glory fills the skies.
   Drawn from every nation,
   People, tribe and tongue;
   All creation sings,
   The wedding has begun.

And the Lamb who was slain shall receive the reward,
Shall receive the reward of His suffering.

1059.

This is my pilgrimage

Ps 84:5; Hep 11:11; 12:2

(Restless pilgrim)

Sue Rinaldi

Gently

This is my pil - grim-age,— to climb— in-to You.—

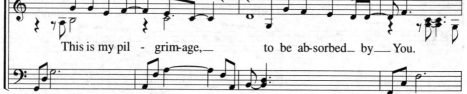

This is my pil - grim-age,— to be ab-sorbed— by— You.

I'm so rest - - less— for more of You,— O— God.—

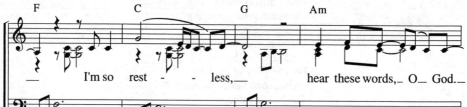

I'm so rest - - less,— hear these words,— O— God.—

Fine

Give me the eyes— of a pro - phet,
Some-times I'm war - torn and wear - y,

1060.
This is the mystery
(Let the Bride say, come)

Song 1:15; 2:10,13; 4:1; 6:4;
Is 62:3,5; Eph 1:9,12; 1Pet 2:9;
Rev 19:7-8; 22:17,20

Phil Lawson Johnston & Chris Bowater

1. This is the mys - ter - y, that Christ has cho - sen you and me,—— to be the re - ve - la - tion of His glo - ry; a cho - sen, roy - al, ho - ly peo - ple, set a - part— and loved, a Bride pre - pa - ring for her King. Let the

Bride say 'come,' let the Bride say 'come,' let the Bride of the Lamb say—

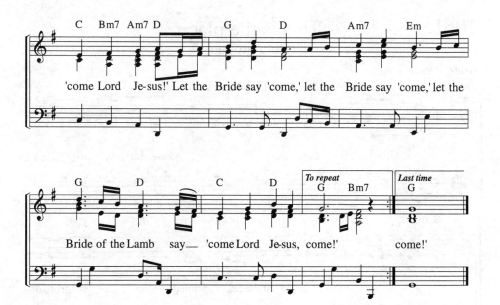

'come Lord Je-sus!' Let the Bride say 'come,' let the Bride say 'come,' let the

Bride of the Lamb say— 'come Lord Je-sus, come!' come!'

2. She's crowned in splendour
   And a royal diadem,
   The King is enthralled by her beauty.
   Adorned in righteousness,
   Arrayed in glorious light,
   The Bride in waiting for her King.

3. Now hear the Bridegroom call,
   "Beloved, come aside;
   The time of betrothal is at hand.
   Lift up your eyes and see
   The dawning of the day,
   When as King, I'll return to claim My Bride."

1061.

This is the place
(Holy ground)

Dave Bilbrough

Gently, with awe

1. This is the place where dreams are found, where vis-ion comes, called ho-ly ground.

Chorus
Ho-ly ground, I'm stand-ing on ho-ly ground, for the Lord my God is here with me.

2. Your fire burns, but never dies;
   I realise this is holy ground.

3. The Great I AM, revealed to man;
   Take off your shoes, this is holy ground.

But for you who revere My name, the sun of righteousness will rise with healing in its wings.

MALACHI 4:2

1062.

This love
(Now is the time)

2 Cor 3:12,18

Geoff Bullock

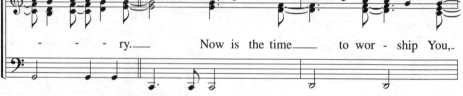

Gently

This love,___ this hope,___ this peace___ of God, this right-
___ and whole,___ and ris - en in___ His right-

- eous- ness,___ this faith,___ this joy,___ this life
- eous- ness,___ I live___ in Him,___ He lives___

1.
- com- plete___ in me.___ Now healed___ _

D.S. 2.
in me,

Dm7   C/E   F

and filled with this hope___ in God,___ re-flect-ing His glo-

F/G G F/G G   C   Chorus   Dm7

- - - ry.___ Now is the time___ to wor - ship You,

1063.

Though I feel afraid
(All I know)

Mt 28:20; Jn 14:18

Moderately

Ian White

1. Though I feel a-fraid of ter-ri-tory— un-known, I
know that I— can say that I do not stand— a-lone. For
Je-sus, You have pro - mised— Your pre-sence in— my heart; I
can-not see— the end-ing, but it's here that I— must start. And
all I know is You have called me, and that I will fol - low is all—

I can say. I will go where You will send me, and

Your fire lights my way. 2. What

Coda

Your fire lights my way.

Your fire lights my way.

2. What lies across the waves
   May cause my heart to fear;
   Will I survive the day,
   Must I leave what's known and dear?
   A ship that's in the harbour
   Is still and safe from harm,
   But it was not built to be there,
   It was made for wind and storm.

1064. Throughout the earth Your glory will come

(Lord, come and reign)

Is 35:5; Ezek 34:26; Joel 2:23;
Mt 6:10; 11:5; Lk 7:22; 11:2; Rev 22:17

James Wright

Brightly, with a 'gospel' feel

1. { Through-out the earth Your glo-ry will come,__
     From Sa-tan's hold this land will be free,__

a day of pow'r, of sal - va - tion.__ To thir-sty hearts Your
the deaf will hear, the blind__ will see;__ to walk in truth, in

1. 3.
ri-vers will run,__ chang-ing lives for the glo-ry of God.__

2. 4.
Chorus
vic - to-ry,__ to__ live for the glo-ry of God.__ Lord, come and reign__

__ by the pow'r__ of Your Spi - rit, show - er this land__

with Your ri-vers of life,___ that Je - sus the Son_____ would be glo-ri-fied___ with - in the heart of Your Bride,___ Lord, come and reign.___

Lord, come and reign.___

Lord, come and reign.___

2. Upon the earth may Your kingdom come.
Within our lives may Your will be done;
Under the reign of Jesus the Son
We will live for the glory of God.
The gates of heaven are open wide,
To bless this land, to turn back the tide,
To welcome in Your glorious Bride,
To live for the glory of God.

1065. Thy hand, O God, has guided

Tune: THORNBURY

Triumphantly

Basil Harwood (1859-1949)

1.Thy hand, O God has guid - ed Thy flock, from age to age; the won-drous tale is writ - ten, full clear on ev - 'ry page. Our fa - thers owned Thy good - ness, and we their deeds re - cord; and both of this bear wit - ness: one

Church, one Faith, one Lord.

2. Thy heralds brought glad tidings
   To greatest as to least;
   They bade them rise and hasten
   To share the great King's feast.
   And this was all their teaching
   In every deed and word;
   To all alike proclaiming:
   One Church, one Faith, one Lord.

3. Through many a day of darkness,
   Through many a scene of strife,
   The faithful few fought bravely
   To guard the nation's life.
   Their gospel of redemption,
   Sin pardoned, hope restored,
   Was all in this enfolded:
   One Church, one Faith, one Lord.

4. Thy mercy will not fail us,
   Nor leave Thy work undone;
   With Thy right hand to help us,
   The victory shall be won.
   And then, by men and angels,
   Thy name shall be adored,
   And this shall be their anthem:
   One Church, one Faith, one Lord.

   E H Plumptre (1821-91)

1066.
Thy word

Ps 119:105; Mt 28:20

Capo 1 (D)

Amy Grant & Michael W. Smith

Thoughtfully

Thy word is a lamp un-to my feet and a light un-to my path. 1. When I feel a-fraid, think I've lost my way, still You're there right be-side___ me. And no-thing will I fear as___ long as You are near; please be near me to the end.___

2. I will not forget,
Your love for me, and yet
My heart forever is wandering.
Jesus, be my guide
And hold me to Your side,
And I will love You to the end.

1067.

To be in Your presence
(My desire)

Ps 27:4

Noel Richards

With intimacy

1. To be in Your pres - ence, to sit at Your feet, where Your love sur - rounds me, and makes me com - plete. This is my de - sire, O Lord, this is my de - sire. This is my de - sire, O Lord, this is my de - sire.

2. To rest in Your presence,
Not rushing away;
To cherish each moment,
Here I would stay.

1068.

To Him who loves us

Rev 1:5-6

Flowing, building in the chorus

Bryn Haworth

To Him who loves us, and has freed us from our

sins by His blood, and has made us to be a

king-dom and priests to serve His God.__ To Him who

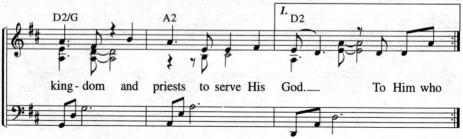

God__ and Fa - ther. (Men) To Him be

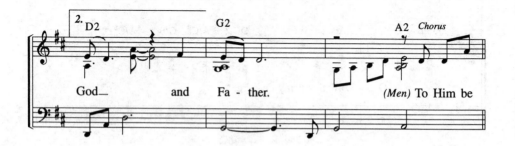

1069. To Your majesty

Sue Rinaldi
& Steve Bassett

Gently

To Your ma-jes-ty,— and Your beau-ty I— sur-ren - der.—

To Your ho-li-ness— and your love— I sur-ren - der.—

For you are— an awe - some God who is migh - ty, You de-

serve— my deep- est praise; with all of my heart,— with

all of my life— I sur - ren - der.—

1070.

Visit us, O Lord

Zech 2:10

Kirk & Deby Dearman

With feeling

Lyrics:

Vis-it us, O Lord,— with Your awe-some pre-sence.—

Dwell in our midst in Your glo ry and pow-er, in Your

strength and in Your love.— This is our cry, O

Lord, let Your pre-sence fill— this place, fill— this—

place. fill— this place.

1071. Waiting for Your Spirit

Jn 4:14

Quietly, with expectaion

Mick Gisbey

Wait-ing___ for Your___ Spi-rit,

thirs-ty___ for Your___ Spi-rit;

touch-ing us, Lord,___ as we pray,___ fil-ling our lives___ with

You a-gain. Fall on us, Lord,___ as we call___ on___ You.

Blessed are those who hunger and thirst for righteousness, for they will be filled.

MATTHEW 5:6

1072.

Wake up, my soul

Capo 4 (D)

Ps 57:8; Rom 8:2
1 Cor 15:56-57; Phil 3:14; Heb 12:2

Brightly

Matt Redman

Wake up, my soul, wor-ship the Lord of truth and life. Have strength, my heart, press on as one who seeks the prize. I'll run for You, my God and King, I'll run as one who runs to win. I'm pres-sing on, not giv-ing in. I will run, I will

1073.

Wake up, wake up O sleeper

Mal 4:2; Eph 1:4; 4:31; 5:8,14; 6:11

With a heavy rock feel

Nathan Fellingham

Wake up, wake up O sleep-er, and rise from the dead.

1. We are His peo-ple drawn by grace, chosen by His glo-rious name, called to give Him all our praise, set a-part
We must be hum-ble now and pray, and turn from all our care-less ways, and in our hearts wait for the hour for Christ to come

(2nd & 4th times)

(2nd & 4th times)

G   Am7   *2nd time D.C.*

— to— wor - ship——— Him.
— in— awe - some pow'r.———

G   C

Re-vere the   name of the Lord,   and He will   shine on   you;

Em   C

He will a - rise with   heal - ing and set   you   free.

2. We are called to righteousness,
   To be like God in holiness;
   So let all slander now subside,
   And flee from bitterness and rage.
   And soon the night will fade away,
   And in its place will come the day;
   So we must clothe ourselves in light,
   The armour that will help us fight.

Wash me clean

Rev 7:14; 22:1

Gently

Maggi Dawn

Wash me clean in that cool ri-ver; wash my soul in the
pure__ wa-ter.____ Wash me clean in that cool ri-ver;
Lord, make me___ new.____

1075.

We are His people
(Shout to the Lord)

Lev 26:13; Ps 42:7; 81:1;
Ezek 34:27; Nah 1:13;
Zeph 3:14; Mt 16:18

Kevin Prosch

We are His peo - ple,_____
But there is a cry___ in our hearts,_____

He gives us mu - sic to sing._____   There is a sound_
like when deep calls__ un - to the deep,_____   for Your breath of de - liv -

_ now,_____   like the   sound   of the   Lord_____   when His
'rance,_____   to   breathe   on the   mu - sic we   so

en - e - mies   flee._____   But with - out   Your   pow - er_____
des - perate - ly   need._____

1076. We are marching in the light of God
(Siyahamba)

A cappella

Tr. Anders Nyberg
South African Trad.

1. We are marching in the light of God . . .

We are marching (marching, marching) oo,
We are marching in the light of God . . .

2. We are living in the love of God . . .

3. We are moving in the power of God . . .

Copyright © 1990 Wild Goose Publications
Iona Community, Commuinity House,
Pearce Institute, Govan, Glasgow, G51 3UU, UK.

Great is the Lord and most worthy of praise.

PSALM 48:1

1077. We are marching to a different anthem
(I love the God of heaven)

With a 'funk' feel

2 Sam 22:35; Ps 18:34
Is 61:1; 1 Cor 15:57

Lex Loizides

1. We are march-ing to a diff-'rent an-them,
   He is mov-ing through the towns and ci-ties,

   we are dan-cing to a dif-f'rent song;—
   He is bind-ing up the bro-ken ones;—

   and our hearts have come a-live with free-dom,
   and His hea-ling hand is work-ing won-ders,

   mer-cy has come,— the God of mer-cy has come.—
   see how they come,— He sets them

   free when they come.— And I sing I love the God of hea-ven,

I love His pre-cious Son;— and in the Ho-ly Spi-rit, He's mak-ing us strong,— and giv-ing us the vic-t'ry. giv-ing us a vic-t'ry song.—

2. He is training up our hands for battle,
   And equipping us to take the land;
   For the promises to us are mighty,
   We will be strong,
   And move together as one.
   We are heading for our finest hour,
   When our Saviour will be magnified,
   And His glory will outshine all others:
   Jesus is Lord,
   Let Him be praised and adored.
   And I sing . . .

The prayer of a righteous
man is powerful and effective.

JAMES 5:16

1078.

We are salt
(Let it rain)

Deut 28:12; Ezek34:26;
Joel 2:23; Mt 5:13-14; 6:10;
Lk 11:12; Rev 22:3,20

Bob Fitts

Rhythmically ♩ = 120

1. We are salt and we are the light; we've come to break the powers of night, and by the love of God proclaim His liberty. We're ambassadors of grace, in His name we take this place; Lord, let Your

cur - ses, let it rain. Hear Your peo - ple

pray - ing, send Your bles-sing, let it rain.

Oh, let it rain.

2. You have won the fight, O Lord;
   By Your death our life's been restored,
   And You have risen now
   To vanquish all our foes.
   Come, abolish every curse
   O'er the nations of the earth;
   In Your name we'll go,
   To proclaim You rose to live and reign.
   Lord, come and reign.

1079.
We are the army of God

Ex 3:14; Joel 2:11; Jn 8:58;
Gal 3:7; Rev 7:14; 19:19

Capo 2 (D)

With a steady rhythm

Kevin Prosch

We are the ar-my of God,___ sons___ of__ A-bra-ham,___
we are__ a cho - sen gen-e-ra-tion.
Un-der a co-ve-nant,___ washed by His pre-cious__ blood,___
filled with__ the migh - ty Ho-ly Ghost.___
And I hear the__ sound___ of the com-ing___

1080.

We are Your inheritance

Ps 3:3; 33:12; Rev 22:17,20

With awe

Paul Oakley

We are your in-he-ri-tance,___ we are Your re-ward.___
Lis-ten, can you hear___ it?___ The Spi-rit and the Bride.___

We are Your in-he-ri-tance,___
Lis-ten, can you hear___ it?___ The

we are Your re-ward,___ and You're our glo-ry___ and the
Spi-rit and the Bride.___ Whis-per "Je-sus!___

lif-ter of our heads.___ You're our glo-ry___ and the
Ma-ra-na-tha! Come!"___ Whis-per "Je-sus!___

lif-ter of our heads.___
Ma-ra-na-tha! Come!"___ O come,

1081.
We ask You, O Lord
(The latter rain)

Ps 85:6; Joel 2:23;
Lk 1:17; Eph 5:26; Rev 21:2

Prayerfully, with strength

Richard Lewis

We— ask You, O Lord, for the rain of Your Spi - rit. We—

ask You, O Lord, for the rain of Your Spi - rit, for— now is the

time, for— now is the time of the lat-ter rain,—

of the lat-ter rain.— Send Your

rain, cleanse us by Your word; let us be Your pure and ra-diant

1082.
We behold Your glory

Is 53:5; Mt 27:26,29;
Mk 15:15,17; Jn 19:1-2;
1 Pet 2:24; 3:19

Thoughtfully

David & Nathan Fellingham

1. We be-hold Your glo - ry,___ foun-tain of life,___ the
Lord Je - sus Christ.___ Lord of the u - ni - verse,___
You die in weak - ness; strong De - li - ver - er,___
how You were woun - ded. Sus - tain - er of life,

2. We behold Your glory,
   Fountain of life, the Lord Jesus Christ.
   Though You were fettered, we are delivered;
   Though You were condemned, we are absolved.
   Though You were exposed to mocking and shame,
   We are established and raised up in honour.
   Though You were laid in the dust of death,
   Though You went down to hell's darkest depths,
   The kingdom of heaven is ours.

1083.
We believe in Hebrews 13:8

Heb 13:8

Ian Smale

Brightly

We be-lieve___ in He-brews thir-teen, eight,___ Je-sus Christ is ne-ver out of date. If it's

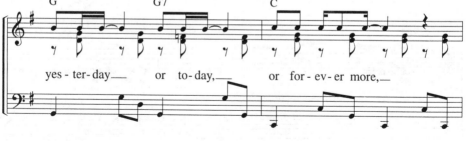

yes-ter-day___ or to-day,___ or for-ev-er more,___

Je-sus stays the same and that is great.

1084.

We bow down

Ps 27:8; 95:6; 105:4; 1 Chron 16:11

Gently, with awe

Viola Grafstrom

We bow— down and con - fess You are— Lord in this— place. We bow— down and con - fess You are— Lord in this— place. You are all I need; it's Your face I seek. In the pre-sence of Your light—— we bow—down, we bow— down.——

Humble yourselves before the Lord, and He will lift you up.

JAMES 4:10

1085. We confess the sins of our nation

(Save us, O God)

2 Chron 7:13-14; Is 56:7;
Mal 3:7-11; Mt 21:13;
Mk 11:17; Lk 19:46

Kevin Prosch

Prayerfully

We con - fess the sins of— our
Turn a - way this curse from— our

na - tion, and, Lord, we— are guil - ty
coun - try; we say that— we've robbed You, and our

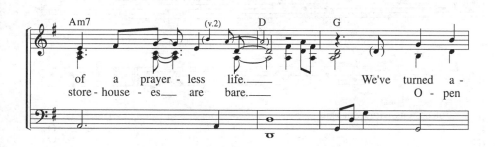

of a prayer - less life.— We've turned a -
store - house - es— are bare.— O - pen

way our hearts from— Your laws,—
wide the flood - gates— of heav - en,

that lifts up— Your name to all— the world._____
let the fear of— the
let the place where— we

Lord be a stan - dard.

live be called— a house_____ of— prayer._____

1086.

We give thanks to You

Rev 4:8; 11:17; 12:10-11

Mark Altrogge

We give thanks— to You, O Lord,— Al-migh-ty— God,— the

One who is,— who was— and is— to— come.—

You've ta-ken up— Your pow - er and— be-gun to— reign,—

— the na-tions bow— be-fore— the Ho - ly— One.—

— Now Your— sal-va - tion,— and Your

1087.

We have a vision

Capo 2 (D)

Mal 3:10; Phil 2:10-11

Chris Falson

Strongly, with a swing

We have a vi - sion___ for this___ na-
- tion;___ we share a dream for this___ land.___ We join with an - gels___ in ce - le - bra - tion,___ by faith we speak re - vi - val___ to this___ land.___

1088.
We have called on You, Lord
(Jubilee song)

Capo 2 (G)

In a rocky $\frac{12}{8}$ feel

Ps 30:2,4-5; Jn 1:5

Stuart Garrard

1. We have called on You, Lord, and You have heard us.
2. You have stretched out Your hand, and You have touched us,

We have called on Your name, and
sent us Your ho-ly fire, and

You have an-swered.
You have purged us.

Mer-cy has
Light has

tri-umphed ov-er judge-ment.
tri-umphed ov-er dark-ness.

Mer-cy has
Light has

tri-umphed ov-er judge-ment.
tri-umphed ov-er dark-ness.

Chorus

We love

Trust in the Lord with all your heart and lean not on your own understanding; in all your ways acknowledge Him, and He will make your paths straight.

PROVERBS 3:5-6

1089. We have come to seek Your face

Ps 27:14; Zech 4:6
2 Cor 12:10

Capo 3 (D)

Robert Newey

Slow and steady

We have come to seek Your face, filled with won - der at Your grace, a-mazed at how You've come and touched our lives. But e - ven as we've felt Your touch, de - sire for You has grown so much, it on - ly serves to make us re - a - lise that the way a - head is in Your strength a - lone. So we

1090.
We have flooded the altar
(Lead me)

Ps 17:8; 149:4;
Mal 2:13,17

Slowly

Martin Smith

1. We have flood-ed the al - tar with our tears;____ we have wear - ied You, Lord,_ with our words.____ Great God, our pro - mis - es____ we've bro - ken, O Lord, for-give me. 2. You are me. So lead me,____ oh__ lead me in - to__ Your arms;____ I will__ be safe in the sha - dow of__ Your wing.

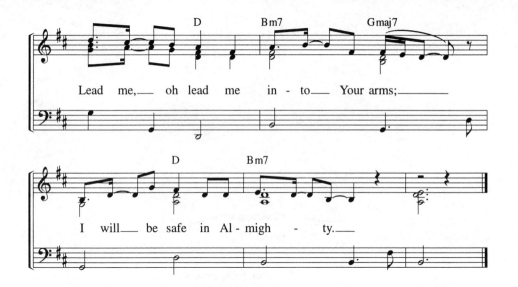

Lead me,— oh lead me in - to— Your arms;———

I will— be safe in Al - migh - ty.—

2. You are breaking the pride of our hearts;
   You have given us tears for the lost.
   You crown the humble with salvation,
   O Lord, humble me.

3. You have paid back our sin with Your love;
   Lover's arms You have offered us.
   Faithful One, raise up a faithful people
   Who find their treasure there.

Be joyful in hope, patient in affliction, faithful in prayer.

ROMANS 12:12

1091. We have prayed that You would have mercy
(Let it rain)

1 Kings 18:44; 2 Chron 7:13-15; Ezek 34:26

Paul Oakley

1092. We have sung our songs of victory
(How long?)

2 Chron 7:14; Ps 68:5;
Is 35:5-6

Thoughtfully

Stuart Townend

1. We have sung our songs of vic - t'ry, we have prayed to You for rain; we have cried for Your com-pas - sion to re-new the land a-gain. Now we're stand-ing in Your pre - sence, more hun-gry than be-fore; now we're on Your steps of mer - cy, and we're knock-ing at Your door. *Chorus* How long be-fore You

2. Lord, we know Your heart is broken
   By the evil that You see,
   And You've stayed Your hand of judgement
   For You plan to set men free.
   But the land is still in darkness,
   And we've fled from what is right;
   We have failed the silent children
   Who will never see the light.

3. But I know a day is coming
   When the deaf will hear His voice,
   When the blind will see their Saviour,
   And the lame will leap for joy.
   When the widow finds a husband
   Who will always love his bride,
   And the orphan finds a father
   Who will never leave her side.

(Final Chorus)
How long before Your glory lights the skies?
How long before Your radiance lifts our eyes?
How long before Your fragrance fills the air?
How long before the earth resounds with songs of joy?

1093. Welcome, King of kings!

Ps 99:1; Phil 2:11;
Rev 17:14; 19:16

Noel Richards

Brightly, with strength

Wel - come,— King of kings!— How great—

is Your name.— You come— in ma-jes-ty— for ev-er— to

reign. 1. You rule the na-tions,— they shake at the

sound of— Your name. To You is giv-en— all pow'r,

and You shall reign.

2. Let all creation bow down
   At the sound of Your name.
   Let every tongue now confess,
   The Lord God reigns.

1094.

We lift up our heads

Ex 15:11; Rev 5:13; 17:14; 19:16

David Fellingham

With strength

We lift up our heads, and we will sing our praise to Him who sits on the throne. We lift up our heads to the King of kings, who reigns in hea-ven and earth.

(Fine)

Ho - - - ly and migh-ty, awe - - - some in pow-er,

Glo - - - rious in ho - li - ness, fear - - - ful in prais-es,

full_____ of com - pas - sion_____ and love.____
work - ing His won - ders_____ in us.____

We lift up our

1095. Well I hear they're singing
(I've found Jesus)

Ps 40:2;Lk 15:24,32; Jn 15:16

Martin Smith

Majestically

1. Well, I hear they're sing - ing in the streets that
   feel like danc - ing in the streets 'cause

Je-sus is— a-live, and all cre - a - tion shouts a-loud— that
Je-sus is— a-live, to join with all— who ce - le-brate— that

Je-sus is— a-live.— Now sure-ly we— can all be changed— 'cause
Je-sus is— a-live.— The joy of God— is in this town— 'cause

Je-sus is— a-live; and ev - 'ry-bo - dy here can know that
Je-sus is— a-live; for ev - 'ry-bo - dy's seen the truth that

Je-sus is— a-live.—
Je-sus is— a-live.— And I will live for all— my days

lifted me from where_ I was, set my feet upon_ a rock,_

humbled that_ You even know_ about me. Now

I have chosen to believe,_ believing that You've chosen me;_

I was lost but now I've found, I've found

1096.

Well, I thank You, Lord
(Times of refreshing)

Ps 40:2; Mal 4:2
Acts 3:19; 1 Pet 5:6

Bob Baker

Brightly

1. Well, I thank You, Lord,— that You are— my Sa - viour;

You're my strength and You're— the Rock on which— I stand.—

(Vs 2.)

You give me life— and a grace— that's great-

- er when I hum - ble my - self— be -

-ing to my soul. 2. For the -ing, You bring times

_ of re-fresh - ing, You bring times_ of re-fresh - ing to my

soul._____

2. For the day will come when we'll all be gathered,
And the sun will rise with healing in its wings;
And all the years of pain won't seem to matter,
When our eyes behold our Teacher and our King.

1097.
We're here for the harvest
(Here for the harvest)

Is 6:8; 61:1-2; Mt 9:37-38;
Lk 4:1118-19; 10:2; Jn 4:35

Chris Bowater

We're here for the har-vest, get rea-dy to reap,_ the call is for ac-tion, it's

here for the har-vest, the yield will be great;_ the fields are now ri-pened, so

1. not time to sleep.— We're **2.** don't he-si-tate.— There's need for more la-b'rers, for

ma-ny,_ not few, the chal-lenge set be-fore_ us is who? And we cry:

Lord of the har-vest, in this day of Your pow'r,_ hear the

an-them of voi-ces: "send me!"_ "Send me,_ send me,

1098. We rejoice in the goodness of our God

Brightly

Ps 145:8; Is 42:7;
Lam 3:22-23; Mal 3:6; Heb 13:8

Carol Owen

We re - joice in the good - ness of_ our God,_ _ we re - joice in the won - ders of_ Your fa - vour._ You've set the cap - tives free,_ You've caused the blind to see,_ hal - le - lu - jah, You give us li - ber - ty,_ hal - le - lu - jah._

Last time to CODA

Verse

1. Al-ways the same,— You ne-ver change,—
and Your mer-cies are new— ev-'ry day._____ Com-
pa-ssion-ate— and gra-cious,— our faith-ful lov-ing God,— slow to
an-ger,— rich in love._____ We re -

CODA

hal - le - lu - jah, hal - le - lu - jah.

2. You give us hope, You give us joy,
   You give us fulness of life to enjoy.
   Our Shepherd and Provider,
   Our God who's always there,
   Never failing, always true.

1099.

We're looking to Your promise
(Send revival, start with me)

2 Chron 7:14;
Ps 85:6; Is 6:5

Steadily

Matt Redman

1. We're look-ing to Your pro-mise of old,___ that if we___ pray___ and hum-ble our-selves,___ You will___ come___ and heal our___ land,___ You will come,___ You will come.___ 2. We're ___ to us.___ Lord, send___ re-vi-val, start with___

me. For I_ am_ one of un-clean_ lips,

and my_ eyes_ have seen the King._ Your glo-

-ry I have glimpsed:_ send re-vi-val, start with

me. We're

(D.S. for verse)

2. We're looking to the promise You made,
   That if we turn and look to Your face,
   You will come and heal our land,
   You will come,
   You will come to us.

1100.
We're reaching out to You again
(Pre-revival days)

Zeph 3:17; Mt 6:21;
Mk 1:26; 9:26; 14:15;
Lk 12:34; 22:12; Acts 8:7

With Anticipation

Ian White

Verse

1. We're reach-ing out to You a-gain._ We're
   kneel-ing on the floor a-gain._ We're

in the up-per room a-gain._ We
cry-ing out for more a-gain._ We're

feel the Spi-rit's wave, we're in___ pre-re-vi-val days.
seek-ing for Your face, we're in___ pre-re-vi-val

We're days. You say where our trea-sure is,_

there is our heart._ You say where our trea-sure is,_

there is our heart.___   2. We're   days.

But a sin-gle_song_ can ne-ver change our_ways,_ so we

cry to You, Lord,_ You are migh-ty to save.___

2. We're looking at our lives again.
   Your love has filled our eyes again.
   We cherish Your embrace,
   We're in pre-revival days.
   We're praying for the lost again.
   The hardened heart is soft again.
   No-one is turned away,
   We're in pre-revival days.

3. We're talking in the streets again.
   You're showing us what to speak again.
   The demons scream with rage,
   We're in pre-revival days.

(Mid section)

4. Jesus out in front again.
   Jesus on our tongues again.
   We're rising up in faith
   To see revival days.
   We're praying for our land again.
   You've stayed Your patient hand again.
   This nation needs Your grace,
   To see revival days.

1101. We're so thankful to You

Mt 28:18; Jn 14:16; 16:7;
Phil 2:8; Rev 1:18; 5:9

Chris Cartwright & Richard Lewis

Steadily

Verse

1. We're so thank-ful to— You, we're so grate-ful for the things You've done,— that You died for us on the cross, – such a pain-ful death, that You paid the price— for us, You paid the price for us.

And we say

Chorus

thank You, Lord. We say thank You, Lord. We say

2. It's so wonderful that You rose,
   Victorious over death and hell.
   All authority is now Yours,
   And the Comforter
   You have sent in fulness to us,
   You have come to us.

1102.

We're standing here
(This is our heart cry)

Capo 3 (D)

Stuart Garrard

Rhythmically

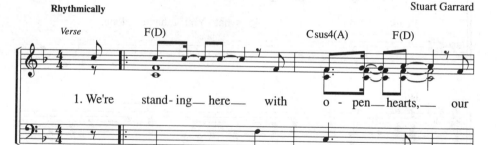

1. We're stand-ing— here— with o - pen— hearts,— our

voic-es— joined— in u - ni - ty.— We know we— don't— lead per-

-fect lives,— and we cry to You— for mer - cy.

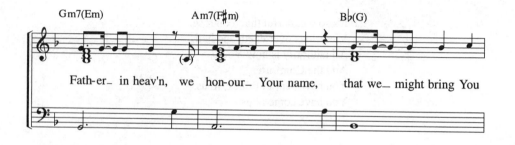

Fath-er— in heav'n, we hon-our— Your name, that we— might bring You

2. We stand before the throne of grace,
   A people for Your possession;
   We hunger and thirst, we seek Your face,
   Come touch us with Your presence.
   Father in heaven, holy and true,
   Stretch out Your hand, let power break through;
   Pour out Your Spirit upon us today,
   To heal and deliver and save.

1103.

We stand together

Mt 25:32; Eph 2:1,5;
Phil 2:8,10; Col 2:13; Rev 5:9

With a heavy rock feel

Lex Loizides

We stand to-geth-er   be-fore our Sa-viour,
We have a vi-sion,   we've been com-mis-sioned

we stand to-geth-er in the cause of our God.___
to raise a ban-ner in the name of our God.___

Once, when we were dead in sin, our hearts were turned a-

way,___ but then the light of Christ broke in and

made us live a-gain. And if You could heal our

blind-ness, You can save our na-tion too, so we give our-selves this

day to fol-low You.

Last time

2. We'll preach the gospel, we'll tell the people
   About a Saviour who has died on a cross.
   With true compassion, without distraction,
   While we have time we will deliver the lost.
   Someday soon the King will come
   With glory, power and might,
   And all the hosts of heaven and hell
   Will bow before the light.
   And the nations will be gathered
   For the righteous Judge will come,
   And the blood-bought church will join the Risen One.

1104. We wanna change this world

With a steady, rhythmic feel

Sue Rinaldi

We wan-na change this world,— we wan-na

change this world.— We wan-na

1. So wave those flags of jus-tice o-ver the
2. So hold each oth-er's hands— a-cross the

na-tions, and hit those drums of peace—
o-ceans, and play those chords of peace—

— a-mong— the peo-ples.
— a-mong— the peo-ples.

1105.   We want to see Jesus lifted high

Jn 3:14; 14:6
2 Cor 10:4; Rev 8:4-5

Doug Horley

Lively

We want to see Je - sus lift - ed high,____ a ban-ner that flies____
____ a-cross____ this land,____ that all men might see____ the truth____ and know____
____ He is the way____ to heav - en. We want to see,
(We're gon - na)
we want to see, we want to see Je - sus lift - ed high.____
(we're gon - na) (we're gon - na)
We want to see, we want to see, we want to see Je -
(We're gon - na) (we're gon - na) (we're gon - na)

1106.
We will give ourselves no rest
(Knocking on the door of heaven)

Capo 3 (D)

Is 62:6

With conviction

Matt Redman & Steve Cantellow

We will give our-selves___ no rest___ till Your king-dom comes___ on earth;___ You've po-si-tioned watch - men on___ the walls.___ Now our prayers will flow___ like tears,___ for You've shared Your heart___ with us;___ God of hea-ven, on___ our knees___ we fall.___ Come down___ in

1107. We will tear down every stronghold

Capo 2 (D)

Is 40:3; Mt 6:10; 2Cor 10:4; Rev 22:2

With a strong rhythm

Dave Bilbrough

We will tear down ev-ery strong-hold through the

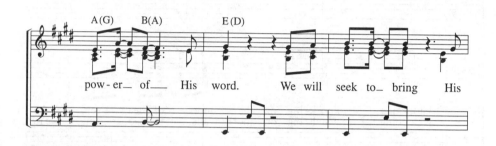

pow-er_ of_ His word. We will seek to_ bring His

king-dom_ in, make a way for_ His_ re-turn. We will

tell of_ His sal-va-tion, for the church of_ Christ_ is

1108. We will worship the Lamb of glory

Capo 3 (D)

Rev 5:12; 17:14; 19:16

Dennis Jernigan

We will wor - ship the Lamb___ of glo - ry,
(Bless the name of)

we will wor - ship the King___ of kings;___
(I bless the name of)

We will wor - ship the Lamb___ of glo - ry,___
(Bless the name of)

we will wor - ship the King.
(Bless the name of)
And with our hands lift-ed high___

___ we will wor - ship and sing,
and with our hands lift-ed high___

1109. What a Friend I've found

Ps 27:10; Prov 18:24

Slow & steady

Martin Smith

1. What a Friend I've found, clo-ser than a bro-ther;
I have felt Your touch, more in-ti-mate than lov-ers.

Chorus

Je - sus, Je - sus, Je - sus, Friend for ev - er.

2. What a hope I've found,
More faithful than a mother;
It would break my heart
To ever lose each other.

"My heart rejoices in the Lord;"

1 SAMUEL 2:1

1110.
Whatever I have gained
(Lost without Your love)

Capo 3 (D)

Moderately

Phil 3:8-9

Geoff Bullock

1. What-ev-er I have gained, what-ev-er I have done,
-tained, the goals I may have gained,

I leave it all be-hind to fol - low You.
a prize or an-y glo - ry

The things that I at- of my own.____

Chorus

For I am lost with-out____ Your love,____

all things are loss____ with-out____ Your love;____

For I am lost with-out___ Your love,___

all things are loss___ with-out___ Your love.___

(Fine) D.%. al fine

2. The won-der of Your

2. The wonder of Your love,
The wonder of Your grace;
To gain You and to know You
As my Lord.
That I am found in You,
Your righteousness alone
Is more than I could dream
Or ever ask.

1111.   What kind of love is this?

1 Cor 2:9; Gal 2:20;
Eph 1:5; 2:8;

Bryn & Sally Haworth

1. What kind of love is this that gave it-self for me? I am the guil - ty one, yet I go free. What kind of love is this,

a— love I've ne - ver known; I

did - n't ev - en know His name, what

kind of love_____ is this?_____

2. What kind of man is this,
   That died in agony?
   He who had done no wrong
   Was crucified for me.
   What kind of man is this,
   Who laid aside His throne
   That I may know the love of God?
   What kind of man is this?

3. By grace I have been saved;
   It is the gift of God.
   He destined me to be His son,
   Such is His love.
   No eye has ever seen,
   No ear has ever heard,
   Nor has the heart of man conceived
   What kind of love is this.

1112. When can I go and meet with God?
(Deep calls to deep)

Gently, but with a rhythmic pulse

Matt Redman

1. When can I go and meet with God? My soul is weak,

my bo-dy tired.__ Can it be here, can it be now?

I need to find that place a-gain.__ __ Where

Chorus

deep calls to deep__ in the roar of Your wa-ter-falls,

You're call-ing me__ with the force of Your love.__

2. When can I come and meet You, God?
   I thirst inside for heaven's touch.
   Let it be here, let it be now;
   I need to find that place again.

3. I want to know Your risen power,
   I need to share Your sufferings;
   And as I die to my own will,
   Lord, raise me to that place again.

1113.

When the music fades
(The heart of worship)

Capo 1 (D)

Mic 6:8

Matt Redman

Steadily

1. When the mu-sic fades,___ all is stripped a-way,___
   and I sim-ply come;___ long-ing just to bring___
   some-thing that's of worth___ that will bless Your heart.___

2. King of end-less worth,___ no one could ex-press___
   how much You de-serve.___ Though I'm weak and poor,___
   all I have is Yours,___ ev-'ry sin-gle breath.___

I'll bring You more than a song,___ for a song in it-self
is not what You have re-quired.___ You search much deep-er with-in___

1114.

When we're in trouble
(Keep on praying)

Eph 6:8

With a strong, steady rhythm

Noel Richards

1. When we're in trou - ble, when there are cares;—
— when faith is sha - ken up,— when we des- pair,— we call on Je - sus, give Him our thanks;— we let His peace— and joy— come to our hearts.—

Prayers for the seek - ers,— prayers for the saints,— pray-ing that peo-

- ple will come to faith.—

Coda

2. When there is sickness, when there is pain;
   There is a healing touch, each time we pray.
   God always listens, cares for our needs;
   Prayers of the righteous one have power indeed.

1115.
When you've been broken
(Kiss the Son)

Job 13:15; 42:6; Ps 2 :12

Steadily, building with strength

Kevin Prosch

1. When you've been bro - ken,_____ bro-ken to piec - es,_____ and your heart be-gins__ to faint, _____ 'cause you don't un - der-stand._____ And when there is no - thing_____ to rake from the ash - es,_____ and you can't ev- en walk__

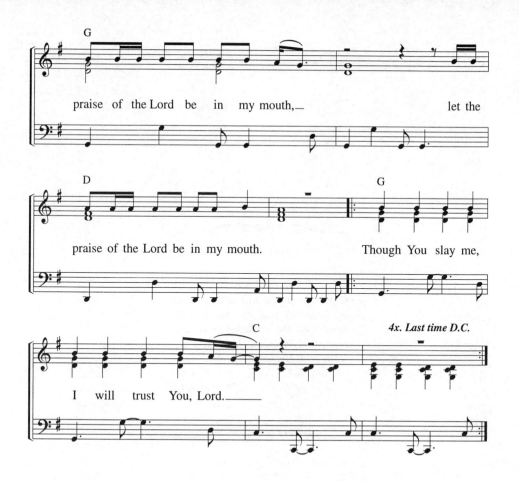

praise of the Lord be in my mouth,— let the

praise of the Lord be in my mouth. Though You slay me,

I will trust You, Lord._____

4x. Last time D.C.

2. When the rock falls, falls upon you,
   And you get ground to dust,
   No music for your pain.
   You open the windows, the windows of heaven,
   And then You opened me,
   And You crushed me like a rose.

I will extol the Lord at all times; His praise will always be on my lips. My soul will boast in the Lord; let the afflicted hear and rejoice. Glorify the Lord with me: let us exalt His name together.

PSALM 34:1-3

1116. Where there once was only hurt

Ps 30:5,11

(Mourning into dancing)

Tommy Walker

Lively, with a 'latin' feel

Where there once was on-ly hurt, He gave His heal-ing hand; where there once was on-ly pain, He brought com - fort like a friend. I feel the sweet-ness of His love piercing my dark-ness.

mo - ment___ in time;___ but His fa-vour___ is here___

___ and will be on me___ for all my life - time.

CODA

1117. Who is there like You?

Capo 3 (D)

Gen 22:14; Ps 71:19; 89:6; 116:12;
Mt 11:28; Jn 14:18; 2 Cor 3:18;
Gal 2:20; Eph 3:20; Phil 1:6

With a gentle rhythm

Paul Oakley

Who is there like You, and who else would give their life for me, even suffering in my place? And who could repay You? All of creation looks to You, and You provide for all You have made.

1118.

Who paints the skies?
(River of fire)

Gen 30:22; Ps 79:13; Is 64:8;
Ezek 11:19; 36:26; Dan 7:10;
Jn 1:3; Rev 5:9; 14:6

Rhythmically

Stuart Townend

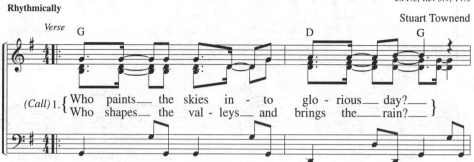

(Call) 1. { Who paints— the skies in - to glo - rious— day?—
Who shapes— the val - leys— and brings the— rain?— }

(Response) On-ly— the splen-dour— of Je - sus. (Call) { Who breathes— His life in - to
Who makes— the de - sert— to

fists of clay?— } (Response) On-ly— the splen-dour— of Je - sus.
live a - gain?— }

Teach ev - 'ry na-tion— His mar-v'llous ways;

each ge - ne - ra - tion__ shall sing His praise.__

G Chorus

He__ is won-der - ful, He__ is glo-ri - ous, clothed__ in righ-teous - ness,

full__ of ten - der - ness. Come__ and wor - ship__ Him,

He's__ the Prince of__ life, He__ will cleanse our__ hearts in__ His ri - ver__ of

fire.

2. Who hears the cry of the barren one?
   Only the mercy of Jesus.
   Who breaks the curse of the heart of stone?
   Only the mercy of Jesus.
   Who storms the prison and sets men free,
   Only the mercy of Jesus.
   Purchasing souls for eternity?
   Only the mercy of Jesus.

1119.

Whose lips will plead?
(This land)

Ezek 22:30-31; 36:26;
Mt 26:41; Mk 14:38;
Lk 21:36; 2Pet 2:17; Jude 13

Steadily

Alex Muir

1. Whose lips will plead for the peo-ple of this land?__ Who'll stand in the gap, and who'll build up the__ wall, be-fore the long day of God's pa-tience is ov-er, be-fore the night comes when His judge-ment will fall?__

2. And

3. And

2. And whose eyes will weep for the people of this land?
And whose hearts will break for the hearts made of stone,
For those who are walking out into the darkness,
Away from God's love, without Christ, so alone?

3. And whose ears can hear what the Spirit is saying
To those who are willing to watch and to pray?
Pray on till God's light fills the skies over this land,
The light of revival that brings a new day.

"Wake up, O sleeper, rise from the dead, and Christ will shine on you."

EPHESIANS 5:14

1120. Will you come and follow Me?
(The summons)

Tune: KELVINGROVE

Scottish Trad.
Arr. Graham Maule & John L. Bell

Not too slowly

1. Will you come and fol-low Me if I but call your name?__ Will you
go where you don't know and nev-er be the same?__ Will you
let My love be shown,__ will you let My name be known,__ will you
let My life be grown in you, and you in Me?__

2. Will you leave yourself behind
   If I but call your name?
   Will you care for cruel and kind
   And never be the same?
   Will you risk the hostile stare,
   Should your life attract or scare?
   Will you let Me answer prayer
   In you and you in Me?

3. Will you let the blinded see
   If I but call your name?
   Will you set the prisoners free
   And never be the same?
   Will you kiss the leper clean,
   And do such as this unseen,
   And admit to what I mean
   In you and You in Me?

4. Will you love the 'you' you hide
   If I but call your name?
   Will you quell the fear inside
   And never be the same?
   Will you use the faith you've found
   To reshape the world around,
   Through My sight and touch and sound
   In you and You in Me?

5. Lord, Your summons echoes true
   When You but call my name.
   Let me turn and follow You
   And never be the same.
   In Your company I'll go
   Where Your love and footsteps show.
   Thus I'll move and live and grow
   In You and You in me.

Graham Maule & John L. Bell

1121.

Within the veil

Heb 6:19

Ruth Dryden

Gently

With-in the veil____ I now would come,____ _ in-to the ho-ly place,____ to look up-on Thy face.____ I see such beau-ty there,____ no oth-er can com-pare,____ I wor-ship Thee, my Lord,____ with-in the veil.____

The sun will no more be your light by day, nor will the brightness of the moon shine on you, for the Lord will be your everlasting light, and your God will be your glory.

ISAIAH 60:19

1122.
Worthy is the Lamb

Is 61:1; Lk 4:18; Rev 5:9,12

With feeling, building in strength

Carol Owen

1. Wor - thy is the Lamb,___ wor - thy is the Lamb,___ wor - thy is the Lamb___ who was slain.___

Last time to Coda

1. 2.

My Lord___ and Sa - viour, my great___ Re - deem - er, Your blood___ has pur - chased me___ for God.___ My

Lord_____ and Sa - viour, my great Re - deem - er, You
came to set the cap - tives free._____

✆ Coda

2. Holy is the Lamb . . .

3. Jesus, You're the Lamb . . .

4. Glory to the Lamb . . .

1123. Yet this will I call to mind
(Because of the Lord's great love)

Lam 3:21-23; Rev 7:14

Carl Tuttle

Smoothly (♩ = 112)

Intro.

1. Yet this will I call to mind,_____ and there - fore I will hope,_____ be - cause of the Lord's great love I've been_____ re-deemed._____ The Lord is gra-cious and kind_____ to all_____ who call on His name,_____

2. I know of His steadfast love,
   His mercy renewed each day,
   Because of the Lord's great love I've been redeemed.
   Washed in the blood of the Lamb,
   Guiltless for ever I stand,
   Because of the Lord's great love I've been redeemed.

1124.

You are merciful to me

Lk 18:13

Prayerfully

Ian White

You are mer-ci-ful to me, You are mer-ci-ful to me, You are mer-ci-ful to me, my Lord. You are

Verse

Ev-'ry day my dis-o-be-dience grieves Your lov-ing heart; but then re-deem-ing love breaks through, and caus-es me to

1125.
You are mighty

Craig Musseau

Rhythmically

You are migh - ty, You are ho - ly, You are awe- some in Your pow-er. You have ris - en, You have con- quered, You have bea - ten the pow'r of death.

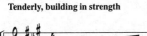

You are my King

Brian Doerksen

Tenderly, building in strength

You are my King, (You are my King) and I

love You. You are my King, (You are my

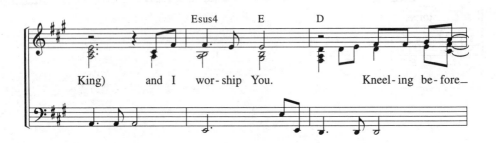

King) and I wor-ship You. Kneel-ing be-fore

You now, all of my life I glad-ly give to

1127.

You are my passion

Song 6:3

Gently, with feeling

Noel & Tricia Richards

You are my pas - sion, love of my life,

friend and com - pan - ion, my Lo - ver.

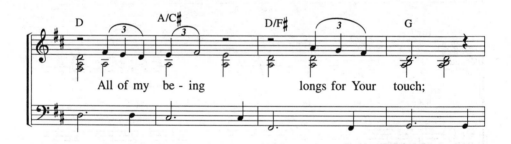

All of my be - ing longs for Your touch;

with all my heart I love You.

Now will You draw— me close— to You,—

gath-er me in Your arms; let me hear the

beat-ing of— Your heart,— O my

Je - sus, O my Je - sus.

You are righteous
(You are good)

Rev 15:3

With a flowing rhythm

Wynne Goss

1. You are right-eous in all Your ways, You are good, You are good. You are truth-ful in all You say, You are good, You are good. And I bow my knee be-fore You, in hon-our of Your name, for You a-lone are wor-thy,

wor-thy of my praise,_____ wor-thy of my praise.__

To repeat

Last time

2. You are

2. You are holy, faithful and true,
   You are good, You are good.
   You are gracious in all You do,
   You are good, You are good.

1129.
You are the great I AM
(Great I AM)

Capo 3 (G)

Ex 3:14; Phil 2:10-11;
Rev 1:17; 2·8; 22:13

Tommy Walker

1130. You are the perfect and righteous God
(I come by the blood)

Heb 1:3,6; 4:15-16;
10:19-22; 1 Jn 3:5

Steve & Vikki Cook

Moderately

1. You are the per-fect and right-eous God whose pre-sence bears no sin; You bid me come to Your ho-ly place: how can I en-ter in when Your pre-sence bears no sin? Through Him who poured out His life for me, the a-ton-ing Lamb of God, through Him and His work a-lone

2. You are the high and exalted King,
   The One the angels fear;
   So far above me in every way,
   Lord, how can I draw near
   To the One the angels fear?
   Through Him who laid down His life for me
   And ascended to Your side,
   Through Him, through Jesus alone I boldly come.

1131.

You are wonderful

Is 9:6; Rev 1:8; 17:14; 19:16; 22:13

Per Soetorp

You are Won-der-ful,____ Coun-sel-lor,____ Might-y God.

You are Prince of Peace,____ our Fa-ther____ for-ev-er more.____

You're the Al-pha and O-meg-a, Lord of____ all

lords.____ You are Won-der-ful,____

Coun-sel-lor,____ Migh-ty God.____

1132. You are worthy to receive

Is 9:6; Rev 5:12-13

John Pantry

1. You are wor-thy to re-ceive all the hon-our and praise. Lamb of God, Prince of peace, we lift high Your name. For Yours is the great-ness, the pow'r and the glo-ry; Lord of the na-tions have mer-cy on us. Though hea-ven be sha-ken, and earth's king-doms fall, we will still wor-ship You.

2. In the footsteps of our King,
   We walk unafraid;
   Though the battle may rage,
   Our praises will ring.

1133.
You bless my life
(Over and over again)

Ps 23:2; 119:176

Terry Butler

Gently, with a lilt

1. You bless my life, and heal me in-side, o-ver and o-ver a-gain.

You touched my heart and brought peace of mind, o-ver and o-ver a-gain. All I can say is I love You. All I can say is I need You. All I can say is I thank You, Lord, for all that You've done in my life.___

2. You've been so kind and patient with me,
   Over and over again.
   When I have strayed You showed me the way,
   Over and over again.

Let us rejoice and be glad and give Him glory! For the wedding of the Lamb has come, and His bride has made herself ready.

REVELATION 19:7

1134.

You came
(Fill the earth)

Is 61:1; Joel 2:23; Lk 4:18; Rom 5:5

Robert Newey

Lively

1. You came to heal the bro - ken - heart-ed;

You came to make the blind— eyes see.

Your light is burn - ing now with - in us, as Your

word of truth sets— us free. *Chorus* And we will fill the earth with the

love of God that's been shed a- broad in our hearts, share with

ev - 'ry na - tion and ev - 'ry land the grace that He im-

parts. And we will sing a new song of joy and peace, a re-

sound - ing trum - pet call, caus-ing hearts to rise, op- 'ning

eyes to see that Je - sus, Je - sus is Lord of

all.

Last time only

2. You come in all Your mighty power,
   You come to bring the latter rain;
   We know You've filled us with Your Spirit
   And a love we cannot contain.

3. You'll come in glory and splendour,
   You'll come to reign upon the earth;
   We know we'll live with You forever
   And declare Your mighty worth.

1135. You have become for us wisdom

(All that we need)

Rom 8:10; 1 Cor 1:30;
Eph 1:23; Col 1:27

Steadily

Verse   G2   C   Mark Altrogge

1. You have be - come___ for us wis - dom;___

Am7   G/D   D   G2

You have be-come___ for us right-eous-ness. You have be-come___our sal-va-

C   Am7   G/D   D

tion;___   You have be - come___ all our ho - li - ness.

Chorus   G/B   C   Dsus4   D

All that we need___ is found in You: oh,___

2. You have become our provision;
   In union with You we have victory.
   In You we have died and have risen;
   You are our great hope of glory.

1136. You have called us chosen
(Take our lives)

Deut 4:24; Rom 8:17; 12:1;
Gal 4:5-6; Heb 12:29; 1Pet 2:9

With reverence

Andy Park

1. You have called us cho-sen, a roy-al priest-hood, a ho-ly

na-tion, we be-long to You. we be-long to You. Take our lives

as a sa-cri-fice; shine in us Your ho-ly

light. Pu-ri-fy our hearts' de-sire; be to us

2. You have shown us mercy,
   You have redeemed us;
   Our hearts cry "Father,
   We belong to You."
   You have shown us mercy,
   You have redeemed us;
   Our hearts cry "Father,
   We belong to You."

1137. You have lifted up the humble
(Holy is Your name)

Ps 107:9; Is 25:4; 40:29; 61:1-2;
Mal 4:2; Mt 5:8; 25:29; Lk 1:51-53;
Jn 4:10,14; Rev 5:9-10; 7:17; 11:15

With awe, building in strength

Alun Leppitt

1. You have lift-ed up the hum-ble, filled the hun-gry with good things; shown Your mer-cy to the fear-ful, You have heal-ing in Your wings. The rich will leave with no-thing, but the poor will have it all, and the pure in heart will see their ho-ly God. Ho-ly is Your name, ho-ly is Your name;

2. You will light the road from darkness,
   As You lead us to Your throne;
   You give strength to the weary,
   And shelter from the storm.
   You pour out living waters
   So we will never thirst,
   And You wipe away the tears from our eyes.

3. You bring justice to the nations,
   Salvation's at Your hand;
   With Your blood You made the purchase
   From every tribe and land,
   To be priests within Your kingdom,
   Your Spirit's on us all
   To show the love and favour of the Lord.

1138. You have taken the precious
(So come)

Is 55:1; 61:3; Amos 9:13;
Hag 2:6-7; Rom 8:22;
1Cor 1:27; Rev 22:17

Kevin Prosch & Tom Davis

Gently, with feeling

Verse

1. You have ta - ken the pre - cious___ from the worth-
cho - sen the weak___ things___ of the world___

less and giv-en us___ beau - ty for ash-
to shame___ that which is strong, and the

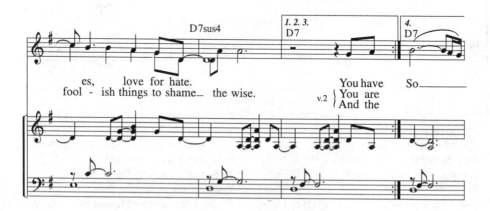

es, love for hate.
fool - ish things to shame___ the wise.
You have So___
v.2 { You are
{ And the

2. You are help to the helpless,
   Strength to the stranger,
   And a father to the child that's left alone.
   And the thirsty You've invited
   To come to the waters,
   And those who have no money, come and buy.

3. Behold the days are coming,
   For the Lord has promised,
   That the ploughman will overtake the reaper.
   And our hearts will be the threshing floor,
   And the move of God we've cried out for
   Will come, it will surely come.

4. For You will shake the heavens,
   And fill Your house with glory,
   And turn the shame of the outcast into praise.
   And all creation groans and waits
   For the Spirit and the Bride to say
   The word that Your heart has longed to hear.

1139. You make Your face to shine on me
(And that my soul knows very well)

Moderately

Darlene Zschech & Russell Fragar

You make Your face to shine on me, and that my soul knows very well; You lift me up, I'm cleansed and free, and that my soul knows very well.

When mountains fall I'll stand by the power of Your hand, and in Your heart of hearts I'll dwell,

2. Joy and strength each day I'll find,
   And that my soul knows very well;
   Forgiveness, hope I know is mine,
   And that my soul knows very well.

1140. You never put a light under a dirty old bucket

Brightly

Mt 5:15-16; Lk 11:33

Ishmael

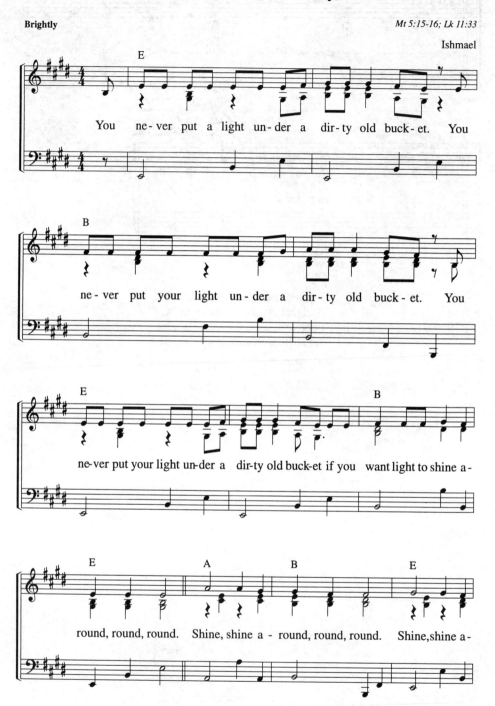

You ne-ver put a light un-der a dir-ty old buck-et. You
ne-ver put your light un-der a dir-ty old buck-et. You
ne-ver put your light un-der a dir-ty old buck-et if you want light to shine a-
round, round, round. Shine, shine a-round, round, round. Shine, shine a-

round, round, round.   Shine a light that ev-'ry-one can   see._____

_____   Lord,   help me let my   lit-tle light shine,   not just Sun-days,

all the time,__ so friends give praise to You__when they see me._____

1141.

You're amazing

Lk 15:20; 2 Cor 1:3

Carol Mundy

Gently

You're a-ma-zing, an a-ma-zing migh-ty God, full of com-pas - sion and true. You're a lov-ing hea-ven-ly Fa-ther to whom all praise is due. You're so a-ma-zing, Fa-ther, I love You.

*O Lord, open my lips, and my
mouth will declare Your praise.*

PSALM 51:15

1142.

You rescued me

Rom 6:22; 8:2; 2 Cor 5:17;
Col 1:13-14; 1 Pet 1:3; Rev 5:9

Geoff Bullock

Flowing

You res-cued me,___ and picked me up,___ a liv-ing hope___
___ You healed my heart,___ and set me free___

___ of grace re-vealed,___ a life trans-formed___ in righ-teous-ness,___
___ from sin and death.___ You brought me life,-

___ O Lord You have res - cued me. For-giv-ing me,___

___ You made me whole,___ O Lord, You have res - cued

me. And You loved___ me be-fore I knew___ You, and You
me, and You sought___ me, Your

1143.
You're the Lion of Judah
(Lion of Judah)

Capo 3 (G)

Eph 6:16-17; Rev 1:7;5:5-6; 11:15,17; 17:14; 19:15-16

Robin Mark

Steadily

1. You're the Li-on of Ju-dah, the Lamb that was slain, You as-cend-ed to hea-ven and e-ver more will reign; at the end of the age when the earth You re-claim, You will ga-ther the na-tions be - fore You. And the eyes of all men will be fixed on the Lamb who was cru-ci - fied, for with wis-dom and mer-cy and jus-tice You'll reign at Your Fa - ther's

2. There's a shield in our hand and a sword at our side,
   There's a fire in our spirit that cannot be denied;
   As the Father has told us, for these You have died,
   For the nations that gather before You.
   And the ears of all men need to hear of the Lamb who was crucified,
   Who decended to hell yet was raised up to reign at the Father's side.

1144.
Your eye is on the sparrow
(I will run to You)

Capo 3 (D)

Zech 4:6; Mt 10:29;
Lk 12:6; 1 Cor 9:24; 13:12; Heb 12:1

Darlene Zschech

Gently

Your eye is on the spar-row, and Your hand, it com-forts me. From the ends of the earth to the depths of my heart, let Your mer-cy and strength be seen. You call me to Your pur-pose, as an-gels un-der-stand. For Your glo-ry may You draw all men, as Your love and grace de-mands.

1145.

Your love looks after me
(For the rest of my days)

Capo 3 (D)

Ps 8:1,9; 90:14

Chris Falson

Contemplatively

Your love_ looks af - ter me,_ it ne - ver_ fails,_

Your word_ takes care_ of me_ and

keeps my mind_ on_ You. You are ma - jes -

- tic_ through all_ the earth;_

I am_ Your ser - vant_ for the rest of my days,_

1146.
Your love, O Lord
(I will exalt You, O Lord)

Capo 2 (D)

Ps 35:5-6; Prov 18:10

Peggy Caswell

1. Your love O Lord,___ it reach-es to the heav-ens;___ Your faith-ful-ness,___ it reach-es to the skies.___ Your right-eous-ness is like___ the might-y moun-tains;___ how price-less___ is Your faith-ful

2. Your name, O Lord, it is a mighty tower;
   Your glory, it covers all the earth.
   In Your hands alone are strength and power,
   All praise be to Your glorious name.

1147.
Your name is peace

Capo 1 (D)

Is 9:6-7; Mt 1:23
Dave Wellington

Quietly, increasing in strength

Your name is peace,— Saviour so ho-ly;—

King of right-eous-ness,— mer-ci-ful and migh-ty.—

God with us,— re-vealed to us,— awe-some
Won-der-ful— Coun-sel-lor,— Ev-er-

and— e-ter-nal God, Your name is peace.—
last-ing Fa-ther, Lord, Your name is peace,—

Your name is peace.—

Every good and perfect gift is from above, coming down from the Father.

JAMES 1:17

1148.
Your voice is like thunder
(House of gold)

Song 1:2; Rom 12:1;
1 Cor 3:12-13; Rev 1:14-15

Paul Oakley

Steadily

Your voice is like thunder, Your eyes like fire;
Your grace is so tender, Your love like wine;

Your throne is for-e-ver, in un-ap-proach-a-ble light.
to You I sur-ren-der,

I lay down my life. And all I want to do

Chorus

is to build a house of gold,
Be my wis-dom and be my strength,

pur-est sil-ver and cost-ly stones;
fill me up with Your faith-ful-ness;

1149. Your will, not mine

Is 42:7; Mt 26:42; Mk 14:36;
Lk 22:42; Jn 10:27;
Rom 12: 1-2;1 Cor 9:24; Heb 12:1

Dougie Brown

Steadily, not too fast

1. Your will, not mine, that is what I___ de-sire to see,

walk-ing in right-eous-ness, and ho-ly li-ber-ty.

Your life, not mine, that is what I___ de-sire to live,

for-giv-ing oth-ers,___ as al-ways You for - give. I

bow be-fore Your ma-jes-ty,___ I fall be-fore___ Your throne; I

2. Your voice, not mine, that is what I desire to hear;
   Speak in the stillness and whisper in my ear.
   Your mind, not mine, that is what I desire to have;
   To prophesy Your word, release the captive heart.

3. Your race, not mine, that is what I desire to run;
   To finish off the work that others have begun.
   Your work, not mine, that is what I desire to do;
   To serve Your purposes, and worship only You.

1150.

You shall be holy

Lev 11:44-45; Jn 15:4
Rom 8:29; 2 Cor 3:18

Steadily

Dave Dickerson

You shall be ho-ly and in ev-'ry-thing be
Stay in My pre-sence, grow strong in My

true, for I, the Lord, am ho-ly, and My
love, with all the gifts I give you from My

word be-longs to you. We are Your
king-dom here a-bove. spired by Your

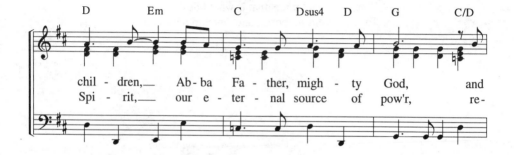

chil-dren, Ab-ba Fa-ther, migh-ty God, and
Spi-rit, our e-ter-nal source of pow'r, re-

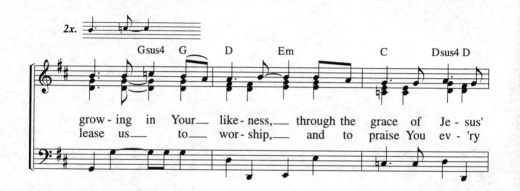

grow - ing in Your___ like - ness,___ through the grace of Je - sus'
lease us___ to___ wor - ship,___ and to praise You ev - 'ry

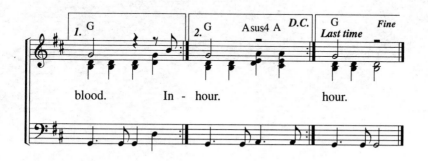

blood.   In - hour.   hour.

Thematic Index

The following index is designed to help church leaders, worship leaders and musicians find songs and hymns appropriate for various themes, settings or occasions. It should be noted that this is by no means an exhaustive listing, and many of these inevitably overlap. If looking for a particular theme, therefore, it is recommended that one looks at several associated categories, rather than just one.

The "seasonal" section has deliberately been kept short. Apart from Easter and Harvest (Christmas songs and carols can be found under the "Jesus: Nativity" section), most other occasions in the church calender will be covered by themes already listed below.

A. GOD THE FATHER
1. General
2. Creation
3. God's love and faithfulness
4. Salvation and protection
5. God's grace and mercy
6. Forgiveness
7. Thirst for God
8. His presence

B. JESUS
1. Kingship
2. Nativity
3. The cross and redemption
4. Sacrifice (the Lamb),
    the blood of Jesus
5. Second coming
6. His name
7. Resurrection

C. HOLY SPIRIT
1. Love
2. Joy
3. Peace
4. Holiness, passion and
    the fire of God
5. Faith
6. Hope
7. Power and anointing
8. Guidance
9. Refreshing and the river

D. CHURCH
1. General
2. Call to worship
3. Praise and thanksgiving
4. Proclamation and evangelism
5. Worship, love and adoration
6. Confession and repentance
7. Communion
8. Commission and revival
9. Commitment
10. Unity
11. Healing and personal renewal
12. Spiritual warfare and deliverance
13. Justice
14. Prayer
15. Church eternal
16. The Bible
17. The worldwide Church

E. CHILDREN

F. SEASONAL
1. Easter
2. Harvest

A. GOD THE FATHER

1. General

2. Creation

3. God's love and faithfulness

4. Salvation and protection

5. God's grace and mercy

6. Forgiveness

7. Thirst for God

8. His presence

B. JESUS

1. Kingship

2. Nativity

3. The cross and redemption

7. Resurrection

C. HOLY SPIRIT

1. Love

2. Joy

3. Peace

4. Holiness, passion and the fire of God

D. CHURCH

1. General

2. Call to worship

3. Praise and thanksgiving

4. Proclamation and evangelism

5. Worship, love and adoration

6. Confession and repentance

7. Communion

8. Commission and revival

9. Commitment

10. Unity

11. Healing and personal renewal

12. Spiritual warfare and deliverance

15. Church eternal

16. The Bible

17. The worldwide church

E. CHILDREN

F. SEASONAL

1. Easter

2. Harvest

Index of Tunes

A more extensive selection of tunes is available in the first
Songs of Fellowship Music edition (Songs 1 – 640).

GUITAR CHORD CHART

The following chord diagrams show the fingering for many of the guitar chords in this songbook.

Key

o = *play open string*   2 = *index finger*   5 = *little finger*
x = *don't play string*   3 = *middle finger* $\text{\scriptsize\NNNN}$ = *index finger bar*
1 = *thumb*   4 = *ring finger*   3 = *fret number*

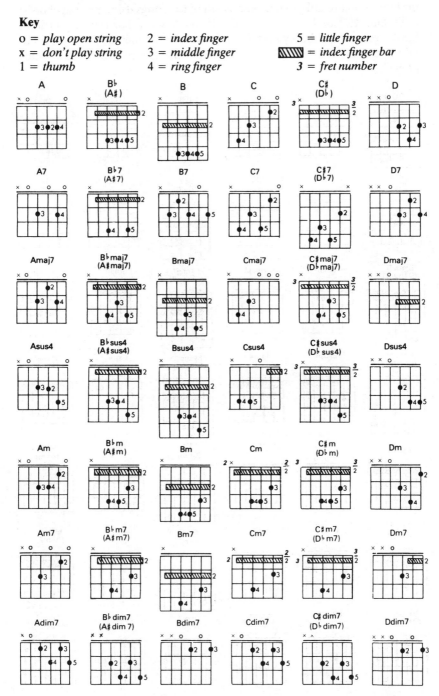

The chords which have been used throughout the book have been carefully chosen with the elementary guitarist in mind. Capo markings, in the left hand corner of many of the songs, allow simple chord shapes to be played with a capo in position. *Capo 3 (C),* for example, means place the capo at the third fret and play the simple chords in brackets, which you will find are in C rather than Eb. If you use these capo markings you will find that you are able to play almost all of the songs using just ten chords: C, D, Dm, E, Em, F, G, A, Am, B7. If you do see a chord which you don't know, you will probably find that it is playable by mentally stripping it of all its 'extras' e.g. Gmaj7, just play G; Dm9, just play Dm; Csus4, just play C.

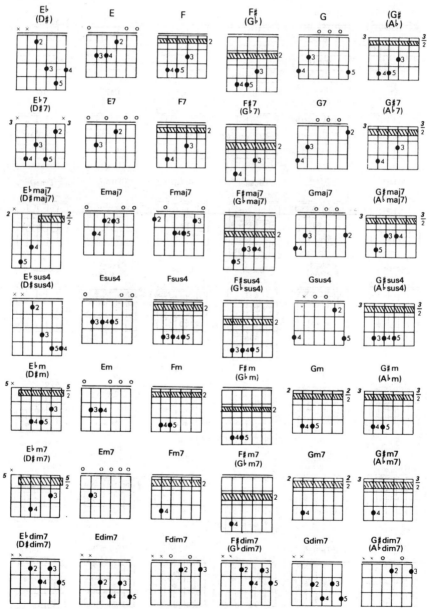

More unusual chords

In this songbook you will come across some more unusual chords—mainly chords with different bass notes. If you see D/A, for example, this means play the chord of D with the note A in the bass. For a guitarist who is strumming, this bass note isn't too important and he can just play an ordinary chord of D, but the A bass note is useful for bass and keyboard players, and for guitarists who are picking and want to add colour to their playing.

The diagram on the right above shows the position of bass notes on the guitar for those who want to learn them. Looking at the diagram you can work out that a D/A is simple (see second diagram).

As already stated, when *strumming,* the bass note (as long as it is a note from the chord) isn't too important as it doesn't sound above the other guitar strings. Because one requires as loud and full a sound as possible when strumming it is best to play chords which use all six strings. This can be achieved by incorporating a different bass note. Use the following full sounding versions of common chords when strumming. For—

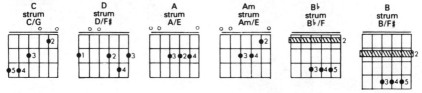

The following are some of the more complex chords you will find in the songbook:

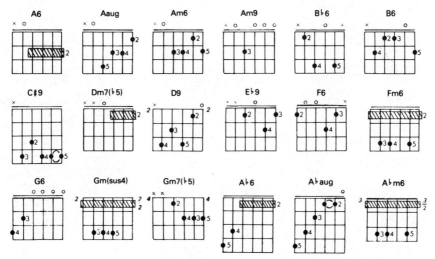

Scripture Index

This index lists Bible passages quoted or echoed in the songs. While not exhaustive, it provides a biblical background for many of the ideas expressed.

Index of Titles and First Lines

Authors' titles, where different from first lines, are shown in *italics*.

KEEP YOUR
MUSICIANS HAPPY!

One of the biggest problems facing today's worship team is finding
suitable parts for all the instruments. That's why Songs of Fellowship
provide their own arrangement service to cover the songs in their books.

Parts for transposing instruments are readily available, as well as four part
arrangements for choirs and vocal groups - all compatible with the piano
arrangements found in the Songs of Fellowship books.

For a list of available parts and prices, please send an A4 stamped
addressed envelope (100 grammes postage), stating what vocal or
instrumental arrangements you are interested in.

The Songs of Fellowship Arrangement
Service
PO Box 4, Sheffield, South Yorkshire, D1 1DU.

Keep in touch!

Kingsway's *Worship Together* is a great way of keeping up to date with new songs and other worship resources. If you would like to find out more about this range of services for you and your church, just fill in your details on the form below, cut it out and send it to us at : Kingsway Music, Lottbridge Drove, Eastbourne, East Sussex, BN23 6NT, UK. Alternatively, you can contact us by telephone on 01323 437708, fax 01323 411970, or e-mail music@kingsway.co.uk, and ask our staff to make sure you are kept informed.

☐ Please send me details of other Kingsway recordings and songbooks.

☐ Please send me details of your worship magazine, *Worship Together.*

☐ Please send me details of the *Worship Together* Resource pack.

☐ Please send me details of the *Worship Together* Seminar programme.

Name (Rev, Mr, Mrs, Miss) _____

Address _____

_____

_____

Postcode _____

Telephone no. _____

Church affiliation (eg. House Church, Anglican, etc.)

_____

DATA PROTECTION ACT
If you do not wish to receive information from other Christian organisations or charities please tick. ☐

Songs of Fellowship Equipping Kids to Worship

- **NEW EDITION:** revised & expanded with 200 popular and lively Scripture based songs for family worship.

- **ACTION SONGS:** unique section with illustrations.

- **NEW SONGS:** from the UK's top children's workers including Jim Bailey, Mick Gisbey, Doug Horley, Ishmael, Mark & Helen Johnson.

- **NEW ALBUMS:** a new series based on the book with 'Backing Track' CD's.

 Available from your local Christian bookshop or in case of difficulty ring 01273 234567
Kingsway Music, Lottbridge Drove, Eastbourne, East Sussex BN23 6NT Telephone: (01323) 437700

THE
Teacher's Guides

CURRICULUM
Student's Activity and Craft Books

THAT HAS
Full-colour Visual Aids

ALL YOU
Theme-linked Songs

NEED!

BIBLE-IN-LIFE

Everything for the busy teacher

- Bible based
- Christ centred
- Activity-based teaching
- Flexible to use
- Easy to prepare

**If you would like further details or would like to take advantage of our 50%
OFF Introductory Offer then fill in the form and send to:**
**Bible-in-Life, FREEPOST (BR641), 26-28 Lottbridge Drive, Eastbourne, East Sussex
BN23 6NT. Telephone: 01323 437749**

Please send me further details of your introductory offer. I understand that when my church purchases Bible-in-Life materials for the first time we will receive 50% discount off the first quarter ordered.

Please send me the following sampler of Bible-in-Life entirely FREE of charge:

☐ 18-36 mths	☐ 9-11 yrs
☐ 3-5 yrs	☐ 11-14 yrs
☐ 5-7 yrs	☐ 14-18 yrs
☐ 7-9 yrs	☐ Adult

SOF2

Name:_____

Address: _____

_____

Post Code: _____

Church: _____

Telephone: _____

Position in church:_____

As far as I am aware, my church has not already used Bible-in-Life curriculum.

Signature:_____

This offer applies to UK churches only.

WORSHIP *together*

Discover the magazine that is equipping worship leaders, musicians and pastors for leading their church in creative, uplifting worship.

It's practical, thought provoking and broad in its scope. From Kendrick to Dudley-Smith, Watts to Celtic Worship, choral to contemporary praise, you'll find it the most in-depth resource available today.

- **Worship Leaders** - Key features on practical and biblical aspects of leading worship.

- **Worship Musicians** - Practical, down to earth advice on musical technique and its contribution to worship.

- **Worship Team Leaders** - How can you build your worship team? How can you enhance the musical arrangements?

- **Worshippers** - Regular biblical overviews of worship. Interviews with key creative leaders.

8 pages of reviews ● In depth Diary ● Personal Profiles

FREE 21 DAY TRIAL
Subscribe now to Worship Together and we'll give you a free 21 day trial. We'll rush you your first issue when we receive your completed subscription form. If you're not totally satisfied, write to us within 21 days and we'll refund your subscription in full.

SUBSCRIBE NOW - ONLY £14.75

Complete the coupon and post to:
Kingsway Communications, Lottbridge Drove, Eastbourne, East Sussex BN23 6NT or telephone: Freephone 0800 378 446 during office hours with credit card details.

☐ I want to receive WORSHIP TOGETHER for six issues. Enclosed is my payment of £14.75*

☐ I want to receive WORSHIP TOGETHER for twelve issues and save £2.50. Enclosed is my payment of £27.00*

Name ....

Address ....

....

....

....Postcode...................

1. I enclose a cheque/postal order for £ ....
made payable to Kingsway Communications Ltd.

2. Please debit my credit card account with £ ....

The Access ☐ Visa ☐ number is entered below

☐☐☐☐☐☐☐☐☐☐☐☐☐☐☐☐

Signature ....

Expiry Date ☐☐ / ☐☐
*This is the U.K price only. All prices include post and packing. Overseas subscribers: please pay by Sterling draft or credit card only.
European subscription £17.75 (£34.00 - 12 issues). Rest of the world £18.90 (£35.00 - 12 issues). Kingsway Communications Ltd, Lottbridge Drove, Eastbourne, East Sussex BN23 6NT. Kingsway Communications is registered under the Data Protection Act 1984, and holds names and addresses on computer for mailing purposes. Details are available on request.

☐ Tick here if you do not wish to receive promotional mailings from other companies.

DISK USERS - PLEASE READ NOW!

Welcome to the Songs of Fellowship Words Disk

Enclosed please find your Songs of Fellowship Words Disk, containing the words to all 1150 hymns and songs in the Songs of Fellowship Combined Words Edition. The songs are laid out simply and clearly, one to a page, and are ideal for 1) printing on to acetates for overhead projectors; 2) making your own customised church songbook; or 3) incorporating in service sheets.

IMPORTANT NOTE. Purchasing this songbook does not automatically grant the right to reproduce the words from the disk. With a few exceptions (indicated below each song on the disk), all songs are covered by the Christian Copyright Licence. Any church or individual wishing to reproduce a song for church use must hold a current Licence for the territory in which the words are to be used. For any other use, permission must be obtained from the individual song copyright holder (addresses given at the bottom of each song in the songbook).

For more information on obtaining a Licence, please contact CCL at one of the addresses shown on the Bibliography page at the front of the book.

REQUIREMENTS AND USAGE

This disk contains no program (except for installation purposes), so there is no new package or series of commands to learn. The words of the songs are saved in .WRI format, which can be installed and operated within your existing word processing package.

This disk is compatible with any Windows-based PC (with a minimum of 5MB of free hard disk space for the installation process) that uses:

Any word processor capable of reading a .WRI file format, eg Microsoft Word, WordPerfect for Windows, Lotus Amipro/Wordpro, etc;

Or the standard Windows word processors: Microsoft Write (for Windows 3.11), or Microsoft Wordpad (for Windows 95).

To install the contents, simply follow the instructions given on the front of the disk. The installation program will create the directory C:\SOFWORDS. Inside this directory you will find three files: README.WRI, INDEX.WRI, and VOLS1+2.WRI. These can be opened using your usual word processing package, by selecting File then Open. Bear in mind that you will need to search for .WRI file types. Then you may save the files in the format appropriate to your program eg. Word document, WordPerfect document etc. If you are uncertain how to open different file types in your word processor, refer to your word processor's manual. Alternatively, you could use the standard Windows word processor (available with all Windows packages) as follows:

Microsoft Write (for Windows 3.11)
1. In Program Manager, select Main.
2. Double-click File Manager icon.
3. Select C:\SOFWORDS directory.
4. Double-click on VOLS1+2.WRI file that appears in the right-hand window. This will automatically load the file into Microsoft Write.

Microsoft Wordpad (for Windows 95)
1. Double-click on the My Computer icon.
2. Double-click Drive C.
3. Double click the SOFWORDS directory.
4. Double-click the VOLS1+2.WRI file. This will automatically load the file into Microsoft Wordpad.

N.B Although Microsoft Write and Microsoft Wordpad accept .WRI files, we recommend you use the dedicated word processing program with which you are familiar, with all the facilities that it provides, eg. Search, Format etc.

For important information on finding songs within the file, and the full Conditions and Terms of usage, please consult the README.TXT file stored in the C:\SOFWORDS directory. The INDEX.WRI file in this directory is an integrated index of all the songs. You may find it useful to print this out for reference before using the songs file.

IN CASE OF DIFFICULTY

If you encounter problems installing the contents of the disk, you may write/fax/email us as follows:

Songs of Fellowship Words Disk, Lottbridge Drove, Eastbourne, East Sussex, BN23 6NT. Fax: 01323 411970. Email: music@kingsway.co.uk.

If you encounter problems in the operation of your word processing package, please refer to your program's manual, or contact the program's Technical Support line.